Lutheran Theology

"Doing Theology" introduces the major Christian traditions and their way of theological reflection. The volumes focus on the origins of a particular theological tradition, its foundations, key concepts, eminent thinkers and historical development. The series is aimed at readers who want to learn more about their own theological heritage and identity: theology undergraduates, students in ministerial training and church study groups.

Titles in the series:

Catholic Theology – Matthew Levering
Anglican Theology – Mark Chapman
Reformed Theology – Michael Allen
Methodist Theology – Kenneth Wilson
Baptist Theology – Stephen Holmes

Lutheran Theology

Steven D. Paulson

t&t clark

Published by T&T Clark International
A Continuum Imprint
The Tower Building, 11 York Road, London SE1 7NX
80 Maiden Lane, Suite 704, New York, NY 10038

www.continuumbooks.com

British Library Cataloguing-in-Publication Data
A catalogue record for this book is available from the British Library.

ISBN13: 978-0-567-48272-3 (Hardback)
ISBN13: 978-0-567-55000-2 (Paperback)

Typeset by Newgen Imaging Systems Pvt Ltd, Chennai, India
Printed and bound in Great Britain

Contents

Contents

Contents

Introduction

Lutheran theology begins perversely by advocating the destruction of all that is good, right, and beautiful in human life. It attacks the lowest and the highest goals of life, especially morality, no matter how sincere are its practitioners. Luther said the "sum and substance," of Paul's letter to the Romans "is to pull down, to pluck up, and to destroy all wisdom and righteousness of the flesh."[1] By the end neither grace nor love is spared this destruction. Take no refuge in thinking that this is mere cynicism regarding *nomos* (law) in the form of custom, like the Greek Cynic Diogenes of Sinope who dropped his robe and defecated in the middle of the Olympic games to prove—what? That the laws of Athens were conventions? That one ought to live according to a higher law in harmony with nature? That he was free? In any case the destruction of the righteousness of the flesh in Luther or Paul is not the search for a higher law that occasionally awakens a desire to shock convention. Nor is this radical attack merely a warning like Socrates' not to practice morality to impress others, but to adhere to virtue and wisdom with a true feeling of the heart come what may—even unjust death by legal means. Lutheran theology begins not as an attack on our lack of knowledge of the good, it is attacking the good itself along with the hearts of righteous people who "proving themselves to be wise, became fools" (Rom 1:22). The first task of theology is to witness to sin and make it great, so great that it kills. This is no less than the task given to the prophet Jeremiah, picked out by a strange act of divine election from the multitude of people of earth and told to 'pluck up and pull down, to destroy and to overthrow' (Jeremiah 1:10a). Paul extended this to the whole world, magnifying sin until it was revealed in the very hearts of the righteous.

1

The second task of theology is to make way for the declaration of a completely foreign, new righteousness that has no law in it at all—"we must be taught a righteousness that comes completely from the outside and is foreign. And therefore our own righteousness that is born in us must first be plucked up."[2] God's call to Jeremiah concluded, "to build and to plant" (Jeremiah 1:10:b). Luther concurred, "Everything that is in us" must be destroyed, and "everything that is outside us" must be planted and built. What is outside us? Is it not life's goals that have not been reached? Is it not the great principles of morality and the very laws that order nature? Is not my striving toward the good the very best thing about me? No. The one thing outside that must be planted is Jesus Christ, the God who is a man. No righteousness that comes from us, from our doings or our heart will endure before God. Only Christ's righteousness lives in the future, "this righteousness which is utterly external and foreign to us." We must become other, foreign to ourselves in the one person of the Jew, Jesus, who was crucified.

This is already no ordinary philosophy about life, nor is it ordinary Christian religion. For thousands of years Christians routinely described life using an allegory of the Hebrew exodus from Egypt. They said life in general, and Christians in particular, were on an exodus out of vice and into virtue. They were on a journey away from badness toward goodness. But Luther bluntly said faith is not a transition from vice to virtue, it is "the way from virtue to the grace of Christ."[3]

Aesthetic ⇒ Ethical ⇒ Faith

The Legal Scheme

Lutheran theology starts where all others end. Virtue is not the goal of life, virtue is our problem. Religion is not given for morality; it is there to end it. The picture of progress upward to happiness is toppled, and in its stead is the apocalyptic end of righteousness in this world so that only Christ remains, who alone is righteous in the eyes of God. Of course this description of religion is a problem for those caught up in the legal scheme of life. That legal scheme assumes there is a law to life (even if no God to give it) and the law must be kept. The legal scheme refers to that

2

teleological picture of life as a ladder on which life is a type of motion from earth's lowest level to the highest heaven by means of the exercise of the free will that either refuses the law and fails to reach its proper goal or accepts the law and fulfills it in order to arrive at the life of glory. Thus the legal scheme has four basic components: (1) God who gives the law, (2) the law which is bestowed as a guide for the journey of life, (3) the free will in the form of human desires which fuels the movement in life by accepting or denying God's guidance, (4) and a judgment by which one either fulfills the law and lives or fails and dies. This law may be described temporally and harshly, as in a Darwinian "survival of the fittest," or it can be softened and spiritualized to incorporate a merciful God and a grace that allows mistakes and even failure, but the basic scheme remains intact so that improvement of desire or some sign of willing agreement with the law must be present. One can forgive an alcoholic, but not if they do not want to change.

Luther was astonished how many Christian theologies accepted the basic scheme of the law and its morality (*opinio legis*), but had nothing worthwhile to say about Christ. Yet it is still more shocking to say that Christian faith is not moving toward virtue, it is taking leave of it. After all, for someone in the legal scheme of life what is left when you say you are taking leave of virtue? Life to them is axial, as philosophers say, and the axis has two extreme poles. If you are moving away from virtue you must be moving toward vice, and if you are moving away from vice you must be moving toward virtue. What else is there? But to say that the "goal" or meaning of life is now Christ is utterly confusing within the legal scheme. How can a person be my goal? Do you mean to imitate him in his virtue? Yes, Christ is to be imitated, but only after virtue is ended. Taking leave of virtue and going to Christ is apocalyptic; it is a new life outside the legal scheme without law at all. It means to have a new life outside one's self, who is dead according to the law, and in Christ exclusively. But, is life without law not chaos? Is it not the opposite of righteousness? Is it not an irrational assertion to call life a crucified man? Where would my motivation be and indeed where would ontology, my being, go?

This is why the apostle Paul started his letter to the Romans with a perverse description of himself: "Paul, slave of Christ"

3

(Romans 1:1 translation altered). An inversion has occurred here much greater than Nietzsche's trans-valuation of morality. Morality, aesthetics, and all knowledge on earth is destroyed. People in the legal scheme will no doubt take this as a recommendation of immorality, stupidity, and ugliness, but the glory of the righteousness of God in Jesus Christ is worth undergoing both a thousand apocalypses and the scorn of those who would protect the law.

Human reason is revolted by the thought that there are two kinds of righteousness, legal and fiduciary, and the two are not complementary. They stand in eternal and deadly opposition so that any striving for virtue ends by crucifying God when he comes to live among us. Divine righteousness destroys the goal of human righteousness through the law, and in its place raises Christ from the dead as its glory and "goal." When the legal scheme is gone, the law ended, and virtuous people are put to death, faith is the only thing that lives by trusting what Christ promises.

To put so much weight upon Jesus Christ for those lucky enough to get a preacher is really too much to swallow for anyone still puttering along in the legal system. When Lutheran theology is worth its salt it is always offensive and perverse in its specific attack on virtue with Christ. No wonder that Hermann Sasse ended his famous book on Lutheran theology *Here We Stand* by saying: "The Evangelical Lutheran Church is a church which has been sentenced to death by the world."[4] Why not, since Lutheran teaching has declared that very world's destruction on account of its very best things?

The key to any theology, especially done the Lutheran way, is to ask what role the law plays in its system. For Luther the breakthrough of the gospel is that where Christ is preached as crucified for our sins and sakes, the law comes to an end. That is the central point of Paul's letter to the Romans (10:4): "Christ is the end of the law." Many fears follow upon this declaration. Is not lawlessness the very definition of sin? Does this not invite immorality? Chaos? Does it not deny God's graceful gift of the law of Moses? So many fearful questions emerge, in fact, that the history of Lutheranism has become the story of attempts to bring the law back into Christian life, like the little Dutch boy putting his finger in the leaking dike. But of course, that is always too late once the

Gospel flood has arrived. The whole Lutheran argument is the work of distinguishing between law and gospel, in a way that the legal scheme does not allow because Lutherans assert that there are two kinds of righteousness, both from God, with only one that stands before God. Let us try to put that argument in one compact paragraph:

We are creatures whose Creator needs no justification. Nevertheless, this Creator seeks justification in his words given to sinners (Psalm 51 and Romans 3). But there are two separate justifications. The first justifies according to the law (which holds among humans awhile), but does not suffice before God—indeed that law was used to kill God's only begotten Son when he came into the world. The second kind of justification is Christ who gives himself to his opponents in the form of a simple promise: I forgive you. These two justifications are called law and gospel, and distinguishing them is the Lutheran passion on earth. The slogan of this way of doing theology is: The Law! . . . until Christ! (Galatians 3:4). God justifies himself by justifying sinners in a simple word.

We do not need to justify God w/ Reason

The Great Misunderstood

The Lutheranism that follows this theology has been called many things: a schism from the true church, a denomination, a reformation, a church, a movement within the church catholic, a proposal of dogma regarding justification, a revolution in thought, a recurring heresy, a religion, a state church, but here we take Lutherans as the product of a particular kind of preaching that delivers God's two words of law and gospel. This book is not a history of Lutheranism, but in laying out the basic teachings of Lutheranism it takes into account a series of major historical variations attempted on the distinction of law and gospel as Luther discovered it. I suggest we think of this history as an attempt to tame the wild animal of the end of the law, consequently an attempt to tame Luther himself. Lutheranism, or as Luther called it, the "evangelical teaching," began as a preaching movement. Luther's student, colleague, and successor, Philip Melanchthon, summarized the project to his students at Wittenberg in lectures that became the first textbook of the Reformation, *Loci Communes* (1521), by saying: "God wishes to be known in a new way, i.e., through the foolishness of preaching."[5] There were certainly other preaching movements in the church before Luther's, but none broke out so far into the public, and none was resisted so stoutly as "another church" (Cardinal Cajetan) and excommunicated by the law of the Empire, the Edict of Worms (1521). What was so upsetting about this preaching? It distinguished the law and gospel and refused any confusion of these two words from God. The law was given in letters in order to kill, and the gospel was given in promises to raise the dead. God first assaulted the pious, then created them a second time—from nothing—by merely sending a preacher to say, "I forgive you."

Luther's early opponents seemed to understand immediately that the Roman church's message over thousands of years was under attack, and indeed Luther himself was aware that he was in the process of overthrowing the careful synthesis that had been worked out between law and gospel that we have called "the legal scheme." Luther insisted on very little but this one point, that God's justice was faith—alone—unaccompanied by any works of law. Consequently he administered forgiveness of sins to actual sinners by preaching it openly, publicly and beyond the law's limit. He then urged the keys of the kingdom to be used liberally throughout the land by preachers in their own places of calling, dispensing a promise from Christ to a sinner that provided the absolute assurance of faith. Preaching was the "means" of the Reformation cause, and could be started immediately, with great freeing effect, anywhere a preacher dared. Overnight a priest could become a Lutheran preacher, and a congregation become a new, evangelical church wherever this freedom was exercised. It was not just that people suddenly began to hear preaching, but the preaching was 'evangelical' because it identified the law's judgment of death as complete, and yet the promise of Christ as victorious over the law's judgment of death. It centered preaching on two words that were normally controlled by a sacramental system with the law at its heart: 'Te absolvo' (I Forgive You). What havoc those simple words created! Dispensing promises required only a call, the Scripture, and boldness to open heaven's gates by using the office of the keys for the ungodly, unjust sinners who abounded wherever the preacher went. Sometimes, with one lecture or disputation, Luther would inspire an evangelical preacher who would then refuse to go back to the old priest-hood—even upon pain of death. Freedom was in the air, and went directly from the ear to the heart so liberty was immediately at hand for many who sought to lose some shackle. Luther taught and demonstrated that these simple words give absolute, indubita-ble certainty, and no one is more dangerous than a person who is *certain*. The certainty was not based on human self-certainty; it was the opposite of that. It was the certainty of forgiveness because of what the Son of God did by taking the sins of the world upon himself and defeating them at the cross. The decisive cosmic battle of God against sin, death, and devil was already waged and won when Christ was raised from the dead to make a new kingdom of people who live with no law, nowhere to go, and nothing to accomplish. They simply were—free.

Four hundred years later, Ernst Troeltsch (1865–1923) summed up the Lutheran way as its exact opposite:

> If to the Catholic it was precisely the external authority
> and the substantiality of grace which seemed to guarantee
> salvation, for Luther's feeling it was . . . purely personal . . . .
> Religion is completely transferred from the sphere of the
> substantial sacramental communication of grace . . . to the
> psychologically intelligible sphere . . . thus Protestantism
> became the religion of the search for God in one's own
> feeling, experience, thought and will.[6]

What happened? There have been movements of reform and renewal many times in the church, and there have been various heresies and schismatic groups, but Lutheranism hit the central nerve of the church because justice before the face of God on the final day was no longer measured by the law. Law had a limit, it came to an end: The law, until Christ!

Luther was the 'the Great Misunderstood,' according to the scout of the army of modernity, G. Lessing (1729–81). What care did Luther have for arcane dogma? Lessing thought he learned from the old Reformer not a dusty dogma of justification, but *the way*—that the search for truth was preferable to possessing it without any search. Luther's was a "method" to get at the truth that should not be choked off by accumulation of church teachings. On just this basis, Troeltsch claimed Luther rejected the old Protestantism and its endless theological arguments that spent Luther's impact and ended up producing the adamant *Book of Concord* (1580) and years of religious wars in Europe. Indeed Luther is the Great Misunderstood. How could he become so contorted into the form of modern Protestantism? One might reasonably take recourse in Luther's assumption that the devil was on the prowl ready to pounce on anyone preaching the gospel. The picture of freedom that developed by the nineteenth century has very little to do with Luther's own theology. On the face of it, Luther's proposal was not of "reform" nor was it modest, though it was excruciatingly simple: it was to replace the papacy with a sermon: "Christ's merit is not acquired through our work of pennies, but through faith by grace, without any money and merit— *not by the authority of the pope*, but rather *by preaching a sermon*, that is, God's Word."[7]

Down comes Christendom, with a word! Preaching is democratized, not in the sense of *emerging* from the people but of being *available* to them all equally—in an instant, rich and poor, male and female, circumcised and uncircumcised, German and Italian. With this the pinnacle of power lay not in Rome or with kings, but at the point of the delivery of a sermon, and so there was no greater authority in the church than the preacher in the act of preaching. Suddenly sacraments ceased being a system of ecclesiastical control or money and became delivered goods in the form of a word to the ungodly. No higher calling, no greater good, no increase of authority could be found than in an absolution that gave life on earth now and in heaven forever to a sinner *in flagrante delicto*. Good work was removed as a sacrifice for God, and was given away to the needy neighbor so that it could not be commoditized as merit, but was released like the modern internet that nobody owns.

The highest office of church became preacher; the service, or slavery, of preaching was for the sake of the sinful hearers. The church itself ceased being an institution of salvation, a factory of the Religious, and became an assembly of sinners gathered around Christ to hear what he has to say. Christ was suddenly present, not occasionally and partially as in the Mass, but wholly and constantly (and all too near to those who were trying hard to be moral), for Christ exercised his own direct Lordship over a brand new kingdom simply by oral proclamation. When the preacher preached, Christ himself was talking right to his flock, gathering his sinners into his own body without need of a *Vicar*, or substitute on earth. The preached Christ was ubiquitous, massive, without need of mediation because He Himself was the one and only Mediator between God's wrath at sin and the sinner. The Holy Spirit poured out like latter-day rain, and even backcountry Germans fresh from the fields found themselves in the shoes of the Jews at Pentecost when Peter, full of the Spirit, did not establish a new religion, and did not send anyone on a mission, or draw up plans for a new institution, nor did he simply come with miracles of healing. What Peter did do, full of the Spirit, was simply to preach a sermon. And when asked by the stunned hearers, "What shall we do?" Peter made them perfectly passive: "repent and be baptized." Their lives would begin and end with this word of promise. What shall we do? Nothing. Listen to Christ, whom you killed; the Father raised him from the dead, and he has come to give you the sole source of new, eternal life by forgiving sin.

It is Luther's great discovery that preaching has always and only been the thing that makes faith, and so justifies—it is not just at Pentecost with Peter, or in Galatia with Paul or Wittenberg with Luther, but with the prophets, with Moses, with Abraham, and was from the beginning with Adam and Eve. The classic picture of the Lutheran Reformation is the Predella of the Reformation altarpiece by Lucas Cranach the Elder (1472–1553) in the Stadtkirche St. Marien in Wittenberg. It depicts Luther dressed in a black robe, leaning out of the old church pulpit in Wittenberg's Town Church preaching with the Scripture opened and with a long finger extended, pointing to Christ (since painting cannot say, it must show), who is in the midst of the assembly, crucified with blood pouring out of his wounds. Those people assembled around Christ stand with equal parts stunned awe and anxious hope waiting for what has finally arrived—the reconciliation, the forgiveness, the end of wrath and enmity between them and God. They are a motley crew of mismatched people, old and young, men and women—rather small in number—but ecstatic as they go out from themselves and live in Christ, and Christ in them. This scene was duplicated in thousands of pulpits almost overnight and made the Reformation a dramatic turning point in history—to say nothing of what was accomplished in the cosmic struggle against evil.

Sermons, after all, are so closely aligned with the preacher, and in turn the preacher is so aligned with mere opinion and insufferable moralizing that one truly does wonder how this could ever be the single divine power, the attack of God on sin, death, devil, and how it could ever work in real life. Preachers are so insipid, so foolish, so lacking in courage, so needy of attention and the desire to be liked that one wonders how it could ever be pulled off. Nevertheless, this is the means by which the Holy Spirit has determined to create in the form of faith the new life that does not die, which is to say Christ himself is grasped by trusting a simple promise. To the world a sermon is either a threat that must be silenced (as when Peter and the Apostles were imprisoned or Martin Luther King Jr. seemed to be stirring up racial trouble with his preaching of temporal freedom), or much more commonly it is perceived as an arcane, boring, silly thing, a crutch for the weak, a waste of time. But a sermon is the cross, which appears as nothing and has no glory in the world even while it is the cosmic power of God to create out of nothing.

Lutheran history has been filled with drama, but unless you understand what occurs in the preaching of a sermon, Luther will always be the Great Misunderstood. Only to the extent that such preaching occurs in the sacraments, and the preaching itself is sacramental (giving all of Christ to sinners without restraint) do we actually have an evangelical, Lutheran "reformation." Lutheran*ism* is a different story since it is the tale from the very beginning of begging off this simple center in proclamation. Too radical, too conservative, too little "reform" or not enough, too much obeisance to the traditions of church, Lutherans have always tried to find some reason that Luther was at the heart of the dramatic changes that occurred and nevertheless they must corral him. Lutheranism is the history of departure from Luther, but this is not a decline or decadence from a golden age, as Jacques Barzun describes the entrance into the modern world, instead bald fear of the Gospel lies at its core. The same charges that were made of

Paul resurfaced among the Lutherans: "Shall we sin the more that grace may abound?" "Is the law to no avail?" "Do I do nothing?" Luther's kind of preaching is a nuclear reactor—so much energy produced from so small a core—and yet the fear always hovers among those who are nearest that the thing will implode and destroy life rather than generate it.

Four Exegetical Episodes of Lutheran History

The only way to moderate Luther's discovery was to turn the sermon back into a moral lesson, and for that the law had to be brought back into the teaching of the Gospel itself. The effect of the attempt to bring the law back into human righteousness before God produced a strange, but predictable result for Lutherans—they repeated the allegorical pattern that had been worked out for Scripture interpretation in the Middle Ages, but now instead of using it spiritually in its fourfold levels of meaning: literal (historically), allegorical (eternally), tropological (morally), and anagogical (Future hope), these were reproduced *seriatim* as episodes of Lutheran history—each new generation reacting to what it saw as a flaw in the previous generation's basis for correcting Luther by re-establishing the law in God's plan of salvation. Luther's position was taken as something like the "literal" position for teaching how to distinguish law and gospel. But fear of the consequences of preaching the law's absolute end prompted an attempt at a universal, allegorical interpretation of God's order or plan as an eternal law into which Christ's cross could be fit. In particular, the leading Lutheran teachers of the seventeenth century concentrated upon demonstrating logically that God's justification of the ungodly does not make God capricious, arbitrary, and therefore untrustworthy. But instead of fidelity to the promise in Christ, God's trustworthiness was fastened to the eternal, objective order of the world provided by God's law.[8] This tendency produced an historical episode of orthodoxy (Lutheran scholasticism) exemplified by John Gerhard (1582–1637) and John Quenstadt (1617–1688) that mirrored the papal scholastics while they were engaged with the public arguments of the Roman counter-reformation in the likes of Bellarmine (1542–1621) and the Jesuits. The orthodox taught by the method of disputed theses arranged according to doctrines in what they called the order of salvation (*ordo salutis*). In order to defend the necessity of the chief article of justification by faith alone, they had recourse to the eternal law and sought an ultimate unity of law and gospel that would enable this order of salvation to be accomplished as with David Hollaz (1648–1713), "The Law and the Gospel practically are united, as if in a certain mathematical point. They concur in producing: (1) the *repentance of sinners* . . . (2) *the renovation of a justified person* . . . and (3) *the preservation of the renewed man*."[9]

When such efforts to defend justification by the eternal law did not work to secure the gospel, a counter-tendency produced a tropological or moral version of Lutheranism that occupied much of the eighteenth and nineteenth century, and indeed continues in some ways to the present. This began with what is called "Pietism" and the desire to have the law give shape to the "sanctified" life in addition to justification, a position that was extended through the likes of Kant and his pietistic upbringing into enlightenment rationalism which held that the Lutheran position was a chastened religion that kept itself within the limits of reason and made of religion a morality of a pure inwardness. In the devotional writer Johann Arndt (1555–1621) and in Jacob Spener's *Pia Desideria (1675)* we find a common point: "The people must have impressed upon them and must accustom themselves to believing that it is by no means enough to have knowledge of the Christian faith, for Christianity consists rather of practice."[10] Lutherans have characteristically chosen the practical over the speculative (if that is all they can choose from), because their theology is meant to produce preaching, but Luther overcame both of those options for how God is known (the scholastic-Aristotelian and the monastic), with his teaching of 'perfect passivity' that does not *do* but *receives* from God. In the moral (tropological) episode, the law was either drawn away from an eternal background into the self and became the hope for autonomy from doctrine or else the law was seen to develop historically toward perfection. Christ became a new Moses and suddenly interest was sparked in rewriting Christ's biography according to the idea that Christ brought in a better law of love than that given by Moses to the Jews. Although begun in the seventeenth century with J. Arndt (1555–1621) and P. J. Spener

(1635–1705), this ethical episode took hold with the Kantians and such theologians as J. C. K. von Hofmann (1810–77), A. Ritschl (1822–1889), and E. Troeltsch (1865–1923) in the nineteenth century.

A backlash against the tropologists occurred by the time of the First World War when the attempt to find freedom through autonomy (using Christ as model of the kingdom of love) was shown to fail. The problem was first detected by Biblical critics who recognized that the new biographies of Christ had little to do with the story of the man in Scripture. People like A. Schweitzer (1875–1965) rediscovered the "eschatological" Christ who is not to be imitated and with whom history cannot truly connect. This episode produced an *anagogical* interpretation by which the law is projected into the future and the present is left to a faith that must trust what it does not really know or grasp, and which lives out of the distance between Creator and creature that the moral law had not been able to bridge. The kingdom of God is not going to be brought through the church and in this time, instead preaching was to cease being a moral exhortation and become a call for an existential decision in the present that depends upon the law reaching its fulfillment in the future kingdom of Christ. R. Bultmann (1884–1976) was the apogee of this approach in the twentieth century.

We will have some recourse in this book to these episodes of Lutheran history, but they all developed a treatment of the law as a way of avoiding the conclusion that salvation was death first and only then resurrection unto new life.

Paul's Letter to the Romans

Lutheran theology is a theology of preaching, and so a theology of the Word of God. The preached word is authorized by Scripture, where the Apostolic preaching of the New Testament came to be written—an unfortunate necessity according to Luther—and the Apostolic preaching was authorized by the promises given to the patriarchs of the Old Testament. For this reason the letter to the Romans, Paul's last will and testament of his Apostolic preaching, stood out as,

. . . summing up briefly the whole Christian and evangelical doctrine, and to prepare an introduction to the entire Old Testament. For, without doubt, whoever has this epistle well in his heart has with him the light and power of the Old Testament. Therefore let every Christian be familiar with it and exercise himself in it continually. To this end may God give his grace. Amen.[11]

Paul's letter to the Romans had everything that is meant by "evangelical,"—which was not doctrine in quite the later sense of the Lutheran scholastic episode, but in the simple sense of

. . . the things that a Christian ought to know, namely, what is law, gospel, sin, punishment, grace, faith, righteousness, Christ, God, good works, love, hope, and the cross; and also how we are to conduct ourselves toward everyone, be he righteous or sinner, strong or weak, friend or foe—and even toward our own selves.[12]

Everything taught at the University of Wittenberg by Luther and the first Reformers was a course on a particular book of Scripture, which was intensely exegetical, often going line by line with attention to details of the translation, and with an eye to the implications of how this was to be preached in the present. But while the letter to the Romans was often thought of as a compendium of doctrine among later Lutherans, the key for Luther was what evangelical preaching required. Paul's letter to the Romans was the best introduction to the Old Testament that a person could have. When Paul says "Scripture" he meant the Old Testament, since the New Testament is something that should always be oral, preached in the present, not written down. What Paul did with the Old Testament, however, was to show that the writing is not primarily God's commands, but a treasure of promises. When the promises made to Adam and Eve, Moses and the prophets—and especially Abraham—were revealed, Scripture took on a whole new light. God has not just one word of law that leads to the destruction of sinners, but he has an even greater word of gospel that produces a new creation. Because Paul showed how to find these promises in the Old Testament, and what to do with them, the letter to the Romans was the wellspring for evangelical teaching.

Ever since, the unfinished business of Lutheran theology is a commentary on Paul's letter to the Romans. Luther was just discovering the evangelical way when he lectured to his students on Romans (1515–16). Melanchthon made lectures on Romans the heart of his teaching at the University and produced from it the first theological textbook of the Reformation called *Loci Communes* (the rhetorical name for Luther's 'things every Christian should know'). For that reason I am organizing this book as a commentary on Paul's letter to the Romans. Lutherans try to say what Paul was saying there, so that Lutheran theology serves as an introduction to the Old Testament.

Accordingly, Luther came to see that our lives are not a series of placid events served up for speculation, or the type of struggle that measures our achievements in life. Rather, human life is the scene of a great, cosmic battle with the forces of evil. God is even now destroying the world he has painstakingly preserved with his own holy law in order to create a new kingdom of heaven. Evil in the persons of death, the devil, and our own sinful selves are in their own death throes since the crucifixion of Christ, and God is at work in the world to destroy and then create through preaching—because he wants not only to be just in himself, but to become just in his words of promise for you. History has meaning as God's incessant search and selection of his chosen for eternal life in the midst of this great cosmic battle. When a preacher arrives, justification of the ungodly is unleashed. Faith ceases being a mere virtue or human activity, and becomes the name for the new creation of the Holy Spirit. Faith arrives in the form of a purely passive gift that kills the old being and raises the new. Luther concludes: "no one can give himself faith, neither can he take away his own unbelief."[13]

The fact that God enters this violent world with a greater violence called "preaching" is shocking indeed, especially when it comes to your own death. It all seems most unbecoming of a good God who established the earth on the ground of law and order to then turn to destroy it. How can a good God destroy that which he has made? Who can bear the truth that God in his mercy is against us? But the fact that his new kingdom has absolutely no law at all is more outrageous still, since Christ rules not by command, but by the faithfulness of his promises. How can there be life without any law? This is what the devil, who is a stickler on the law, cannot understand. If the goal of life is not our fulfillment of the law, and if the law is not the very being or mind of God, then the goal of freedom is nothing other than freedom itself; Paul was adamant about this proclamation: "for freedom, Christ has set you free."

Theology is therefore broken into two parts: life *without a preacher* in which you are found to be a sinner under God's eternal wrath; and life *with a preacher* by which you are justified despite yourself according to Christ's own word of forgiveness—free of death, free of the devil, free of yourself, free of the world and even free of the most holy law.[14]

When Luther taught Paul's letter to the Romans he did it by identifying the key words that distinguish life without and with a preacher: sin, death, justification, faith, and freedom. Paul organized things himself by describing God's justice in a single sentence: "He who by faith is righteous shall live" (Romans 1:17). He then described life without a preacher and with no righteousness—since you cannot give yourself faith (Romans 1:18–3:20). Then he preached God so as to bestow faith, concentrating on the first part of his little sermon: "He who by faith is righteous . . ." (Romans 3:21–5:21), followed by a detailed description of what the latter part of the sentence, "shall live," means in terms of a series of remarkable freedoms: freedom from wrath (Romans 5), freedom from sin (Romans 6), freedom from law (Romans 7), and freedom from death (Romans 8). He concluded the argument with a justification of God in his words (*deum justificare*) that hangs everything on the faithfulness of God to his promises (Romans 9–11). Paul concluded with the fruit of good works that comes from faith, including the way Christians relate to the old world and its sinners (Romans 12–14). Paul concludes as he began, with his own call as Apostle to the Gentiles which ensures that even the worst of sinners will not be without a preacher (Romans 15–16)—even dirty Gentiles shall become free of wrath, sin, law, and death.

For Lutheran theology, at least, this is the whole of Christian doctrine in brief, and "it leaves nothing to be desired" because it announces where law ends. Of course, the commonest and simplest of arguments against the Lutheran teaching is that it is merely Pauline and cannot account for all of Scripture. Paul is not everything, but he is the proper entrance into Scripture, especially the Old Testament. No philosophy on earth, including the many Christian kinds, has ever been so radical as to say that the goal of life is to become lawless. Who would ever want to claim that the law comes to an end? How would one then distinguish good and evil? How would one reward the good and punish the bad? If I have no law in eternity then what will be my motivation in life? Christ always provoked questions just like this, and seemed finally to be a terrible threat to good order, holding up the law in his left hand and overcoming it with his right: "For truly I tell you, until heaven and earth pass away, not one letter, not one stroke of a letter, will pass from the law until all is accomplished" (Matthew 5:18 NRS); "The law and the prophets were until John; since then the good news of the kingdom of God is preached, and every one enters it violently" (Luke 16:16 translation altered). Nevertheless, here we have the bass note of Paul's argument, the slogan of Lutheran theology and the crux of the distinction of law and gospel: The law! . . . until Christ!

Chapter 1

The Preacher

Romans 1:1–15

Defend Thy truth, O God, and stay
This evil generation;
And from the error of its way
Keep Thine own congregation.
The Wicked everywhere abound
And would Thy little flock confound;
But Thou art our Salvation.

Luther, *O Lord, Look Down*

The Bombshell

"Paul, a slave of Jesus Christ, called to be an apostle, selected out for the gospel of God which he promised beforehand through his prophets in the Holy Scriptures" (Romans 1:1–2). Before Paul was, there was God. Theology always begins with God, unlike philosophy or any other sciences that order thought. This makes theology unique and frankly offensive. Before there was Paul, there was God and God selected him, separating him out from all others for the purpose that lies deepest in God's heart, his "proper work" as Isaiah put it, the *Gospel*. God's predestination is all appointed for the Gospel, and for this purpose he elected Paul (and no one was more surprised by this predestination than Paul), which very election authorized everything Paul says.

Predestination is meant to be the greatest comfort given to humans because it reveals what God's precious promises are—but instead it has become the single most troubling assertion of theology (and life), so troubling that it has knocked theology out of the sciences altogether in the modern world, and banished it from the society of reason.

18

The first thing in Lutheran theology is God, who is almighty, and so naturally a predestinating God and thus we come upon the inexorable, logical conclusion: God's will is free; yours is not; everything happens by divine necessity. Therefore the first lie that must be exorcised from theology is the *Liberum Arbitrium*—the myth of the free will. It is not Scripture that proposes such an imaginary creature, but Aristotle, with his little word 'will' (*voluntas*), which concerns choices in external things. But as Melanchthon observed, it is not external choices by humans that concern God, whatever they may be, but the *heart*. Scripture is always interested in the heart because it is the heart that God judges, not external acts. One could take up psychology immediately, as Melanchthon did, dividing the human into parts—like a cognitive part by which a person comes to know something, and an affective, appetitive part that "follows or flees" the thing one has come to know.[1] Thus, throughout philosophy, and especially in the scholastic theology, the interaction of reason and will was considered crucial, especially when it came to how these relate to God's judgment and grace. In one way or another will is added to knowledge and cooperates with grace in what then is called "free will." But the will is not only unfree, it is a tyrant, as Melanchthon called it. Luther loved his young colleague's *Loci* precisely because it dared to begin with the bondage of the will. One can hardly claim such a thing as *voluntas* psychologically, since the imaginary will is never able to overcome the simplest impulse or emotion. But leaving that aside, the real issue is theological: "Since all things that happen, happen necessarily according to divine predestination our will (*voluntas*) has no liberty." That is a truly theological starting point. Lutherans, at the beginning at least, were the most uncompromising monotheists around and took Jeremiah at face value: "I know, O Lord, that the way of man is not in himself, that it is not in man who walks to direct his steps" (10:23).

Perhaps it would have been better not to start theology in this way with God, since it is appalling to think that all things happen by almighty power, and none from the choices of our will. But this revolt against God's being God is not caused by omnipotence itself, it comes from living under a delusion perpetrated by the legal scheme that requires free will in order truly to be free. When this myth strikes the reality of God it must rebel—it has no choice.

God is omnipotent; your will is not free. Even if it is true, who wants to trouble themselves with this knowledge? Often people don't even want to know if they carry the gene for Alzheimer's disease, to say nothing of beginning with this slap to the face of what we call fate. Melanchthon said, "But I may be foolish to discuss the most difficult point, predestination, at the very outset of my work. But still, what does it matter whether I take it up first or last in my compendium that which must intrude into all parts of our discussion?"[2]

Free will must be the first discussion because it is the operating assumption of nature, reason, philosophy, all false theology, and so of the entire legal scheme. Free will refuses monotheism, omnipotence, and predestination and therefore is in open revolt against God the minute it is created in the mind of the sinner. The revolt is so strong, so basic, and so carefully hidden from view that it really must be brought out into the open. Luther had a name for this that comes from his theology of the cross—a theology that refuses the legal scheme. He called it, "calling a thing what it is," as opposed to what it wants to be or should be: "A theologian of glory calls evil good and good evil. A theologian of the cross calls the thing what it actually is."[3] The law speaks in the language of what "should be," but its purpose is not to accomplish that, it is to reveal what *is*, but should *not be.*

Almighty means almighty, and is the proper attribute of God's nature without which God is not God and one must go look for another. When Lutherans argue against free will they confess as Israel has always done, "The Lord our God is one God." There are no other gods; God is unique and alone God. He is omnipotent, and so Christians confess openly and absolutely that God is "the Father, almighty" in all the creeds. What God wills—is. Isaiah says, "My counsel shall stand, and my will shall be done" (46:10). So God chose Paul out of all others to be set aside for a Gospel that he promised beforehand, therefore it had to come to pass. This (and all things) happens by divine necessity. There is no free will, no choice, no decision, no acknowledgement, acceptance or any other verb you could try to give the human in relation to the Creator. His is not a passing conjecture of Paul's; it lies at the heart of all theology, and so not only is assumed by Paul's call, but also is expressed in the great conclusion to his argument in Romans:

20

O, the depth of the riches and wisdom and knowledge of
God! How unsearchable are his judgments and how
inscrutable his ways! 'For who has known the mind of the
Lord, or who has been his counselor?' 'Or who has given
a gift to him that he might be repaid?' For from him and
through him and to him are all things. To him be glory for
ever. Amen (Romans 11:33–36).

Lutherans do not suppose that you must go to Scripture or receive
a special revelation to find an almighty God. They were aware
from the beginning of the great attempts by the philosophers, and
especially the dramatists of Greece, to reconcile themselves to fate.
Experience in life proves the absence of choice in anything that
really matters—that which concerns the heart rather than simply
irrelevant, 'external,' passing things. One of the most arresting
developments of the modern world is Charles Darwin's open,
logical, scientific discussion in *Origin of Species* (1859) of the fact
that nothing happens by free choices of the will. It is an argument
cold as ice, and yet it seeks to have one escape from reality in order
to accept this truth, which is that God is not almighty—otherwise
the bondage of the will would be unendurable. Luther liked to
quote Virgil's *Aeneid* on the score, "By changeless law stand all
things fixed."[4] And who could miss the point of *Oedipus Rex*?
Even in daily speech people still say, "God willing," and mean just
what Lutherans mean. Both the existence of God and predestination are natural knowledge for people, who then, as Freud taught,
proceed immediately to deny this. Even knowledge that over-
whelms human ears is nevertheless natural and universal. Denial of
God and his almightiness, even when it seems all that we can do, is
no proof against these things; to the contrary it is the evidence of
them. If Freud took his patient's denials as facts there would be no
analysis and no change. It is this combination of the *necessity of the
knowledge* and the *inevitability of its denial* that makes humans what
they are, creatures of their Creator in rebellion by denying their
own deaths. What is a therapist to do, to say nothing of a theologian? Denial of death is necessary because death is inevitable.

The almighty will of God that necessitates all things is not used
in Lutheran theology as a point of speculation. The reason I address
this at the beginning is not to agonize over fate or peer into the

abyss of non-being to see if there is a loophole. Nor is the point to agitate you and make you rebel, since of course that kind of rebellion will simply set aside Lutheran theology—as if that rejection were a solution to this pesky question of fate. Luther accused Erasmus on that score: "You reek of nothing but Lucian, and you breathe out on me the vast drunken folly of Epicurus."[5] Luther himself knew that "necessity" in relation to God was too harsh a term for what he was after, because it is heard by a will (supposing itself to be free) as "compulsion," thus being forced to do something it does not want to do. Nothing could be further from the truth; the point is that fate is to do only and always exactly what you want. But what your heart desires is to rebel against the Almighty and kill God. The pot always wants to say to the potter, "Why have you made me thus?" The Lutheran pastor's son, Friedrich Nietzsche (1844–1900), got this entirely wrong, though he had caught enough of the theology to know that the simplistic descriptions of a free will were foolish. But he ended by seeking to love his fate, embrace it, desire it—including his own death in what he calls the oldest desire for *amor fati*, making your personal fate your eternal goal to repeat your life and death endlessly. He taught us that the greatest desire of all is to love your own death.

Such is not what we are speaking of here. Paul says that he was selected, predestined, for the *gospel*, and here is the key word—*promised* beforehand. Fate is what we call knowing that nothing happens by chance, all things occur by divine necessity, and yet not to know what your particular fate is—other than to note that in general we all die. Fate is having an almighty God who never speaks. In the middle of great suffering and atrocity, and even your own earthly death, this God is unspeakably silent. Has there been a better depiction of this since Sophocles than another Lutheran pastor's son, Ingmar Bergman's *Winter Light* (1962) and *The Silence* (1963)? But an almighty God who gives a promise prepared for you beforehand puts God's necessitating power in an entirely different light. No greater contrast exists between a predestined *silence* and a predestined *promise*. Against the first we rebel; to the latter we cling for life. Can God, having made a promise, keep that promise no matter what? But we wait in theology for the unfolding of that promise. At the beginning of our work we simply drop the bombshell: "It is fundamentally necessary and wholesome for

[margin handwritten note: Fate is bound up with Natural theology / Predestination / any leads to despair]

Christians to know that God foreknows nothing contingently, but that He foresees, purposes, and does all things according to His own immutable, eternal and infallible will. This bombshell knocks ✗ 'free-will' flat, and utterly shatters it . . ."[6]

The crucial development in the history of Lutheran theology is that Melanchthon was the champion of this bombshell in his early teaching days having just learned the gospel from Luther. Gradually, however, he became frightened of it and warned often of "Stoical madness," offering hedges and alterations in edition after edition of his *Loci*, until he began experimenting with a free will cooperating with grace under the scheme of the law—surreptitiously while Luther was alive, and openly when Luther had died. This development in Melanchthon has deeply affected Lutheran theology over time, and subsequently opened the way for a very different kind of reform to emerge under the name "Protestant." What certainly is the case is that Lutheran theology, along with every other kind, has qualified God's omnipotence. Modern theology is finally the wholesale rejection of omnipotence, the refusal of predestination, and the reworking among Lutherans of the central medieval scholastic attempt to unite divine and human work in salvation under the rubric of grace.

The question of all theology is whether or not you have free will. If you have it, then God is not omnipotent and therefore you have something to render to God for which you must be recompensed. God would then be under legal obligation to justify you, for therein lies the goal of the myth of free will: it is to bring the almighty God under the law and so oblige the divine if you fulfill his law. But if you do not have such free will, then everything depends upon how God is disposed toward you, that is, whether or not you have a gracious God. That is why, when the legal scheme began to crumble under the weight of reason and Scripture, Luther went on his famous search for just such a gracious God. What else could he do, but attempt some futile *amor fati*?

Preached God and Not-preached God: "Paul, slave . . . Apostle . . ." (Romans 1:1a)

Theology is the work of making distinctions, and the most important distinction Lutheran theology makes is that between

God not preached and God preached as Luther did in his debate with Erasmus:

> When now Diatribe pertly asks, "Does the good Lord deplore the death of his people, which he himself works in them?"—for this really does seem absurd—we reply, as we have already said, that we have to argue in one way about God or the will of God as preached, revealed, offered, and worshiped, and in another way about God as he is not preached, not revealed, not offered, not worshiped.[7]

All creatures have a relation to God not preached, but only those who have a preached God experience His mercy. For that reason, the ground on which the church stands or falls is not an objective doctrine of justification, it is the advent of the preached word. The only way to get a gracious God is for God's silence to end, and so your predestination must involve a preacher: "For everything rests on the preaching of the Word and with it stands or falls the decision of the legitimate reformation of the Church as well as the foundation of a pious life."[8]

But getting a preacher appears in life to be utterly contingent— haphazard, here today, gone tomorrow—and so entirely a matter of chance. Humanly speaking, preaching is utterly contingent upon historical accident, and so *a priori* it is not necessary. But once one has arrived, and we look back with God's eyes, then the arrival of the preacher is the height of necessity and entirely non-contingent. The fact that the almighty God works predestination through historical means is part of the genius of Lutheran theology. Another part is to see that free will works only with a legal scheme; it clings to the law as its hope, not to God. Upon first hearing this, people protest, as Luther noted,

> At this point they cry out in protest and say: 'So, then, one is innocently condemned because he is bound to the commandments and yet is unable to keep them, or one is obliged to do what is impossible.' To this the apostle replies, 'No, O Man, who are you to argue against God?' (Romans 9:20). For if your argument is valid, it follows that preaching, prayer, exhortation, yea, even the dying of Christ, are

24

not necessary. But God did not predestine the elect of salvation in this way, *but through all these means.*[9]

That is, the means of predestination are through preaching and sacraments. Predestination is a confusing term for this, since it appears as if God chose Paul and all his elect by some "military muster," going down the line pointing at this one, not at that, determined before time and space—that is before history. We do not know that, and God does not want us to know, since it is not predestination itself that is ever to be trusted. It is not an abstract term like "predestination", with the various horrors it connotes, that is ever the thing you have faith in. God has a destination that he is heading for, with a specific delivery of a promise to make, come hell or high water, and this is (to use the preacher's language)—necessarily *for you.* God has an *unthwartable divine destination* in time and space, and the way he arrives for the event is via preachers. Preachers do not come with information about an election done elsewhere, outside of time; preachers actually do the electing here and now, in the present, as Christ did for the thief on the cross, "Today, you will be with me in Paradise." We will get too far ahead of the story if we go much further here, this kind of proclamatory predestination will be treated in its proper theological place in the third chapter of Romans and "everywhere else," as Melanchthon once said, but this teaching will mark the difference between various Protestant treatments of predestination and will have a decided impact on the teaching of the sacraments of baptism and the Lord's Supper.

Theology is not so much for speaking of God, but to speak for God—to announce God's words, rather than to exchange human opinions. Everything about theology then depends upon what that Word of God is in contrast to mere human words. What makes Lutheran theology Lutheran is the discovery that this preaching of Word rests not on a first principle or an original being, or a future unity of the many parts into one whole—but all life depends upon a *distinction* that permanently marks everything in the cosmos—including God. When we say "the Word," there is not one Word from God, but two; the first kills and the second creates new. This distinction has been given a slogan for easy reference, it is the act of distinguishing *law* from *gospel.* Lutheran theology leads to preaching the Word that elects the ungodly by applying first the law and then the gospel. Uttering the words "law and gospel" however is not the same as making the distinction. Nor is "discovery" or "reformation" quite the right word for what began with Luther, since the distinction is not like finding a shipping route to India, or remolding a lump of clay that is already there. This is really the distinction between death and life, and it must be made while God is actively killing you with his holy and precious law instead of justifying you by it. Distinguishing law and gospel is an act that opposes your feelings, your ideas, indeed your own self, because a sinner naturally seeks one word from God in the form of a law that has the potential to justify. This explains why the urge in thought has always been to Monism, to speculation that seeks the one word of law that has the potential to liberate, rather than proclamation of law and gospel. Even doctrines of the Trinity usually succumb to Monism of one of the persons.

The distinction between law and gospel is dynamic and ultimate. Failure to distinguish is not an excuse—and not really even possible—so that one can do it badly or well, but do it we must. Theologically we find ourselves in a life and death struggle to find out what is due to God. This doubtless is a struggle to find meaning, but more to the point, a struggle simply to live and not die before the wrath of God. The fight takes place individually, but is cosmic in scope, since it involves everyone in all places and times. The model case in Scripture is Job who struggles with God while having no preacher; but the most revealing is Jacob, who was set to cross the Jabbok when he was accosted by an unknown being of great power with whom Jacob wrestled through the night, refusing to let him go until he squeezed out a word of blessing from this mute opponent. Getting a silent God to speak is what the struggle of faith is all about, but this is literally out of our hands, depending completely upon whether or not a preacher is sent by the Holy Spirit. It is exactly beyond the power of the human will.

Apostolic Preaching

For this reason the very first thing encountered in any of Paul's letters is Paul's call as apostolic preacher of Christ at the end of the

The Preacher

age of the law: "Paul, a slave of Jesus Christ, called to be an apostle, set apart for the gospel of God . . ." (Romans 1:1). Without a preacher there is no good news, no gospel, and so no distinction between law and gospel. The arrival of a preacher is the *sine qua non* for faith, since "faith comes by hearing" and no one can hear without a preacher (Romans 10). Romans is a letter, and a letter begins with a greeting from its sender, but Paul presents his authority to preach not because of formal etiquette; he does it for the sake of his churches since without an apostle they cannot live. The two bookends of Romans in Chapter 1 and 15 have Paul telling of his call, which is not through any one person or group of persons, but "through Christ and God the Father" (Galatians 1:1). An Apostle is first and foremost a preacher who stands in the long line of the prophets who say, "Thus says the Lord," but an Apostle comes after the prophet's message ("The Messiah is coming") has ended. "The law and the prophets were until John" (Luke 16:16 translation altered). The Apostle then says, "Here he is," and so with this the New Testament is no longer anticipated, but received. He delivers God's predestination in the form of an unthwartable promise that is not dependent upon the righteousness of the receiver. This is what makes Apostle the most powerful office in the world, but at the same time Paul calls himself a *slave*. Luther and Melanchthon liked to contrast Paul's office to that of bishops and kings who held power in the world, since Paul had no worldly power. His is the purely spiritual power that is not yet seen, but heard. Paul's calling is ministry or service in the form of slavery to Christ, and so is the exact opposite of a tyrant in this world. When church people confess in their creeds that they believe in an apostolic church they are not referring to bishops or kings, but to the reason Paul wrote the letter to the Romans— which is to give the content of the true preaching of the New Testament. If what is preached in Rome fits with this preaching, Paul rejoices. If not, he must correct, even if it means confronting other Apostles like Peter as he did in Jerusalem and Antioch. *Romans* is then saying: "This is the Gospel, is it not? I trust this is exactly what is being preached in Rome," and Paul seems to have every confidence that was the case. Apostles preach the Gospel, and so all preaching in the church aligns with this—or it is not apostolic.

Paul begins his letter by telling the church in Rome that, "hence my eagerness to proclaim the gospel to you also who are in Rome" (Romans 1:15 NRS), indeed, he is a "slave" of Christ and so "a debtor" to the wise Greek and the foolish barbarian alike (Romans 1:14). What the preacher brings, and no one else has, is the gospel and the gospel is expressed entirely in terms of Christ: "the gospel of God which [God] promised in the holy scriptures, the gospel concerning his Son, who was descended from David according to the flesh and declared to be Son of God with power according to the Spirit of holiness by the resurrection from the dead, Jesus Christ our Lord" (Romans 1:3–4 NRS). The Gospel is the man/God Jesus Christ, and this gospel gives power to the preacher to preach and the hearer to hear so that the second description of the gospel is anthropological—about the person who receives it: "For I am not ashamed of the gospel; it is the *power* of God for salvation to every one who has faith, to the Jew first and also to the Greek. For in it the righteousness of God is revealed through faith for faith; as it is written, 'He who is righteous by faith shall live' (Romans 1:16–18 translation altered). It was this second, anthropological, prescription of the gospel that caught Luther and worried him to death. It was the very benefit of Christ that upset him. The Trinity is no problem to believe, even for a non-Christian, and the same holds with Christ's two natures, but Paul was speaking about the most frightening thing in the world as if it were the very hope and freedom of the world— God's almighty power, his eternal wrath, our bondage in which we have no free will, and so God's divine election apart from the law—in which case some are chosen and others apparently not. Paul spoke as if Christ who was crucified by ungodly men was given all power to rule the new world as he sees fit. Who wants this as our hope?

Lutheran Method

The radical implication of apostolic preaching for the ordering and outline of theology was set forth in Melanchthon's *Loci* in his *Hypotyposes theologicae* that began the book with a "sketch" of the whole in contrast to previous theology texts—most notably the

"Eastern" *De fide orthodoxa* of John of Damascus (675–749), and the "Western" *The Book of Sentences* compiled by Peter Lombard (1100–1160). Instead of speculation like the neo-platonic ontological philosophy of John or the compilation of tradition in the rabbinic form of "human opinions" in Lombard, Lutherans intended "to set forth the meaning of Scripture."[10] Yes, they held there is a meaning, and that it can be set forth. This led them immediately to a new starting point in theology, since normally one began with "God" in the form of the mysteries of the Divine, in particular the doctrine of the Trinity and unity of the one God in three persons. Even the "manner" of the incarnation was not the place to start, although it is the incarnation that provided the proper beginning: "The Lord God Almighty clothed his Son with flesh that he might draw us from contemplating his own majesty to a consideration of the flesh, and especially of our weakness."[11] Yet this "consideration of the flesh" could also become sheer speculation, merely beginning with one's logical inferences from below rather than from above—as anthropology rather than theology. Such was the mistake of the liberal Christology that emerged among Lutherans in the nineteenth century, which was enamored with a speculation of anthropology rather than divinity.[12] Instead Melanchthon held to Paul's method in 1 Corinthians 1:21: "God wishes to be known in a new way, i.e., through the foolishness of preaching, since in his wisdom he could not be known through wisdom."[13]

The Scholastics, the school teachers of the middle ages who used the basic texts of John of Damascus and Lombard, made a mess of the "exalted topics" of the Unity and Trinity of God, Creation, and Incarnation because they did not work by means of the foolishness of preaching. Melanchthon simply considered them stupid, because whenever they attempted to make an argument, say, for the existence of God, or the reason God must be triune, they actually ended up overthrowing the true doctrine, arguing against it (and for a heresy), because they substituted a speculation according to human reason for a word from Scripture. That means they made inferences about human power based on the principle of the legal scheme that if there is a law, then humans must have the power to keep it. Consequently, the attempts to argue before Jews and Muslims, and even Christendom, that God is necessarily three while yet being one ended up in Modalism or Tritheism. They are "ignorant of the fundamentals" according to Melanchthon. Any science has fundamentals which comprise the *scopus* of a discipline which is the target aimed at in studying something. The proper *scopus* for theology is not Trinity, incarnation, and deification, but law, sin, and grace, for when law and gospel are properly distinguished then and only then will the doctrines of Trinity, incarnation, and deification come to true expression. Preaching is not neutral inquiry, nor is it merely thinking ideas or feeling emotions—and it cannot wait interminably for investigation into mysteries of being; it announces sin by using the law, then it bestows new life in the form of freedom by using grace.

For all the power there is to renew theology in this reorientation, there is a lurking danger in Melanchthon's brief description of the *scopus*, since grace can easily be drawn back into a scheme of law. It would have been better for theology if Melanchthon had finished the parallelism of law and gospel so that the fundamentals were four: law and sin, grace and *new creation*. Nevertheless, Melanchthon is quite right in thinking that from the point of view of proclamation the only thing needful is "to know Christ," not as a doctrine, but in the biblical sense of the Hebrew *yada* (יָדַע) —to be known rather than to know—the form which Luther had learned from the book of Genesis. It is from the state of being known that Melanchthon uttered one of the most famous phrases of Lutheran theology, and one of its most controversial: "to know Christ means to know his benefits."[14] Melanchthon intended this phrase to counteract an old Aristotelian problem that put in place of the distinction between law and gospel the "historical" mode of distinguishing form and matter. The matter remains; the form changes, and so when this was applied to Christ one then erroneously teaches that the incarnation is a *change of form* (a mere transformation of being). As innocent as it sounds, this has led to a host of problems in preaching where faith became something like agreeing to an otherwise impossible ontology—that Christ maintains two contrary forms of being at once divine and human. The master illustrator, Melanchthon, suggested thinking of the difference between passive and active 'knowing' in theology like you would a pharmacist who knew all the plant classifications—shapes, colors and the like—but had no idea how to apply even one of these plants to the healing of a sickness. Such was Peter Lombard's book, and likewise for John of Damascus. If you were sick, which would you rather have: someone who knew the classifications of plants, or someone who knew how to heal you with them? To be known rather than to know means that Christ cannot simply be known as form. It is mere history to state the truth about Christ, that he is God, and that he became man, but what is necessary to know in order to preach is his *power* in order to apply Christ to the healing of a sickness. Preaching is not interested in the history of Christ for its own sake, nor is it interested in the internal history of the Triune being; it is interested in applying the power of Christ to the people who need it, for only the sick need a physician; "it is therefore proper that we know Christ in another way than that which the Scholastics have set forth."

Melanchthon himself did not hold very long to what he did next, yet it is the key to Lutheran theology that uses preaching as its method. One begins with the sick person, diagnosing that sickness by means of the law. What does the law demand and what power in humans is there to do this law? This question diagnoses the sin, then (and only then) can the proper medicine be applied, which is the grace of Christ to cover the sin. But sin cannot be known in relation only to the law; it must be placed in relation to the crucifixion of Jesus Christ. For this reason there are three "fundamentals" of law, sin, and grace which encompass the sum of Lutheran theology. Melanchthon and Luther both recognized that they were doing what Augustine did, which was to reach back to Paul in this matter of theology's ground, not to Aristotle or Plato. Paul was the great preacher of Christ, and neither the dogmatician of Christ nor the originator of a new religion. "In his letter to the Romans when he was writing a compendium of Christian doctrine, did Paul philosophize about the mysteries of the Trinity, the mode of incarnation, or active and passive creation? No! But what does he discuss? He takes up the law, sin, grace, fundamentals on which the knowledge of Christ exclusively rests."[15] Theology is a knowledge of Christ, for as Luther once said in a phrase that became part of the public confession of all Lutherans, "apart from this human being there is no God . . ."[16] Often in Lutheran theology various articles of the creeds are played off one another—the

31

first about the Father and creation, the second of Christ and redemption, and the third about the Holy Spirit and sanctification. One of the common Lutheran criticisms of Karl Barth (1886–1968) was that his theology was "christo-centric" and needed to be tempered or preceded by a robust theology of creation. There are reasons Lutherans have criticized Barth, but it is a misunderstanding to fear "christo-centrism" when Christ is spoken of out of the *foolishness of preaching*. It is not a matter of pitting creation against redemption, but of diagnosing the human problem from the reality of the cross, instead of orienting theology by means of speculation about human powers. If Christ died on the cross, the problem we all inherited must have been grave indeed. When we turn our minds from the immediacy of proclamation a common problem results, as Melanchthon observed, "Most people seek in the Scriptures only topics of virtues and vices." They go to the Bible to find out what they are to do to be right with God. This misses everything, because it misses Christ. But what if this inquiry considers Christ as a model of the godly life who shows us the way from vice to virtue? Then, even when it speaks of Christ, it misses Christ *and his benefits*. When the legal scheme is in place, we miss Christ because he has no power other than modeling good behavior. Be like Christ! But that is not the power of Christ. Christ forgives sin. Forgiveness is *the* power the law does not have, and marks the difference between speculation and proclamation. The one speaks admiringly of Christ who sits on a pedestal, the other unleashes his power to be applied to the truly sick who need it. Speculation keeps Christ on the shelf to contemplate; proclamation applies him actively.

It was Rudolph Bultmann, the towering figure of Lutheran theology in the twentieth century's anagogical episode, who used Melanchthon's "to know Christ means to know his benefits," to re-orient modern theology to proclamation and away from Idealism. It was Bultmann who also brought theology back to the concentration on the text of Scripture so that today he is primarily known as a Biblical scholar rather than a systematic theologian. It was Bultmann who identified why Christ's apocalyptic preaching was not an embarrassment, as Schweitzer taught, but was the very stuff of theology instead of the legal form of concentration on being and completion of creation. But it was also Bultmann who misconstrued the crucial first assertion of Lutheran theology after applying the distinction of law and gospel. He made of preaching a "moment of decision," taken out of ontology, to be sure, but made into an existential act of freedom that stepped out of human potential in direct denial of the bondage of the will.

[handwritten margin note: From Heidegger, Pietism!]

Instead, Melanchthon began all of theology with the astounding claim that before God there is no free will. Imagine beginning your theology with that claim—especially since Melanchthon was a humanist. No wonder Luther loved this first, 1521 edition of Melanchthon's *Loci*. Luther had not even entered his famous debate with Erasmus on the free will by that time, but already the implications of a preaching theology that rids itself of the legal scheme were clear. Hearing a preacher is God's choice, not yours. Specifically it is the work of the Holy Spirit who bestows Christ's benefits only when and where he will—not where the hearers will. The theological side of this new beginning in theology is to say Melanchthon began with predestination, "But I may seem foolish to discuss the most difficult point, predestination, at the very outset of my work."[17] Melanchthon learned not to be so blunt later when he wrote the basic, public confession of Lutherans, the Augsburg Confession (1530) where he prided himself on keeping predestination and bondage of the will hidden from the Roman theologians: "throughout I speak as if predestination follows our faith and works."[18]

Now it is one thing to take up predestination and the bound will in the legal scheme; there it is sheer horror, a "Stoical madness," that freezes the mind and soul before the thought of sheer fate, and God's all-working power. It is quite another, in fact it is freedom itself, to take up God's election by preaching with the gospel beyond the legal scheme. By starting with the preacher, one comes quickly to the truth of the hearer—the will is bound, it has no freedom to choose God, the law, or righteousness for itself. This is not so much an ontological statement as it is an historical one, or better yet, an eschatological one. By the time the preacher arrives it is too late for any moment of decision; the decision is God's and it is already made once and for all.

In Lutheran theology we begin as Paul did, that is with the arrival of a preacher. From the hearer's side this appears accidental, just as it appeared to Job, Jacob or Abraham. Why me? Why now?

33

It is a shock that God chooses by some other art than humans can divine naturally, working outward from the required principles of the law. Yet from God's side—theologically—Paul was "set apart beforehand," as was Abraham, and all things in the cosmos are just so tuned to the arrival of the Son of God in flesh. The cross of Christ is where everything was always heading in history and creation. However, without a preacher, Christ is not revealed; he slips back into the course of history as one more event in a steady progress toward fulfillment of the law alone. His death is at best a speed bump on the road to something else—like justice for all or the second law of thermodynamics. So Paul lays out what a true preacher preaches upon arrival, and second, he takes up the bleak case of what life is like without a preacher.

Chapter 2

The Sermon

Romans 1:16–17

'It should not bore you if we repeat here what we teach, preach, sing, and write at other times and places. For if we lost the doctrine of justification, we lose simply everything.'[1]

That One Word: *Iustitia Dei*

Paul first established his apostolic office, then he gave the content of his preaching: "I am not ashamed of the Gospel . . . the one who is justified by faith shall live" (Romans 1:17). Luther called "justification by faith alone" the chief doctrine of the church, but by the nineteenth century Wilhelm Wrede argued that Paul's religion can be articulated without even mentioning this doctrine of justification since everything Paul says depends not upon some revelation of gospel by faith alone, but upon historical polemics that Paul waged against his enemies at the time, either "Judaizers" or Gnostics. Most modern, historical critics have simply followed suit, so that later in the century Albert Schweitzer called justification merely a "subsidiary crater," in the mysticism of the apostle.[2] The secret of this liberalism three hundred years after the reformation is that at heart it is deeply conservative when it comes to the law as the means of righteousness—for Jews first, then Greeks. Liberality technically means being liberal with the law, applying it freely and equitably to all. The contrast with Luther is what makes him so interesting today, the revolutionary par excellence—an excessively apocalyptic and earthly man at the same time—so that few, Lutherans especially, are willing to follow him at the central point.

What exactly is the Gospel, and how is it different than the Law which came before? Since evangelical theology is not simply a new set of doctrines it has been difficult to summarize briefly. Often a formula is tried such as "justification by faith alone," which indeed can shed light on what made Lutheran theology evangelical, but when Luther tells the story it becomes clear that what happened was no mere change of mind or a new idea. Luther called it a new birth, just like the one Jesus described to the befuddled Nicodemus, "unless you are born anew . . ." (John 2). One day God forgave the sinner Luther, apart from any works of the law—and it worked.

During his last university lectures on Genesis Luther came upon the story of the elder brother Esau having sold his inheritance for pottage and Esau's belated prayer for a consolation blessing from the Lord. Selling a birthright for pottage prompted Luther to think back to the inauguration of the Reformation when he received God's undeserved blessing like the thief Jacob. Luther recollected how one word from Romans 1:17 took over his life in his lectures and in a *Preface* he wrote for a collection of his Latin writings published in 1545: "Meanwhile, in that same year, 1519, I had begun interpreting the Psalms once again. I felt confident that I was now more experienced, since I had dealt in university courses with St. Paul's Letters to the Romans and to the Galatians and the Letter to the Hebrews." How "experienced"? Luther had gone through all of those Scriptures before, and yet he could not fathom why Paul made this little phrase "*iustitia dei*" the centerpiece of the whole letter and the content of the Gospel itself. Luther assumed what the church had taught him was true, that God's justice was the *law*. He assumed that law was the substance of God, and the goal in life was to restore lost fellowship with God by loving this righteousness above all things in heaven or earth. He knew the legal scheme and was ready for the challenge, but something about that phrase *iustitia dei* (Romans 1:17) bothered him. It seemed like an accusation to him, not an affirmation of his religious efforts.

As a good scholar, he set the problem aside for the moment, assuming the fault was his ignorance rather than the church's teaching. He went to the other places in Scripture that speak prominently about God's righteousness like the Psalms, Galatians, and Hebrews before returning to tackle the Himalaya of Romans 1:17. Paul had not coined the term *iustitia dei*; the phrase wound like a scarlet thread throughout Scripture, but was especially prominent in the Psalms as the foundation for the prayers of deliverance or lament: "In thee, O LORD, do I put my trust; let me never be ashamed; *deliver me in thy righteousness*" (Psalm 31:1 translation altered). Isaiah, Ezekiel, Jeremiah, and all the prophets followed suit: "but with righteousness he shall judge the poor, and decide with equity for the meek of the earth . . ." (Isaiah 11:4 NRS). To call upon God's righteousness was to hope for life in the midst of death.

Luther realized that the bible presented a *sufferer's* version of justice quite different than Aristotle's cool, philosophical definition of "giving each his due." With this in mind Luther returned to Paul, who seemed to want to communicate something about this *iustitia dei* which unnerved Luther. Almost all interpreters agreed that God's justice was law, and the law was God's will by which he punished the wicked and preserved the righteous—but that required love of God's *wrath*. Perhaps loving wrath is possible in some abstract sense, like people who attempt to embrace their deaths, but for Luther, when the wrath poured out on him it was not a desirable goal toward which he was drawn by love. So he continued his recollection, "I had conceived a burning desire to understand what Paul meant in his Letter to the Romans, but thus far there stood in my way, not the cold blood around my heart, but that *one word* which is in Chapter 1: 'The *righteousness of God is revealed in it.*'"

Somehow, everything had come down to this one letter, one sentence, and even one word: *iustitia dei*. Luther is so often misunderstood here that it bears clarification. His intense concentration on the phrase was not a result of psychological guilt. He was not, as the great misunderstanding of the twentieth century has it, suffering from "the introspective consciousness" of Western Christianity produced by the Roman Church's preoccupation with penance.[3] What stood in Luther's way was not his *heart*; he was not a cold man unable to love, nor was he guilt-ridden. The trouble was not an inner *feeling*, it was a *word* in the text of Scripture, and a single word at that: "I hated that word, 'justice of God.'"

How did he come to hate a word, especially one as important as God's justice? That phrase was decidedly external to him, read on the page of Scripture and regularly chanted by him in the

Psalms in the daily office. Such words in Scripture are what Paul calls "letter" that kills (2 Corinthians 3). Letters like this are not scribbling or symbols. They do not stand in for some other greater things like thoughts, ideas, concepts, or even substances. The letters of Scripture, unlike human concepts, are very worldly means used by the Holy Spirit to communicate to creatures or get through to them. Scripture is the way God publishes his will and the words have a way of going to work on people like Luther. Now, it is true that the external letters *iustitia dei* produced a feeling in him but it was the very opposite of a "cold heart." It did not produce guilt, it produced hatred. He knew that the psalmists, who were in the midst of suffering and death, used God's righteousness as the name in which to trust and by which to plead for help. For them, God's righteousness produced hope, not hate. Luther was *in extremis* about this because something in that word was prohibiting him from true lament. He could not approach the one visiting the suffering upon him since hatred seeks separation. Yet even this feeling of hatred in Luther did not produce any introspection in him; he was led by the words to something decidedly outside, which until that very moment was an unquestioned assumption about God's justice. "I hated that word, *iustitia dei*, which by the use and custom of all my teachers, I had been taught to understand *philosophically* . . ."

Luther had been the victim of a legal framework—a schema or paradigm—that was assumed by all his teachers as "custom" and passed on as if its presuppositions were the same as Paul's. The scheme understood justification philosophically, which meant "formal or active justice, as they call it, that is, that justice by which God is just and by which he punishes sinners and the unjust." Philosophy provided this definition, and no one sang its praise better than Aristotle, "Neither the evening star nor the morning star is more beautiful than righteousness." Righteousness was the discipline of noble virtue, the goal toward which humans aspire for happiness. To be right is to do right. To do right is to enjoy one's own possessions; to be unjust is to rob the possessions of others.[4] This philosophical definition is called "distributive" justice where balance accounts are kept in the matter of who owns what, what belongs to each, and so whenever there is a controversy a judge decides "justice" on the basis of possession or "ownership." This often worked in solving disputes between people, but when God was put into this framework, he was set up as the final judge who sees to it that in the end all get exactly what they deserve using the law as the means of restoring equity—and Christ was that divine judge. But what exactly is owed God? Everything! Our very possession of life has robbed him, and the conclusion is that God's righteousness is none other than his wrath and destruction of such robbers.[5] How can a sinner survive this conjunction of *iustitia dei* with law, judgment, and God's eternal wrath? Luther hated the word *God's justice* because it was law, and by that law Luther himself was condemned along with the whole world—although he was blameless according to that same law. He had done what it asked of him, right up to the point of concluding that the legal scheme simply agreed that God was right even in destroying a righteous man, as had happened with Job, Paul, and the rest of the Bible's subjects. How do you love the law when it means loving God's wrath, not in general, but against your own self?

When Luther came upon this phrase in Scripture, God's righteousness was assumed to be God's way of judging the world, and the standard of judgment was the law. Psalm 119:142 seemed to confirm this: "Thy righteousness is an everlasting righteousness, and thy law is the truth." Luther was quite willing to participate in such a divine plan since, like Paul, he knew he was blameless. Where the law taught to reach higher to God's goodness, he reached higher. Where it taught that he ought to reach lower, to be humble, he did. Luther used a system that originated with Augustine that recognized two kinds of righteousness, divine and human, each of which worked together seamlessly as two parts completing a whole. Luther summarized the plot of this drama in his first lecture on Psalm 71: "And Thy righteousness, O God, even to the highest." There he taught that, "the righteousness of God reaches up to the heavens of heavens and causes us to reach. It is righteousness even to the highest, namely, of reaching the highest."[6] This is a simple and powerful, Platonic idea. It says God is our goal. Life is a journey of love's desire upward. If you did not know God's goodness, how could you aspire to do it? God's righteousness is his goodness, and pure goodness *attracts* the less good to aspire to the higher. Righteousness is a ladder to God, and

God is the ultimate goal, the highest good. God's righteousness "to the highest" in the Psalm seemed to fit in a perfect, Platonic fashion.

Augustine assumed that the power that moves upward toward God is none other than desire, and like any source of power, it is a dangerous thing in the wrong hands. Desire is the love the Greeks called *eros*, and is rightly connected in English to eroticism. He then went a step further, linking erotic desire, *libido* or *cupiditas* to Paul's use of coveting in Romans 7 in order to illustrate that sin somehow remains after baptism. That meant that desire was a double-edged sword. It was the way to bliss and also the temptation to perdition. When used rightly it directed a soul to God, but when desire was disordered (when the creature is loved for itself and God is used as an instrument to procure that creature), perversion results. A perverted will chooses badly by putting itself at the center so that even God is used as an end for the sake of the self. The self sets itself in the place of God, becoming a law unto itself (autonomous). In the end, the evidence of a defective use of the will was that one actually *hated* God instead of desiring Him above all others. Luther did not expect it of himself, but that is where he ended up: "I hated God." He was a pervert.

Contemptum Dei and Odium Sui

There was a theory that accompanied Augustine's system that said the cause of the illness of hatred of God (*contemptum dei*) was excessive love of self (*amor sui*), and naturally the remedy was the reverse—hatred of the self (*odium sui*). With this, human righteousness entered the picture. Unlike *God's* righteousness, the human form does not reach higher, "it reaches down to the lowest." Initially it seems strange, but paradoxically the way to reach up to God was by first reaching down—humbling one's self, following Christ's own example. This was taken to be the "baptism" of Plato and Aristotle, but Luther soon found that this theory could not escape philosophy's monovision.

How does one reach down? Pride destroyed the attempt to reach up, and so its opposite, humility, was deemed the counterintuitive path to true elevation because it chastened disordered

"s. u as "misplaced desire"

desires, while keeping the motor of desire alive in order to ascend to God. What is humility? Monasticism's ascetic life sought pity from the eternal judge (Christ) by anticipating his guilty verdict before it becomes official (and final), and nothing accepted the guilty verdict like hatred of the self. Yet something was awry, since Luther knew that his *odium sui* was pure: "But I, blameless monk that I was . . ." As much as he had come to hate God, he hated himself even more, and still no resolution came of it. Luther's disease had progressed from hatred of the word *iustitia dei* to hatred of God himself, but the normal treatment failed.

Luther then made his famous confession: "blameless monk that I was, I felt that before God I was a sinner with an extremely troubled conscience." This was not guilt ("blameless"), but something worse. Luther was not failing the system; the system was failing him. The problem was not failure to fulfill the law, but law did not produce love of God, it produced uncertainty. So Luther concluded, "I couldn't be certain that the just God was appeased by my satisfaction."

The church failed him because it caused him to put faith in his *satisfaction* of the law (his self-hatred). Luther presented humility in imitation of Christ, complete with self-hatred and pursuit of the higher good—what more could God want? Confusing God's justice with law was understandable. Romans 1:17 was followed immediately by the revelation of God's wrath that seemed to undo the Gospel: "For the wrath of God is being revealed from heaven against all ungodliness and unrighteousness of humans." This made sense in the old system of the law, because righteousness of God was his wrath at sin; God's anger and justice were synonymous. But Luther had to admit that wrath covered even the humble. If God stayed with the scheme all would be well, but then Luther realized that God veered!

If even the humble monks, who used the sacrament of penance and made satisfaction are cursed, what hope is there? Luther said, "I did not love, no rather I hated the *just* God who punishes sinners. In silence, if I did not blaspheme, then certainly I grumbled vehemently and got angry at God." What do you do with a God who will not be bought off with sacrifice? As long as God's anger at sin, his law, is his righteousness then his righteousness is in the process of destroying the whole cosmos. Is the destruction of the cosmos not the very definition of evil? Luther was encountering the hidden God, who worked destruction of the cosmos and did so even above and beyond his own law (the "problem of evil," as it is called today). God's wrath was supra-legal, bigger than it should have been according to the law; it operated outside reason, outside the free will, outside the process of going down in order to go up. When this dawned on Luther he was forced to conclude that God's *will*, the *good*, and *law* were not synonymous, So, Luther lamented, "Isn't it enough that we miserable sinners, lost for all eternity because of original sin, are oppressed by every kind of calamity through the Ten Commandments? Why does God heap sorrow upon sorrow through the Gospel and through the Gospel threaten us with his justice and his wrath?"

What a mess. Luther had come to hate the gospel precisely because it was outside the law. A decade later, when Luther finally took up the pen to respond to Desiderius Erasmus, Luther saw a kindred spirit who was in the process of taking offense at God as he once had. However, Luther had learned that taking offense at the Gospel itself was a terrible spot. What a sorry state when the gospel itself, the electing promise of Christ apart from the law, becomes the enemy for fear of losing God's justice in the form of law. So in his *Preface* Luther gave three escalating complaints. First, that we are all blamed for original sin so that we are without free will, prior to our birth—through no fault of our own. Then, God added insult to injury by piling on the law in the form of the revealed Ten Commandments that shines a light on *actual sin*, as if God's punishment for original sin were not enough. Then to top it off, God "heaped sorrow upon sorrow" by the *Gospel* (Christ's teachings of love). Luther had learned that law was supposed to be God's gracious gift, which made a covenant with Israel. Then Jesus added to Moses the sublime teaching of the Sermon on the Mount: "You have heard that it was said, 'You shall not commit adultery.' But I say to you that everyone who looks at a woman with lust has already committed adultery with her in his heart" (Matthew 5:27–28). Is this the Gospel? No wonder the "gospel" was making Luther angry, since it literally added the demand to change not only external behavior, but one's own heart.

So Luther recalled: "I constantly badgered St. Paul about that spot in Romans 1 and anxiously wanted to know what he meant.

I meditated night and day on those words . . . ." Eleven years after this Luther was to write one of his most powerful descriptions of faith, which he gave as a gift to his Father and a help to Melanchthon and the other Protestors who were presenting the Augsburg Confession to the Roman officials. It was based on Psalm 118, *The Beautiful Confitemini,* "out of my distress I called on the Lord; the Lord answered me and set me free" (Psalm 118:5). By 1530 Luther had been set free because he got a preacher who delivered the promise of forgiveness directly, and at last his faith had something to believe in beside himself and the law. So he comforted others by saying that the "little group of Christian faithful," has "anxiety as its abode." Therefore,

> faith does not despair of the God who sends trouble. Faith does not consider Him angry or an enemy, as the flesh, the world, and the devil strongly suggest. Faith rises above all this and sees God's fatherly heart behind His unfriendly exterior . . . Faith has the courage to call with confidence to Him who smites it and looks at it with such a sour face . . . that is skill above all skills. It is the work of the Holy Spirit alone . . . the self-righteous are ignorant of it . . . let everyone become a falcon and soar above distress.[7]

Ah, to become such a falcon! But this is a meta-skill, beyond human capacity to effect, solely the work of the Holy Spirit. Then Luther recalled how the Spirit's apocalypse finally arrived to him, "until at last, by the mercy of God, I paid attention to their *context.*" But what was that context?

The End of the Legal Context

Before we can understand Paul's context, we must address two false legal contexts taught by the church which Luther called "useless fables." In its older, scholastic form, the issue of Christian righteousness was believed to mirror God's righteousness as works correspond to law. If you were ever going to be right before God you had to be right in relation to the law. The discussion of the article of justification was then preoccupied with human works that precede God's grace and those that must follow it (merits of "congruity" or "condignity"). These scholastics recognized that no person is justified by deeds of the law (Romans 3:20), but they assumed that Paul meant no one was justified by deeds *alone*—grace had to be added. Such theologians could not grasp that God's word of promise all by itself justified the ungodly; they assumed there had to be an ontological change in the being of the Christian that accounts for God's good judgment so that the law remained intact. A word/sign did not have sufficient reality to make this change because God's justice could not forgive without actual fulfillment of law in the person who was then being "made" right.

Super cogatia

The scholastics called this "formal righteousness," which meant that when someone did a good work God accepted it, despite its limits, and on account of that work infused the person's heart with the love called *caritas*. God infused charity by grace, on account of the imperfect merit, and so it became a real quality that attached itself to the heart in the same way that white paint on the wall becomes an actual quality of that wall. What color is the wall? It is white. What makes this man righteous? The quality of love infused in his heart. Luther derided this claim once he properly considered the context of Paul's words, "they cannot climb any higher in their cogitations," so that "nothing is more intolerable to them than to be told that this quality that informs the heart as whiteness does a wall is not righteousness."[8] The sophists, as Luther called them, tried to assure people that grace meant God would legally count any love applied to the soul for inadequate merits as "formally righteous." In other words, on the last judgment day, such Christians would get off on a technicality. Still, it was God's *techne*, (making) and so even though the wall was old and decrepit, it had a fresh coat of paint and that was sufficient. God would not count anyone as righteous without love in the heart—even if it had to be infused into a sick heart by grace. Luther finally called this "the opinion of the sophists—and of the best among them at that." The conclusion: love makes a person righteous, not faith.

There was another group of scholastics called "Nominalists" who sprang up in partial opposition to this teaching. They had a new theory both of words and law because they recognized the problem with the first argument, but they simply made

44

everything worse. Luther's assessment was terse: "Others are not even that good, such as Scotus and Occam." They agreed that no one could be made righteous unless they had love in the heart, but that it was not necessary to get that love artificially from God's grace, as an addition or loan from God, since then righteousness would always depend upon the mere whim of God. Paradoxically the new scholastics took seriously God's freedom (even from law), but then saw to it that that such freedom never really functioned outside the law. Luther summarized Scotus' teaching this way: "If a man can love a creature, a young man love a girl, or a covetous man love money—all of which are a lesser good—he can also love God, who is a greater good."[9] If bad men can love lower things by nature they merely show that good men can love God by nature too.

To avoid simple Pelagianism, the Nominalists had to increase the demand of the law so that in addition to "natural" love given to all creatures, "Christian" love must be added by grace, otherwise there would be no need for Christ or church. So, Luther thought, the church went from bad to worse. Not only must I *love* (as the law of Moses demands), I must now love with the *right intention*. Luther scoffed at this: "It is as though the lady of the house were not content that her cook had prepared the food very well but scolded her for not wearing precious garments and adorning herself with a gold crown while she prepared the food." Lutherans who later thought they heard the gospel in Kant should take note, since Lutheranism is not merely considering the motive of a good work.

The spiral downward into legal chaos landed Luther in the opposite place than scholasticism intended: Luther had tried to cook by the book, and then put on an apron and gold crown while cooking, but not only did he fail to love God as the greatest good, he hated him for God was simply law, a cruel tyrant who by grace always demands just a little bit more: "be ye perfect as I am perfect."

God's Justice is by Faith (Habakkuk's Oracle)

Despite his troublesome synthesis of sin, grace, law, and especially his theory of words as mere signs, Augustine helped Luther overcome the first hurdle in the legal framework of Romans 1:17. Even if all the other interpreters of Scripture missed Paul's point, Augustine recognized that *iustitia dei* was not paired by Paul with *law* and *wrath* (as Luther had been taught by his church), but rather with *grace* and *faith*. Luther then took this one step further by using Paul's letter as his introduction to the Old Testament that provided the two important contexts for *iustitia dei*, one the "close" context of the sentence in Romans 1:17 that sets God's righteousness together with faith in the oracle of Habakkuk 2:4; the other was the broad context that appears in Paul's argument in Romans 3 where *iustitia dei* (God's justice) was put together with *deum justificare* (justification of God) in Psalm 51. God's justice is in the justification of God—by sinners no less. Furthermore, Luther found that God is not justified abstractly by *speculation* into his inner substance, but *verbally*—concretely in an external word delivered by a preacher. These two contexts free God's justice from the law alone and make the gospel something completely different than the law.

How did Habakkuk set Luther free? Luther recalled that he first took *iustitia dei* 'abstractly'—that is as a universal law (*lex aeterna*). His framework for the simple phrase righteousness of God was a legal one where God lays out his will in the form of ideal, abstract commands. If free wills were then moved to do what God commanded, they would become just in the same way that God is just. Plato's old rule—like likes like—fit this abstract sense of justice perfectly, but it could not give certainty. The law can provide an abstract shape for your aspiring life by telling you what must be done, but it never quite reveals when this has been accomplished. There is no "beep" when the cooking is done. Meanwhile equating God's justice with law makes God abstract, distant, impersonal, or "totally other," as the anagogists (dialectical theologians) of the twentieth century like Bultmann, Gogarten and Barth liked to say.

Then Luther attended to Paul's context for *iustitia dei* that was categorically concrete. Instead of an *ideal*, Paul gave a *promise* in the form of one Old Testament oracle. It began to dawn on Luther that the phrase "God's justice" was found especially in the Psalms and prophets where it took not the form of a command, but served as the ground for the most aggressive laments of the suffering and

Scholastics took this up again

dying who demanded immediate redemption: "Deliver me, in thy righteousness!" (Psalm 31:1). God's righteousness was not a goal to aim at, but the concrete, relational ground on which to plead to our Creator. This is like a child who pleads to her father: "But you are my father, whom else my I turn to?" "God's justice" as used in Scripture did not function like a law; it functions like a promise of mercy, and a promise comes from a father's kindly heart. Paul preached a simple sermon to the Romans in the form of the Oracle of Habakkuk 2:4: "the one who is righteous by faith shall live." Once Luther saw that it was *fides* (faith) that was joined to *iustitia dei*, and not a work of the law, then the old spell was broken. Even a thing as holy as God's law would eventually have to give way to "Christ who makes promises." Only then could he summarize this teaching: "where they put love, we put faith."[10]

Habakkuk's oracle has two claims: one is that righteousness is paired with faith—not law ("the one who is righteous by faith"), and the second is "shall live," which makes the oracle a promise—apart from any law.[11] Now if that promise were based on the law then it would apply only to certain Jews who, by trusting the law in Habakkuk's day would escape the menace of Babylonian captivity, but because faith has a different object from the very beginning (Christ himself and alone), the "shall live" applies to all those who trust him, and life is now a new creation ruled by Christ without the law. Law and Christ are not the same, which was of course a fearful shock to Paul—before it became the Gospel to him.

For Paul to claim that the promise is Christ seems impossibly "Christian" to modern historians of religion. But Habakkuk would be the first to tell you he is not the source of the oracle, and though it always comes as a surprise, especially for those who are legally righteous, all God's promises have their "yes," in Christ (2 Corinthians 1:20) without any law. Paul takes the oracle away from any who would interpret it according to law's righteousness (including himself before he came to faith). We know that the Qumran community interpreted this by the law when it added, "because of their suffering and because of their faith *in the Teacher of Righteousness*" (QpHab 8:1:31). But Paul could hardly ignore Christ once he had been apocalypsed in a new Aeon that lived without any legal framework. Even the Septuagint version made

47

a famous alteration that would have been available to Paul if he had wanted it, "the just will live by my [God's] faith." Perhaps the old, Greek translators sensed the problem and wanted to make sure that *God's* faithfulness was indeed the promise given by Habakkuk, and not human faith as some type of work. They took faith to be God's own instead of a reference to a human virtue. But Paul knew that even making faith into God's own faithfulness provided no escape from the legal scheme, and so he removed the pronoun belonging to faith altogether, and freed the oracle of Habakkuk to be heard in the context of Christ's doctrine of justification—not the other way around. Habakkuk's deliverance of God's promise belongs entirely to the ones who are righteous by faith alone. Faith that is in Christ is the only kind that finally escapes putting trust in the law. Faith, it is promised, *shall live*.

Luther discovered that once you break out of the legal framework it is finally possible to hear an unthwartable promise from God, such as "he who believes and is baptized *shall live*" (Mark 16:16). It would not take long before he returned to penance, and there recognize that the purpose of the sacrament was not the law's satisfaction, but the bestowing of a promise. Paul's sermon is not synthetic—it is not adding a promise to the legal system. Faith is polemical. It breaks with the legal framework as the proper context for interpretation, which means that faith is not moral; it does not fit with works; it cannot be assumed under the law, and needs no love to fulfill it.

Of course that was a shock to the blameless monk, Luther. Later, we will take up the proper relationship between faith and love, but never in the doctrine of justification itself, for in laying out how we are justified, love must be neither seen nor heard. The polemical nature of faith alone does not immediately strike one in Romans 1:17, since the remainder of Paul's letter is the polemic. However, it is unmistakable that in the Galatians churches, where Habakkuk's Oracle first arose in Paul's preaching, *iustitia dei* is a fighting word.[12] There Paul purposefully set the two basic words from Scripture in direct opposition: "The one who is righteous by faith shall live," and, "The one who does the commands will live in them" (Leviticus 18:5 translation altered). The law can even appear in the form of a promise, as there in Leviticus, so that it suited Paul's argument exactly. Its type of promise depends upon something abstract, ideal, and potential; it promises life, but with a condition that the things demanded are actually done.

Now if Paul had left things there we would have a great problem. Habakkuk 2:4 and Leviticus 18:5 are saying opposite things—yet they are both in Scripture. We would have two words at war in Scripture that cannot be resolved or synthesized into a greater whole. One would appear to be forced to make a choice between these two words or to externally divide up the Scripture and God as Marcion once did in a simple dualism. But the matter is not left with a dualism for the free will to make its choice. In Galatians Paul added another word from Scripture: "Cursed is everyone who is hanged upon a tree!" (Deuteronomy 21:23). Where do you suppose we would all end up if these promises were left to us to activate? Neither the law nor the promise of faith can be grasped rightly apart from telling the story of Jesus Christ that drives to the cross. Justification is not an abstract doctrine, as it would certainly be without the story of Christ's crucifixion. The law, doing its appointed job of accusing sinners, was found one day to have laid its curse on Christ because he was hanged upon a tree. This was law's end; but instead of being the end of humanity's story, Lutheran theology begins at this point: "The law of God, the most salutary doctrine of life, cannot advance humans on their way to righteousness, but rather hinders them."[13] The law is the most salutary doctrine of life! Leviticus 18:5 could not be truer; nevertheless, this law does not advance humans to their righteousness, contrary to every expectation of what Melanchthon called the *opinio legis* (the legal scheme) which cries out: "If law is a salutary doctrine of life, giving us the proper goal for our desire, then must it not be God's divine path to eternal life?" The cross of Christ is the emphatic answer: "No."

But with this teaching the basis of reason and morality itself was overthrown—as Quintilian's dictum shows: "the law cannot be in conflict with itself," and thus the conflict between these two "promises" in Leviticus and Habakkuk is eschatological. Leviticus 18:5, the strong word of *law*, speaks of one life—the created life in which we are all descended from the one man, Adam. When law is taken up it must be taken up whole, and God's wrath at sin extends from Adam to the destruction of this old, evil world. Habakkuk 2:4 with its "weak" word of *faith* speaks of another life

[margin note: "opinion of the law"]

[handwritten margin note: Essence of Law and Gospel]

altogether: two lives, two worlds, two lords, two kinds of right-eousness—and one God who wins righteousness in the new world by losing in the old. The whole of Scripture must come into play in order to have this revealed; specifically everything in life and Scripture must be seen to converge on Christ's death on the cross.

Sola fide, gratis, passiva

Thus when Paul put together God's righteousness and our righteousness (*iustitia dei* and *iustus ex fide*) he did so not by law, but by faith—and thereby delivered the power of Romans 1:17. The righteousness by faith stands (now we have our key) *alone*, apart from any addition or synthesis with the law. The *alone* is not the reduction of human contribution to the smallest particle (faith as a very small work); *alone* is the eschatological proviso that the new life in Christ shall be lived without any law—not a renewed law, not a revised law, not a law at all. As long as God's righteousness was paired with the law, Luther hated it because it was cold, abstract, demanding and, in the end, disregarded works anyway and simply elected apart from the law—as if God were merely playing with us. This made God capricious, irrational, and unfaithful to his own system, "I had formerly hated the expression 'iustitia dei' . . ." Then the apocalypse: "I now began to regard it as my dearest and most comforting word, so that this expression of Paul's became to me in very truth the gate to paradise." Faith, not law, was God's purpose and with that, everything turned around. Luther's "goal" had found him. Life ceased being a pilgrimage, reaching higher, and became God's movement to bestow his favor upon sinners without regard to the law. Lutheran theology often attempts to express itself through this *sola*:

> Thus we must learn to distinguish all laws, even those of God, and all works from faith and from Christ, if we are to define Christ accurately. Christ is not the Law, and therefore He is not a taskmaster for the Law and for works; but He is the Lamb of God, who takes away the sin of the world (John 1:29). This is grasped by faith alone, not by

love, which nevertheless must follow faith as a kind of gratitude . . . . Victory over sin and death does not come by the works of the Law or by our will; therefore it comes by Jesus Christ alone. Here we are perfectly willing to have ourselves called 'solafideists' by our opponents, who do not understand anything of Paul's argument.[14]

Modern attempts to reach agreement on justification between Lutherans and Rome have often turned on the *sola*, which Roman theology is pleased to put with grace, but not with faith. The reason should now be clear, since *sola gratia* (grace alone) is able to keep the law as God's justice, where faith banishes law. However, the *sola* cannot by itself secure the Lutheran teaching on justification.

The first definition of anything is negative: Faith is—not the law. But faith also has a positive description: "I began to understand that in this verse the righteousness of God is that by which the righteous person lives by a gift of God, that is by faith." A gift (*donum, gratis*) is the opposite of a command. Because God gives it, this gift is also the opposite of a sacrifice. But what is the content of the gift? It is not the transference of owned substance and possessed property. The gift is God's essence which is not there to be sought out, imitated or even participated in, but something which God bestows. God does not sit waiting to see if you will find him. God is in essence the Justifying God who does not wait for repentance or merit, but takes the bull by the horns and makes the unjust just by an authored act of forgiveness that creates out of nothing. God is creator, and the gift of God himself is to become a new creation. Justification IS creation.

Justification by faith alone replaces substance logic (who owns what) with relational and eschatological logic (how God creates out of nothing). God's justice is not what he owns and what we must strive for, but it is *whose* we are, or the category of "belonging." At this point Luther could open up the nature of the genitive in the phrase *iustitia dei*, and it is this grammatical discovery which he used as the marker of his breakthrough. A genitive phrase like *iustitia dei* can be objective (referring to what God possesses,) or subjective (referring to what he gives, called the "genitive of the author"). Better even than the word "give," this genitive is what

[handwritten marginal note: Contra theology with strong scholasticism, Anselm, Calvin, Barth]

51

the author *creates out of nothing.* The first way of taking the genitive made God passive, a goal to reach, and humans were the active ones seeking to find this God. Instead, Luther learned to make the sacramental reversal with the authored sense. Justification's movement is the opposite of Thomas Aquinas' definition of justification as "a certain motion of man." It is God's movement to the static human, and the source of God's movement is decidedly not desire or attraction (love). God does not pursue that which he finds lovely, but that which is unrighteous, unlovely, the direct and determined opponent of God. God loves the unlovely by bestowing faith where there was none.

It would be better if we translated *iustitia dei,* not as "the righteousness of God," but as "the righteousness *from* God," as Paul's letter to the Philippians clearly does: "not having a righteousness of my own, based on law, but that which is through faith in Christ, the righteousness from God that depends on faith" (Phil. 3:9). God gives! Paul Tillich used this to say that God is a verb, not a noun. A new group of Lutherans have set their flag here in attesting to God's gift of grace as the central matter in Luther theology, but a caution must immediately be added.[15] The simple fact that God *gives* is not what made the Lutheran doctrine of justification. As Ernst Käsemann observed, everyone agrees today that God's justice is an authored genitive concerning what God gives, but trouble resurfaces when God's gift is taken back into the law to say that God's gift is *love,* and this love is to have one's desires ordered properly (according to the law). God's gift is not ordering our loves properly; it is faith. It is not the fulfillment of desire, but desire's end. The righteousness from God creates faith where love has gone after idols.

Augustine

The next step then opened for Luther. "I began to understand that this verse means the justice of God is revealed through the Gospel, but it is a *passive* justice." Augustine was right. There are two kinds of righteousness, one active and the other passive, but they do not function as the two parts of a whole (humility first, and then reaching higher to love God above all). They are antitheses—active righteousness (which is the law requiring you to do something) and passive righteousness (God's creation) that will never be resolved into a higher synthesis. Luther was effulgent:

The Sermon

Here I felt that I was altogether born anew and had
entered paradise itself through open gates. There a totally
other face of the entire Scriptures showed itself to me.
Thereupon I ran through the Scriptures from memory.
I also found in other terms an analogy, as the *work of
God—that is, what God works in us*, the power of God, that
which makes us powerful, the wisdom of God, that which
makes us wise . . . . And I extolled my sweetest word
[*iustitia dei*] with a love as great as the hatred with which
I had before hated the word righteousness of God.

God gives, and what God gives is no less than his own self. "God's
self-giving" has been an important point in modern Lutheran
theology. God does not operate simply as a great "Cause" with
many little effects. The post office also gives, but what it gives is
this or that letter or package, not itself. What God gives is not
merely various gifts, as if these expressed some affection, or
stood as signs of his care as in a birthday card. God gives not just
"things," or "effects," but his own self. When Adam and Eve ate
the good fruit from the garden, they consumed not just an object
of creation, but God himself. When God gives, he gives sacramen-
tally, not figuratively; he does not give signs of his affection, he
gives—Him.

Who then is the "self" that God gives? He is not the law—not
even the glorious outpouring of love that inspires others to love—
God's self giving is his Son, Jesus Christ, so that God's essence is
verbal, sacramental, and Christological: "God was in Christ reconciling the world to himself" (2 Corinthians 5). When Christ is
bestowed there is an "effect" in humans, but it is too much, too
eschatological, to be captured by that term. This gift puts to death
the passive receiver as she was, and raises a new creature from the
dead. His giving effects the most drastic exchange possible so that
Christ's life becomes mine, and mine becomes his. This exchange
Luther called "imputation."

Later I read Augustine's *The Spirit and the Letter* where
contrary to hope I found that he, too, interpreted God's
righteousness in a similar way, as the righteousness with

which God clothes us when he justifies us. Although this was heretofore said imperfectly and he did not explain all things concerning imputation clearly, it nevertheless was pleasing that God's righteousness by which we are justified was taught.

Augustine showed Paul's meaning to Luther, that God's justice was faith, but an imperfection remained because Augustine thought Christians in themselves became righteous, and would be judged so by the law at the end. Luther would remove this last shackle of law.

Deum Justificare (David's Psalm 51)

There was a wider context for Romans 1:17 which kept Luther from making faith into a virtue, or mere diminutive work of the will. That broader context takes its critical turn in the third chapter of the letter where Paul addressed the question, If the law does not make anyone righteous, what advantage has the Jew? Answer: Much in every way, since Jews have words from God; Gentiles have only an unpreached God. What Luther discovered next was that faith is created *ex nihilo* (out of nothing) by *words*. God's own justice becomes passive because God wants to be justified *in his words.* With this discovery, *iustitia dei* was joined with a second crucial Scripture: "That Thou mayest be justified in thy words" (Psalm 51:4 and Romans 3:4 translation altered). It is no coincidence that this Psalm is David's great psalm of repentance and forgiveness, since he learned that justification depended entirely upon getting a preacher like Nathan who could give a divine promise.

If the law was never given to make anyone righteous, what advantage do Jews have being chosen by God? Jews have a preacher, many preachers in fact, and so they have been given God's words. The Gentiles had none, until Paul—Apostle—and thus before the preacher arrived they were reduced to investigating a fallen creation for clues as to who their hidden God was (Paul found them in Athens worshipping a statue that said, "To the unknown God"). Usually God is known by his mighty acts of the *past* so that even Gentiles could learn something of God this way. The words that gave Jews an advantage in life were promises by which God could be known in terms of the *future*—as faithful or unfaithful to a promise. When one is able to trust God by means of a word one speaks very differently to him—in the way husband and wife speak to one another as opposed to the way an advertisement addresses an unknown client. The stories of Abraham, Jacob, Joseph, and Moses hinge on God making a promise from which a surprising, dynamic relation is built. Gentiles had no basis for trusting God; they were left with a hidden God of fate or fortune, and no way to justify what this divinity did. They could only get used to the pitfalls of fortune and settle for the lugubrious business of reconciling human will with its fate. Yet, once the preacher Paul arrived, God gave even the worst of sinners a promise of the forgiveness of sin. Once faith has a promise, it clings to it for its life because it gives an "advantage" unlike anything else in the world—it allows one to turn to God, the justifier (*iustitia dei*), and justify him (*deum justificare*). This is an astounding reversal. It calls God "right" for making a sinner "right" merely by the declaration of the forgiveness of sin. At the same time this allows one to demand that God be righteous, which is the basis for lament in the Psalms.

God *is* just in his inner being, and so God is always and ever God whether someone believes in him or not; lack of faith does not reduce God's righteousness even an iota. But now, Paul says, even among Gentile sinners from birth, God wants to *become* just—and in a mere word! God who is above time and space now enters the world with a steely determination. Theology suddenly ceased being what philosophy thought—the endeavor to see the unchanging, eternal God above history and beyond death, through the nature of things. History, with all its accidental twists and turns, suddenly came to its proper place in the sinner's justification of God: *deum iustificare*. Trusting a promise from God is the justification God seeks for himself, and he intends upon getting this justification come hell or high water so that stories of God's arrival to sinners make the great tales of Scripture (Abraham, David, Mary) and our own lives like Augustine's *Confessions*.

This realization was rarely grasped even by Lutherans, until it reentered in response to eighteenth century Deism's unhistorical

God and the moral episode of Lutheranism in which Kant (1724–1804) had banished God from history for the purposes of removing faith from predestination and the dicey proposition of getting a preacher. Hegel (1770–1831) was the champion of the return of faith and God to history, by which rational humans went about justifying God in the face of evil. But all that was still a failure to grasp Luther's discovery here. It is not just that God acts in history, enters it, and even suffers the cross of it, or that God is justified by the playing out of history itself, but that God specifically, concretely seeks historical justification in his *words*. It is the fact that preaching is the location of God's justification by sinners that is so mind-boggling—and ultimately freeing. *Iustitia dei* does not seek *deum iustificare* for his own sake. God could not cease being God even if sinners took it upon themselves to convict God of every evil known to humankind, to kill him, and then to declare that "God is dead!" By what or whom does God need justification? Does the pot say to the potter, Why have you made me thus? Nevertheless when a preacher comes with the words of forgiveness God wants the hearers to justify him for that act. That is what *deum justificare* means, to "give God his due." What is due God? Not a sacrifice or a work of law, but trust in his promise alone.

Faith has the power and burden of justifying God, which is the *creatrix divinitatis* (creator of the divine), as Luther said. Luther recognized his discovery of faith was not unlike the Greek myth of Prometheus stealing fire from the gods, "as you believe, so you have him," only in this case God gave it freely, and with full awareness of the devastation it would cause when sinners determined to call God a liar. The masterpiece of theology in which Luther lays out this teaching is his *Large Catechism*, the first commandment. Luther had discovered what made humans human— it was not thought, or will, or even love; it was faith alone. He learned that the heart is not made for itself; it is made to go outside itself and cling to that which speaks to the heart. Humans are therefore "hearing" creatures whose heart is always clinging to some word or other. Unfortunately, words from the preacher are easily drowned out by other voices, and especially imaginary voices of what one sees or feels internally. Faith alone is that which justifies us, but faith is never a virtue or attitude of a person, or some instrument or power which the person possesses. Faith goes outside itself, since faith requires some*thing* to believe in, and that something is God's word as a promise—or else what faith grasps ends up being an accusing law.

Now humans in themselves are sinners, they are makers of idols who snatch the opportunity in the word to make a god over which they can be a god. They use faith to raise themselves over God in his word and defeat him there, which is what the crucifixion of Jesus Christ is. The cross was the act of taking God—who became his incarnate word, Christ, in order to be justified there—and destroying him by ridiculing the promise. Faith as the power to make god is the source of the great shift in "modern" theology to anthropology. Lutherans like Ludwig Feuerbach (1804–1872) are to be blamed for discovering this power of faith from Luther, but they missed his point and used faith as the way to rid themselves of a preacher (which was the Enlightenment's version of freedom). Take away the preacher, and it is true that what Luther says about faith is monstrous; in fact it is none other than the original sin. However, when a person gets a preacher the point is not to justify God outside his words—but in them. It is not to discover the power of faith as the power to doubt, and the power to doubt as the power of critical thinking that can actually make its own God. Faith is not there to glorify itself. Faith is not ever faith in its own faith, which is the fundamental problem with modern theology. Faith goes outside itself and exists in the word of promise that depends—against experience—upon God keeping the promise.

Penance and Forgiveness

In order to justify God in his words one needs a preacher, and for this reason Luther's search for a gracious God centered upon penance and the word of forgiveness. There he discovered that underneath Augustine's synthesis of faith and law lurked a troublesome theory of words that forced one into a philosophical understanding of God's justice. Faith could not be in a word for

Platonism

Augustine because words were merely "signs," so that one had to fly from the sign (*signum*) to the real thing (*res*) that resided elsewhere than in earthly things like bread and wine. Faith flew to the "real thing" by turning inward to the heart, then upward to God. Reality appeared to be in the abstract idea of law as divine love, where mercy was offered under certain restricted conditions—like humility being demonstrably real. This abstraction infected penance with a disease. Both priest and penitent were caught in a web of signs that did not allow the words of forgiveness themselves to be trusted, and so a legal "reality" called "satisfaction" had to be substituted for the words. How does one know if true repentance is present? Look to the *res* of a penal satisfaction. But God does not want to be justified in the payment of penalty; he wants to be justified in the words his preacher gives. Because God's justice was joined to faith instead of law, an entirely new face of penance appeared to Luther. In penance God is giving his own self, Jesus Christ, who is the justifier that has full power to forgive (as only God can), and at the same time, God has arrived to the thing that needs forgiving in a sacramental reversal of the legal scheme, having become sin itself for us. All of this is done by means of one little, earthly thing—a simple preached word in the form of a *promise*. This word is received not by any work or attitude of a person, but in the perfectly passive anti-work, anti-attitude, called faith.

Where did Luther finally find a gracious God? He found God hiding in the word of promise delivered by a preacher in the real word of penance: *Te absolvo!* I forgive you. That word is not a sign pointing somewhere else for its truth, but is the power of the Holy Spirit to create out of nothing. Luther had discovered what he called *promissio*, by which God creates a new person in a new world with faith that hears the promise *for me*—and trusts it. In doing so the believer justifies God in his words and has a gracious God. So Luther taught in his Small Catechism that "where there is forgiveness of sin, there is also life (now) and salvation (eternal life)."

Faith and *words* (promise) had coalesced at Romans 1:17. As Luther said in his *Preface*, "I extolled my sweetest word with a love as great as the hatred with which I had before hated the word 'righteousness of God.' Thus that place in Paul was for me truly the gate to paradise."

Protestant Failure

Among Protestants, it has been a common mistake to forget the preached word (*deum justificare*) and have faith become an act of self-reflection. The question then becomes "Do I have faith?" with no recognition of what it means to go outside the self and cling to a promise. There has been a long history of revisionism that treats words as husks of wheat and the kernel as some religious idea that always ends with the same phenomenon. Let us consider two illustrations of the problem in Lutheran theology.

Albrecht Ritschl (1822–1889) summed up the work of theology, not only for his own nineteenth century (dominated by Schleiermacher), but also the preceding eighteenth century (dominated by Kant) when he defined the chief article of justification as "active trust in God as the highest good."[16] He meant "active" because faith combines feeling, knowing, and willing of the subject (ridding himself of passive justice). "Trust" was the basic teleological reorientation of the human (which the previous Lutheran theology had discarded). "In God," meant the teleological life requires God in the form of the highest of goals (which is none other than love). Ritschl thus unlinked justification specifically from the preached word and brought it back under the trans-historical law of love, thus negating both of Luther's discoveries in one fell swoop.

Paul Tillich's (1886–1965) revision of justification summarizes the twentieth century of Lutheran theology: "Since 'justification' is a biblical term it cannot be rejected . . . but it should be replaced in the practice of teaching and preaching by the term 'acceptance,' in the sense that we are accepted by God although being unacceptable according to the criteria of the law . . . and that we are asked to accept this acceptance."[17] For Tillich non-acceptance and acceptance remain firmly under the law: "Accepting our acceptance while unacceptable" is faith turned into itself. Modern Lutherans routinely psychologize justification by making faith into an inner (existential) act of "accepting my unacceptability," but for Luther at least, faith does not trust its own power to believe. It takes leave of itself by hearing the promise from the preacher and justifying God for saying it—in contradiction to one's own experience of death (not just unacceptability).

Even the scholastic, orthodox Lutherans of the seventeenth century (against whom these "new Lutherans" were speaking) fell into this problem with technical distinctions they introduced into justification like two "energies" of faith (passive and active) one receiving Christ's merit, the other the power to love. These sturdy theologians in the century following Luther fell to the temptation of the great teacher Melanchthon, allowing themselves to be drawn back into the legal scheme in terms of Aristotle's categories of cause and effect. Whether one makes faith a cause of justification or an effect of it, the heart of Christ and the preacher's word are removed so that only a carcass remains.[18]

It took Luther's *Smalcald Articles* (prepared for a possible Church council on the Lutheran question, 1537) to give justification the simple form of the story of Christ preached to sinners:

> Here is the first and chief article: That Jesus Christ, our
> God and Lord, 'was handed over to death for our trespasses
> and was raised for our justification' (Rom 4); and he alone
> is 'the Lamb of God, who takes away the sin of the world'
> (John 1); and 'the Lord has laid on him the iniquity of us
> all' (Is 53); furthermore, 'All have sinned,' and 'they are
> now justified without merit by his grace, through the
> redemption that is in Christ Jesus . . . by his blood'
> (Rom 3). Now because this must be believed and may not
> be obtained or grasped otherwise with any work, law, or
> merit, it is clear and certain that this faith alone justifies us,
> as St. Paul says in Romans 3.

In Christ's story faith and word are properly fit. Faith alone justifies; faith comes by hearing the promise of Christ: "I forgive you." But Luther concluded his Latin Preface with a haunting reminder: "I was all alone."

Chapter 3

Life Without a Preacher

Romans 1:18–3:20

> *Theirs was a false, misleading dream,*
> *Who thought God's law was given,*
> *That sinners might themselves redeem,*
> *And by their works gain heaven.*
> *The Law is but a mirror bright,*
> *To bring the inbred sin to light,*
> *That lurks within our nature.*
>
> Paul Speratus, *Salvation Unto Us Has Come*

The Foolishness of Preaching

Paul wrote his letter to the Romans as a preparation for the preaching he intended to deliver upon arrival in the city—God willing. It is not a collection of doctrines (*corpus doctrinae*), but practice in making the distinction between law and gospel. It circles relentlessly around the two *loci* (commonplaces) of the preacher's trade, which are resistance to and reception of the gospel—wrath and promise. Systematically put, once he revealed the content of his preaching (Romans 1:17), only then did he take up the *a priori* of preaching (Romans 1:18). Paul had never been to Rome when he wrote his letter, yet he knew that in every church true preaching is followed willy-nilly by infiltrating preachers who refuse to give only the gospel (1 Timothy 6:3). So Paul began correcting, clarifying and simplifying before his arrival to clear the deck so that when he gave them forgiveness of sin there would not be the stock attempts for an addition, subtraction, or confusion of the law and gospel: Is that all there is? Can it be so simple? Who will try to be good? Paul knew that were he merely attempting to persuade free wills of his opinion he would despair, but he also knew the only preparation for hearing the gospel is that there be real sinners and a preacher sent by the Holy Spirit. As a result, there are no prolegomena to Lutheran theology except the *foolishness* of preaching.

Preaching is foolish when it opposes the basic presupposition of morality: "ought" implies "can." It is foolish when God elects sinners merely by a preached word so that eternal fate—predestination—depends upon whether you have got a preacher or not (which is surely the strangest accident of history). But what can be more foolish than to preach to bound wills that cannot hear? Scripture repeatedly publishes this strange fact: "But I am like the deaf, I do not hear; like the mute, who cannot speak" (Psalm 38:13 NRS). In the scheme of the law, preaching to bound wills is illogical and self-defeating. Yet preaching operates beyond the scheme of the law saying ironic things: "Hear, you deaf!" (Isaiah 42:18), and "Hear this, O foolish and senseless people, who have eyes, but do not see, who have ears, but do not hear" (Jeremiah 5:21). Paul preached just as these prophets, but as the Apostle to the Gentiles he spread his impossible, "Hear you deaf," over the whole cosmos. Luther likened Paul to the Nile that inundates all Egypt with a flood because Paul preached *after* the apocalypse of the dreaded last judgment and is aware that his hearers are already dead before God. The preaching is foolishness because it is declared to deaf people, and you cannot be deafer than dead.

Teaching God's Wrath

When Paul prepared to preach he knew a universal truth about his hearers: "There is no fear of God before their eyes" (Romans 3:18). Knowledge of God's wrath does not precede a preacher, it must be taught. Melanchthon defined sin accordingly in the second article of the Augsburg Confession (1530) as "to be without fear and without trust in God . . . ." People are by nature without fear of God, but this is not a wholesome lack. "Natural theology" is what we call the attempt to find some vestige of life not already condemned by God's wrath that can be used to make a case for sparing one's life. The typical defense assumes a tiny spark of the "image of God" that is imagined to remain in "nature" by which a sinner could become good again. The best hope in this way of thinking is a stay of execution that seeks more time to fulfill the law's demands. But Paul teaches God's wrath very differently, by placing "the sweetest word" in Romans 1:17 next to the bitterest word: "For the wrath of God (ὀργὴ Θεοῦ) is being apocalypsed from heaven against all ungodliness and unrighteousness of men, who by their unrighteousness obstruct the truth" (Romans 1:18 translation altered).

The first lesson in teaching God's wrath is that we are not dealing with a pending possibility, but the wrath "is being revealed" (present tense). Paul began with the end so that the *apocalypse now* disabuses sinners of thinking they have more time for amendment of life. Why teach this wrath if it is inevitable and *ex post facto*? Even Jonah preached God's wrath to Nineveh as a warning to repent and turn to the true Lord: "Yet forty days." Paul preached wrath after the fact so that we who are without might in fact gain fear of God, yet he does not use fear as a psychological motivator, as in the legal scheme, but it comes as a deadly shock. Fear induces flight, not movement toward a goal. Luther calls this learning how to flee the unpreached God. There is a point of connection between Lutheran theology and the strange, negative, irrational, line of mysticism from the likes of John of the Cross and Eckhart, which was absorbed into Lutheran theology through J. Arndt (1555–1621), and especially J. Böhme (1575–1624). Their modern offspring was Rudolf Otto (1869–1937) who, instead of teaching flight from God's wrath (called, "the fury" or "*mysterium tremendum*"), taught God's anger as the point of highest attraction—a *fascination*. So Otto's wildly popular book, *The Idea of the Holy* tried to use God's wrath as an attack on the moralism of Lutheran orthodoxy of the sixteenth century, who taught purely rational doctrines allegorized in terms of the eternal law:

> For the Lutheran school [orthodoxy] has itself not done
> justice to the numinous side of the Christian idea of God.
> By the exclusively moral interpretation it gave to the
> terms, it distorted the meaning of 'holiness' and the

'wrath of God', and already from the time of Johann Gerhardt and onwards Lutheranism was returning to the doctrine of divine ἀπαθεια or passionlessness.

However, it was not apathy they taught; it was wrath proportional to law, and Otto merely transformed God's wrath into the flip side of Kant's morality in the form of the Romantic experience of the *sublime*. For Luther the strange attraction people have to death is not the purpose of publishing God's wrath.[1] Lutherans preach God's wrath not in order to launch a search for the source, but so that one learns to run from this angry God in naked majesty—but where does one run from wrath? Jonah found no escape. Paul takes away every place to run from God—including the law—so that only the preached word of promise remains. People must learn to flee from God—to God; sinners learn to run from the unpreached, absolute, naked God of wrath who hates them, to the preached God clothed in the new word of the Crucified, who is pleased with them. Only in this flight does God change relations from *iustitia dei* (which Luther hated) to *deum justificare* (which gave him his whole new face of Scripture). Once he had learned this, Luther turned Aristotle's search for happiness (*eudaemonism*) on its head. All attraction to God ceased, curiosity, love and the other imaginary motivations were removed, and nothing remained on the last day's judgment—but the foolishness of preaching.

Without a preacher God's wrath is the only theological truth of life, but divine wrath must be revealed, the heavens have to be ripped open, and the apocalypse of wrath actually delivered because it is not directly known or experienced, even though death encircles us. In fact, what makes this divine wrath so awful is that it lies outside human reason and feeling, not because it is never felt or thought, but the truth of wrath is obstructed or suppressed. Freud noticed that even the truth of our own desires is suppressed, and if we cannot stand our own desires, what will we do with death and divine wrath? Yet Paul revealed to the Romans exactly what was first revealed to him. God's wrath is personal (not theoretical or legal); it is zealous beyond any proportional limits of law; it is universal in breadth (since God shows no partiality); it is relentlessly eternal. Most offensive of all, this wrath is hidden so that it must be revealed for what it is, the total destruction of this world with no hope for a change in plans—the apocalypse *now*.

How God could be so revolting in one revelation (1:18) and gracious in the other (1:17) has troubled Christians from the beginning. God must remove faith deposited in wrong places before it can locate the right place, and so God made life without a preacher a sickness unto death, and made himself hate-able. So, Luther taught in his *Small Catechism* that we are to "fear and love God," in a repeated opening line for each commandment. Fear and love do not mix, and so they force either a separation between two gods or a synthesis in the form of two psychological steps in a process of moral transformation (first I must feel sorrow, then I must feel joy). Most theologies prefer the approach of the ancient heresiarch, Marcion, who tried to liberate God from the stain of wrath by removing his name from Romans 1:18 altogether, saying simply, "for wrath is revealed." He assumed that no God worth pursuing could exercise such destruction, even against a faulty creation, and so he proved to be the opposite of a Pauline theologian. The ethical episode of Lutheran theology followed suit, rejecting outright the teaching of God's wrath, and consequently Lutheran theology devolved into one more legal defense of God's inner essence of love. Schleiermacher's (1768–1834) "new Protestantism" could not find a place for Paul's proclamation of wrath in the experience of the church lest Christ and church lose their appeal of love, and Albrecht Ritschl (1822–1889) followed suit, warning Lutherans that preaching God's wrath was merely a failed attempt by Paul to approach the issue of justification from the point of view of humans and their feelings, but, Ritschl argued, this obscured the true essence of God which is love, not wrath.[2] Has something evil befallen you? Don't blame God, he is nothing but love. Theologians routinely make God into an abstract wish for pure goodness in the form of undifferentiated love, and consequently there is no fear of God.

There is every reason to hate God's righteousness apart from faith, and Luther knew it better than any modern atheist. If you cannot grasp hatred of God, you will never fear him, and cannot love him. In fact, the religious attempt to love God through the law has always been disastrous and explains the well-intended theologies of the Middle Ages that Luther called "sophistry" and their practitioners "disciples of Aristotle, the dead, damned heathen." Aquinas (1225–1274) taught that love of God was possible, with plenteous help by grace; Scotus (1264–1308) that even created nature could love God without any help from grace. Their common mistake was to remove fear and the infinite extent of God's wrath beyond law in order to make God a proper object of desire. It was Philip Melanchthon who recognized that the entire system of penance and the preoccupation with the second table of Moses' commandments typical of the Middle Ages (moral casuistry) came from the belief that humans had *capacity for love* of God, thus losing "the chief maladies of human nature: ignorance of God, contempt for God, the absence of the fear of and trust in God and the inability to love God . . . in conflict especially with the first table of the Decalogue"—all because they lost the truth of God's wrath.[3]

Trying to make God lovable and convince sinners "to deal with God as though God and our nature were good friends of each other," created Luther's own problem in the first place.[4] Human nature and God are not friends. When theology attempts to justify God apart from his words a "natural" theology results that replaces the distinction of law and gospel with a synthesis of nature and grace summarized in the scholastic phrase: "grace perfects nature." Instead, Lutheran theology holds that grace *frees* nature precisely from this need or desire for perfection or transcendence simply to *be human*. Luther put this in a formula to contrast Aquinas: "to be human, that is the summa." The "goal" of human nature is not to fulfill desires, but have desire extinguished; in its place is found grateful reception of all things needed for life from the hand of the heavenly Father, or "doxology"—the Amen to God's words-in-things. But before this freedom is unleashed, God's wrath apart from his words must be revealed.

Reason revolts at the very idea of God's wrath, since God's anger cannot be confined to the law, and thus is immoral and unjust. Divine wrath undermines morality, destroys faith in God's law, and (adding fuel to the fire) God intends it that way. God's greatest enemies are his friends who package him and sell him as "the greatest good" and our heart's highest desire. This is why the wrath of God has to be revealed, since suppression of it is deeper than even Freud knew.

Fear of God

Just as wrath is taught, so also its anthropological counterpart, fear, must be taught. Fear concludes with the greatest shock of all: "through the law comes knowledge of sin" (Romans 3:20 NRS). Law belongs with sin, not righteousness, and so the *opinio legis* is burst. The law was never intended to make anyone righteous; to the contrary, it was meant to make sinners truly sinful. So the law is an expression of God's wrath; it certainly is not grace for anyone, including God's own Jews. This is why Luther's *Bondage of the Will* inspired fear and continues to do so, despite Luther's assurance that the book is meant to comfort. Fear engulfed even Melanchthon, who in later life could not stop warning his students against the "stoical madness," of addressing "divine necessity" and the hidden God as Luther did. The generations of Lutheran teachers following Melanchthon, including the likes of G.W. Leibniz a century removed (1646–1716), could not help but offer the same caution (despite a fascination) about Luther's teaching of God's wrath:

> Hardly had I gained some tolerable understanding of Latin writings when I had an opportunity of turning over books in a library. I flitted from book to book . . . I was charmed by the work of Laurentius Valla against Boethius and by that of Luther against Erasmus, although I was well aware that they had need of some mitigation.

Mitigation indeed! He went on to say, "Melanchthon, a man of sound and moderate ideas," curbed the wrath of Luther against Aristotle, and finally in the *Apology*, "allowed a favourable mention of Aristotle and his *Ethics*."[5] How far from Luther (and Paul) this had come is evident in Leibniz' thesis: "It is clear that Jesus Christ, completing what Moses had begun, wished that the Divinity should be the object not only of our fear and veneration but also of our love and devotion . . . God is all order; he always keeps truth of proportions, he makes universal harmony; all beauty is an effusion of his rays."[6]

Against such aesthetic, legal dreaming, Luther simply pointed out the truth of our life without a preacher: "The law in the end is not able to say anything else to you than this: 'You have not fulfilled. You are not able to. Nevertheless you should. Therefore, you are rightly sentenced to eternal death.'"[7] Here is the awful summary of Paul's revelation: You have not! You cannot! You must! Your past and your future have been reduced to a present judgment which no work or regret can change. God requires what no one can do, and executes his wrath because they nevertheless should do it. Paul says, "Why, then, does God find fault? Who can resist his will" (Romans 9:19 NRS)? Luther calls this, "that awful will of the Divine Majesty," and having this will of God revealed is what makes true fear: "And it is not for us to ask why he does so, but to stand in fear of God who both can do and wills to do such things," and further, "Reason thinks she is mocked by an impossible precept, whereas we say that [a person] is warned and roused by it to see his own impotence."[8]

Life without a preacher is life with a silent God whose will is immutable, and who stands on a high mountain, like Zeus on Olympus, hurling thunderbolts called fate, judgment, and death that eclipse the dream of free will:

> Here is a thunderbolt by which free choice is completely
> prostrated and shattered, so that those who want free
> choice asserted must either deny or explain away this
> thunderbolt, or get rid of it by some other means. . . .
> everything that happens . . . happens in fact nonetheless
> necessarily and immutably, if you have regard to the will
> of God.[9]

To be sure, necessity is not the word here—things are worse than "necessity"; they happen because God willed them that way.

Fear that has no end turns into hate and hatred of God makes the human heart a hell. Luther himself had had enough of that in his years as an Augustinian friar, yet one of the students of Philip Melanchthon, Johann Arndt, reproduced this monasticism with certain Lutheran rubrics, and so was dubbed the "prophet of interior Protestantism" by his famous devotee, Albert Schweitzer. Arndt became the spiritual father of the only real movement Lutherans ever produced called "Pietism," whose secret was to cultivate fear as a weapon against the fleshly, lower desires—but to do so, Arndt had to reduce God's wrath to the scale of the legal scheme as mere punishment for disobeying laws. That is not the apocalypse of wrath revealed by Paul. Arndt taught Protestant asceticism to the laity by telling them they had no need of a cloister, but they did need repentance that cultivated the fear of God: "if [becoming a true Christian] is to occur, dear Christian, you must continually live in a childlike, subservient fear of God and not be so free in your mind to do what gives the flesh pleasure."[10] Down through the ages this "Lutheran" way of teaching fear was echoed even in the greatest of Lutheran minds, like Johann Gerhard (1582–1637) in a Christmas sermon: "The angel proclaims: 'You, be not afraid.' So also Christ becomes spiritually born in us as slavery's fear is dispersed, so that contrarily, that child-like, love-enriched fear be in us."[11]

For Luther, fear is not "love-enriched," but must be taught only so that it can be extinguished so that one will flee *from* this God, not *to* him. We are to fear God who has no words (unpreached), and run from him to the place where he has given himself in words—that is to the preacher. Only there do fear and wrath end in Christ incarnate as he gives himself to sinners. Luther learned this strange Christian flight from Paul's argument that God's eternal and immoral wrath (Romans 1:18) ends only where he wants to be found in his words of promise (Romans 3:4).

What is life like before a preacher arrives? Life is filled with voices that are "passing judgment" (Romans 2:1), their words are forensic so that life comes under constant judgment. The judge could be outside one's self like a father telling you to live up to your potential, or a written law that says, "thou shalt not steal." The judge can also be inside, called a conscience, holding itself to a standard of judgment. Life without a preacher is life with a knotted collection of voices that either accuse or excuse, but in either case end up used in the service of self-justification.

Because judgment stands ever at hand, this *forensic* life becomes a search for an escape. When judgment becomes too severe people are driven to elude it. By the time a preacher arrives people have long been on the run from God's judgment, seeking shelter where they can, deep in a rut of some "false, misleading dream" (Speratus), and if you care to listen they will fill your ear with their attempted self-justification. Unfortunately, self-justification never works in the end. Paul teaches that this life has become old, and so is known not by its beginning but by its end in death. The final judgment of all is announced ahead of time according to the Gospel of Jesus Christ (Romans 3:16). The universe ended with a whimper, with every mouth shut up while the whole world stands guilty before God (Romans 3:19). By the time the preacher arrives, the law has not only failed to produce an escape, but has put the last nail in the coffin: "For by the law comes only the knowledge of sin" (Romans 3:20 translation altered).

In the face of God's wrath, two means of escape are attempted. The first uses creation (the typical refuge of the Gentile since it is all they know), and the other uses law, which is the common refuge of the Jew: "For Jews demand signs and Greeks desire wisdom" (1 Cor. 1:22 NRS). Paul therefore proceeds to prosecute God's case against both failures.

Paul's Prosecution of the Ungodly

The initial word from the preacher prosecutes God's case by delivering a curse: "You have no excuse" (Romans 1:20 and 2:1)! There are three levels of accusation, the first, lying nearest the surface, tells us what everyone already knows: God's wrath is against the wicked. (Romans 1:18–32). The second goes deeper by condemning those who judge the wicked by means of the law (Romans 2). The third confirms the "Repugnant Thought" that God says, "You Must!"—precisely so that you cannot. That means that the "law came in to increase the trespass" (Romans 5:20) so that "you have no excuse."

Paul's first accusation is reasonable: God hates the unrighteous: "For the wrath of God is apocalypsed from heaven against all ungodliness and unrighteousness . . ." (Romans 1:19 translation altered). But we ought not to be lulled asleep, since Paul's point is that God's wrath is not a reflex against sin. It is true that there is no excuse for unrighteousness, but wrath is never reduced to retribution (lex talionis). God does not wait in heaven for a sin, then meet it with an apportioned amount of wrath; humans build their court systems that way, but it is not so with God's wrath.

70

Augustine attempted to teach a wrath proportional to the error of sin in hopes of preserving God's law, but Paul did not. When God's wrath is revealed it is too late to sit on the sidelines telling the wicked that, after all, they got exactly what they deserved. When Paul concludes there is "no excuse" for the unrighteous/ungodly he does not mean simply "deserves," he means *no escape*.

God's wrath is apocalyptic, cosmic in scope, under whose bright light unrighteousness and ungodliness are seen for what they are: an anti-God, deicidal mania that attempts annihilation of God by proxy. Curiously, Gentiles would at first appear to have an odd plea since they had no one to give them the law as Moses did to Israel. However, ignorance is no excuse, since indeed even Gentiles without prophets knew what God demanded, "since the creation of the cosmos his invisible things . . . have been known and seen in the things made . . ." (Romans 1:20 translation altered). Gentiles have no loophole because they got no law; indeed creation proves it. Luther often observed that all creatures know three things by their own living—that God exists (so Lutherans do not spend time on proofs of God's existence), that God has a law, and that God will judge everyone by that law. But the crucial information "nature" cannot provide is precisely what this God thinks of you in particular—what his final judgment is concerning you. Paul, the preacher, came to fill in that unknown judgment. Gentiles cannot turn the tables and put God on trial by claiming that his election of the Jews is unfair, or that if only they had Moses it would have been different. The apocalypse of wrath means the last and highest court has denied every claim; no excuse means the end has already come.

Now Jews had long known of Gentile wickedness in flagrant opposition to the Creator, especially in sexual perversions. They anticipated the destruction of Gentiles, and agreed with God that it was just: "But judging them little by little you gave them an opportunity to repent, though you were not unaware that their origin was evil and their wickedness inborn, and that their way of thinking would never change. For they were an accursed race from the beginning" (Wisdom of Solomon, 12:10–11 NRS). But Paul knew also that the evil Gentile birth is not the *cause* for God's wrath, it is wrath's *conclusion*. The only question worth asking in the end is, Accursed from the beginning as Gentiles obviously are—bad seed—can they excuse themselves by saying: "I could do no other"? But Paul closes that door: "no excuse."

What exactly is unrighteousness/ungodliness that demands universal destruction of creation, if it is not disobedience to a written code of law like Moses' commandments? What is the problem with human beings from which they cannot extricate themselves? Paul says that unrighteousness/ungodliness is *idolatry*, and although Gentiles are the professionals, Jews are not immune. Gentiles are the ones who especially fall back upon created goodness as a defense because they have no preacher. They take creation as a "likeness" of God who leaves tracks here below to allow himself to be tracked back to his high dwelling place. Creation becomes a grand window through which spiritualists look to find the hidden truth "up there." That is, they became speculative idolaters: 'They have exchanged the truth of God for a lie and offered worship and service to the creature instead of the Creator— blessed be he forever. Amen!' (Romans 1:25 translation altered).

What is the 'truth of God'? God made humans in a garden to communicate with them through the things of creation, not to test and judge them according to the use of their free wills. Luther once told his friends,

> We recognize the might of his Word in his creatures, how powerful it is. For he spoke and it came to be [Ps. 33:9]— even through a peach stone. Even though its outer shell is very hard, in its own proper time it must open up because of its soft center, which is inside. Erasmus passes over this artfully and looks at creatures the way the cow looks at a new [barn] door.[12]

No one really believes that God is known *in* created things; in fact this is repulsive to people seeking a worthy goal on high to which they can aspire. You cannot aspire to a peach, you can only eat one. The world wants a transcendent God rather than a deeply present one—if they could only get a distant God without the wrath. Abstraction from created life has always been the problem Lutheran theology has with "metaphysics," or "ontology." Paul says, "For what can be known of God is plain to them" (Romans 1:19a NRS). This was not due to an inner, human power, it was because God showed it to them plain as day. Paul continues, "Ever since the creation of the cosmos, His invisible things, his eternal power and deity, have been known in the things made so they are without excuse" (Romans 1:20 translation altered).

What kind of knowing is this? It is not the Stoic religion's "the eye of the understanding," which was presumed to be a divinely given capacity for transcendence to see through things of creation and upward to the invisible God. Nor is it the Existentialist *nous* (mind) as the "critical, evaluative understanding, which recognizes the claim of a situation or of a demanding will."[13] Bultmann, and many in his wake, misunderstood what Luther was after here and tried to reject metaphysics by means of existential moments of decision. Instead, it is knowing God *in the things made.* Stoics like Seneca thought God's invisibility in the world led to the act of thinking that raises humans above the level of mere worldly things, "he has escaped our sight; he has to be perceived in thought."[14] But God is not perceived in thought, he is perceived in things. God is actually in the peach, not in a sign of peachiness or the thought of the abstract category "fruit." Nor is God seen as making a claim by using critical judgment in relation to things, as if God were using a peach to create space for an event, or a moment, in which a person could chose him or not—thus becoming authentic in existence (Bultmann). No, God is known in his intimacy in things bent toward human use.

How do we know him there in creation? By using the God-given senses as they manifestly provide for life in the things—seeing, smelling, touching, hearing, tasting. So Luther declared in his *Confession* of 1528: "The Father gives himself to us with heaven and earth and all creatures, so that they can serve us and be useful."[15] God is Creator—a materialist, not an idealist—and so he is not far, far off, but *deeply present.* Luther reformulated Augustine's slogan, "God is nearer to me than I am to myself," by saying God is "deeper, more within, more present than the creature himself."[16] Consequently Lutherans have often been attracted to the kind of pantheism envisaged by Baruch Spinoza (1632–1677), but even that is too slight for divine presence as if God were simply immanent as the sum total of all things. God is deeply present, meaning not just there, but personally, in things, freely (not of some ontological necessity), fully in complete, sacramental self-giving *for you*. "Present," for this God is not just "being there," but he is full of speech in which every "thought" is already a spoken word, and every word is instantly a material thing: "For he spoke and it came to be [Ps. 33:9]–even through a peach stone." God is in the peach, more yet, in the stone (even "the soft middle"), and he will be heard and eaten—in space and time. Of course all these matters must return when we discuss sacraments, but here in Romans 1, the deep presence of God did not produce faith, it proved revolting. Eve and Adam did not want God in the peach (God's word-in-thing), but preferred to seek God without things or words—transcendentally, metaphysically—as if God were hiding from them rather than manifesting himself to them in the lowly fruits of the garden. We could say that God came too close, and approached his creatures crudely *from below*, but they were deluded and repulsed: "they did not give him worship or thanks [eucharist as God-in-things-for-you] so they became empty in their thoughts and their foolish hearts were darkened" (Romans 1:21 translation altered).

We Did Not Want Him There: Idolatry

In the garden, God could have been grasped "in the things that have been made," and having been grasped there would indeed have been a loving heavenly Father who gives all that is needed for life. Had Adam and Eve not been revolted by being creatures of a Creator, we would know God today in the peach, and so we would also be divinely known by eating the peach, but we did not want him there. We wanted God "above," which is a metaphor for *in himself, without his words,* in the purest form of mathematical law, and thus the Fall is "upward," not downward into sin. Sin in its original, and only, form eschews God's word/things and pursues idols instead. In its briefest form sin is seeking to have God without a preacher, and so to have God *immediately*, apart from created things. So God is sought where he does not want to be found, and is not found in the created things he gives for life: "When a greedy man, who worships his belly, hears that 'man does not live by bread alone . . .' he eats the bread but fails to see God in the bread; for he sees, admires, and adores only the mask."[17] That is where Stoics end up, after all, with the grandiose natural theology in the grand, ecumenical, catholic law (*nomos*) by following the inner eye (looking through created things as through a mirror, and upward to the divinity beyond the world). The Stoics found the law in nature, which they believed drew God, cosmos, and self together in one "ecumenical" whole.[18] However, the attempt to see through things to the higher power of God fails to transcend creation and gain access to the mind of God; instead it pulls God down into idols made of *images* of things: "analogies of mortal man or birds or animals or reptiles" (Romans 1:23 translation altered). Seeking to transcend through created things, Greeks only succeeded in making perfectly good, earthly things like wood or stone into idols shaped to look like a created thing—by analogy. They made an image of the peach rather than eating it. Then they tried to secure themselves against anthropomorphism (lest they be the creators of God) by distancing God from created things. They thought that "to give God his due" meant to elevate God beyond time and space. If we failed to find him in the peach, perhaps he wants us to search for him outside all created things in highest heaven? So even Jews in Diaspora like Philo learned to approach God this way: "they have advanced from down to up by a sort of heavenly ladder and by a reasonable calculation happily inferred the creator from his works."[19] Created things became a ladder to the distant God. Yet, God is not thanked and worshiped by projecting him infinitely above creation and so as "wholly other," as we find in those anagogical Lutherans of the twentieth century like Gogarten (1887–1968) and Bultmann—along with Karl Barth—who tried to follow a line from Soren Kierkegaard in this matter.

But certainly the other side of idolatry is also untenable. God is in the things, true enough, but when you make images of the things and then try to use this abstraction as worthy of the glory that belongs to God alone, you have withdrawn God from being-in-the-thing, and now dwell in a symbolic world separate from God and his creation at the same time. We could say that once we refused God-in-things-for-us (Creator) one could either become a negative idolater that infinitely separates God and creation, or a positive one that tries to get back into God's good graces by manipulating the created things as a sorcerer. Luther was attuned to the demonic magic that attracts religious people to use things as symbols of God. He warns of this in the *Small Catechism*: "You are not to misuse the name of your God. What is this? Answer: We are to fear and love God, so that we do not curse, swear, practice magic, lie, or deceive using God's name, but instead use that very name in every time of need to call on, pray to, praise, and give thanks to God."[20] This is one reason why Luther refused sacrifice in worship, even in the form of the historical, eucharistic prayer (canon of the mass). Sacrifice and idolatry misuse created things as if their priests are vicars (stand-ins) that can present an appeasing victim, burned up for the sake of an absent God to assuage his wrath, but *God* intended to make the gifts to creatures in daily life, not the reverse.

Paul says they have "exchanged" the truth for a lie. Idolatry is an "exchange" or commerce that takes the things God made for intercourse with his creatures, and turns those "things" into images. Images are imagined to be "seen" by an inner eye, not heard, and are used by creatures as the means of escaping communication with God by communing only with themselves. The external business that should be transacted between Creator and creature has become an inner business, and is no more than a personal Ponzi scheme. God's true business is communication. From the beginning God has sought communication through his words that make things for the creature's own benefit. The garden of Eden was bent entirely toward humans so that all creation served them and all communication was with their Creator—which Paul calls "God's glory." The true exchange begins with God making a thing by speaking it to his Man and Woman and hearing back the thanks and praise that makes for true worship. True worship is to receive all that is necessary from God, who withholds nothing— even communicating his own self in the intercourse of the divine words as gifts—and humans having their mouths opened to speak the glory of God's words in praise of this glory. This "dialogical" worship (true communion in words) that makes created things perfectly suited to the need and delight of the Man and Woman— was exorcised in the world of shamans and magicians as if it were a demon: "they did not honor him or given him thanks"

(Romans 1:21 NRS). God's communion through the things of creation was treated like an evil spirit, sucked out, so that the word was given up for images, glory for darkness, truth for a lie, and wisdom for foolishness. God's words were exchanged for images, and images emptied things of God in order to make an idol that told the maker God was not there, but could be sought and placated elsewhere. Seeing with the inner eye then replaced hearing by faith and their stupid minds became clouded with darkness. Now, what happens to idolaters in the real world?

Three times Paul repeats that God "gives up," or "hands over" idolaters to their own fantasized idol (1:24, 26, 28). God gives his Spirit, and withdraws it as he desires. When he withdraws his Spirit, he hands over his creatures to the enemy, betraying them into exactly what they want—God hands them over to their own desires. Lutherans resist spiritualizing nature on this account; they do not look for the inner light; they do not seek a remaining image that can serve as a starting point to participate in the divine; they do not "make themselves a gracious God," as they imagine and desire their God to be.[21] Any attempt to spiritualize nature ends up in destruction of creation. Not wanting their Creator, humans now meet their Judge instead. Rather than finding the world a friendly place, a garden, the world has become a minefield of forensic judgments. Created things are then "used" by a will desperately seeking to escape God's judgment. Luther liked the distinction Augustine brought to theology between what ought to be "used" (and so is beneath us), and what is to be "enjoyed" (and is above us). When these are confused they are no longer gifts for creaturely life, but rungs on a ladder—or merely picture windows through which we look longing for a return of the distant Creator. For this reason, "God gave them up . . ." (or 'handed them over' Romans 1:24 NRS). Let me make this clear: someone who hands you over is called a "traitor," and so God has become the sinner's Traitor.

Once God withdraws his Spirit, people without a preacher are left to trust images rather than divine words. Thus, the ungodly treat words as secondary to sight and humans become deaf to God altogether. Still the original impulse of faith remains, but with nowhere to put it, since the heart is a trusting factory, so the abandoned, lonely creature makes something of his own (an image) and puts his faith in it—a resemblance of a bird, or a reptile, or some animal. When faith has gone wrong nothing is left but the heart searching for something to love, and love becomes a driving desire that seeks an object worthy of replacing the Creator. In fact, their own love seems to idolaters as something divine itself, and the object they find most worthy of this "divine" love is ultimately themselves. Even their own bodies are made into an "image" and worshiped instead of the Creator, so that sin curves in upon itself in grotesque self-love. To this narcissus, "God gave them up to their shameful passions. Their women exchanged natural intercourse for unnatural and the men likewise gave up natural intercourse with women, were consumed with desire for one another, men committing shameless acts in men, and received the reward for their delusion (as was necessary), in their own persons" (Romans 1:26–27 translation altered). Idolatry eventually turns inward and seeks itself in the form of its desires, free will, or love. Seeking the law in love paradoxically produces only hatred of God, since humans, it turns out, can love anything—except their own personal Traitor. Thus, God's wrath at sin is revealed by *giving the wicked free will*, not taking it away. So if we were to ask how wrath feels, the answer would be: it feels like freedom of will. God betrayed them into their own hands. Yet, God does not agree that they are righteous in doing what they desire; death stalks them, and they know their own personal death is finally God's own "decree", or even more pointedly, "the justification of God" (Romans 1:32).

God knows that the pursuit of desire is neither freedom nor the true glory of God in this world; it never leads to happiness (*eudaimonia*), even when God is reputedly the goal of the desire. Instead, the goal is death, since God refuses to let anyone have any other gods. So God cursed the ungodly with free will, withdrew his Spirit and bound us forever to ourselves. From then on love, not faith, makes us the kind of sinners we are. Whatever we love leads us around, Luther said, "like a ring in a cow's nose" until death consumes us. Now we can understand why Luther calls sin *incurvatus se*, being curved back into the self, or simply "The Belly" when in fact creatures were originally fashioned to open like a flower toward the sun of their Creator.

The Second Accusation: The Judge is Also Judged

Next Paul embarks on a second, deeper accusation in Romans 2:1–16 concerning the case of those who side with the law, judging others for their obvious idolatry. It seems at first blush that the law would provide an escape from God's wrath where creation failed, just as an umbrella shields from the rain. Does anyone not know that God opposes the wicked? But the fact that the wicked stand in opposition to God's law leaves behind a temptation: if wickedness *opposes law*, then goodness, logically, must be *agreement with law.*

But those opposed to wickedness end up being worse off before God, whether Jew or Gentile, because they judge others using the law without knowing that the law accuses them also. Neither having, nor doing, the law provides a loophole in God's wrath. God gave the law to limit wickedness, but not to make anyone righteous—Jew or Gentile. Consequently, the law, "the most salutary doctrine of life, does not help, but hinders our salvation."[22] Those without a written law will perish without a law; but just so those who have the law will perish with it (Romans 2:12). Interpreters sweat here over whether Paul is speaking to Jews or Gentiles, and the answer is of course both: "whoever you are" (Romans 2:1 NRS).

The problem is deep indeed. Morality and reason both rest on the attempt to limit God's wrath by making it arithmetically proportional to wickedness, and therefore by implication, if one does what the law demands (whether written in the heart or on tablets of stone), God's wrath should cease. In this way of thinking, if one day you awoke to God's anger—and death threatened—there would be one remedy: to flee to the law, repent and do what it commands. Obedience to law would then be the "gospel." Until the Apostles came preaching a different word, this was too often understood to be the role of the prophet who called Israel back to faithfulness in the covenant of the law given through Moses. In light of this history of God with his people Israel, Paul took up the special case of the Jews and the law: "If you call yourself a Jew and rely upon the law [the embodiment of knowledge and truth] . . . do you dishonor God by breaking the law?" (Romans 2:17,23 NRS).

Paul cuts to the chase. The law is not done by circumcision—an outward, bodily matter—but is "a matter of the heart—a matter of spirit, and not letter" (Romans 2:29). Even the "second table" of the law, which Paul rehearsed in brief (Romans 2:21–23), exposes simple hypocrisy and may get the defendant to admit that in teaching against adultery he may have committed the same.

It is true that Paul's mission to the Gentiles to bring the Gospel was met with blasphemers against the true name of God *on account of the Jews* (Romans 2:24). Gentiles heard Jewish condemnation of their perverted sex and immediately cried, "Hypocrite!" Do not the prophets of Israel themselves tell of the Jews' hardened hearts? Gentiles naturally asked, "What good is bringing Moses to us if Moses has not brought righteousness to the Jews?" Paul knew his personal burden of preaching as a Jew to Gentiles, but his theological point is made at the culmination of his case against all judges and every law. The real issue in the law is the first table that concerns the sinner's relation to God, not her neighbor. That relation comes down to the first commandment that demands a good, clean heart. One is either good in heart or not; there is no cherry picking by Jews or Gentiles for which law accuses and which one excuses. Judges point the finger rightly at the wicked, but miss the point about their righteous selves. The real matter concerning the law is the heart, and the heart cannot be made good by the law. The law is not spiritual, meaning that it cannot create anything, especially not a new heart. The law reveals your heart as good or bad as light reveals what hides in darkness, but Paul now claims that the law has already made its universal judgment and come to its fatal conclusion: there is no good heart anywhere.

But how did Paul know that there is no such thing as a righteous Gentile, to say nothing of a righteous Jew, according to the law? Had he investigated each life before making the accusation? How does Paul condemn the world without presenting case-by-case evidence in the prosecution of a defendant; are we all lumped together in a class-action suit? The reason is that the wrath of God has been *revealed*, the end of self-justification and the law has come in the cross of Christ; Christ's forgiveness alone, not the law, makes someone righteous—Jew or Gentile. No heart, no inner Jew or Gentile, was, is, or shall be found righteous—otherwise Christ died to no purpose. Paul's entire argument is from the cross of Christ, not from the law. Paul was not counting every person's works; he was not looking into their secret hearts by some power of spiritual perception. What Paul found was more astounding than that none is perfect in relation to the law. God was found outside the law in the cross, making sinners righteous who have faith in Christ (Romans 3:26). Faith, not love, makes a person's heart good. The law has no role to play in making anyone good because it cannot make faith and faith is everything when it comes to the heart.

There are three common misunderstandings of Lutheran theology, and Paul, at this point. One is the observation that the law for Jews never demanded perfect obedience, so that Luther set the bar too high and misunderstood the Rabbis' claim that the law is grace and kindness. Yet Paul was not prosecuting anyone by attempting to make every Jew into an adulterer or a tomb robber (Romans 2:22). That would assume that God's wrath is only a reflex to sin and arithmetically proportional to it, but that was precisely what Paul purged from his hearers. The wrath of God is against our hearts, and there is no escape from the wrath by using this law. Even when judges are right to accuse others of wickedness, they reveal their own hearts are in the law—and the law is simply not Christ.

A second misunderstanding thinks that when Paul says one must be a Jew "inwardly, not outwardly," he separated the law into "ceremonial" and "moral" parts—saying that only the first comes to an end. Nothing could be further from the truth. Paul is simply arguing that if Jews condemn Gentiles by the law, a law-abiding Gentile (even without the written letter on tablets of stone) will end up judging Jews—and in the end everyone will come under accusation. There is no way out of the wrath once it has been revealed, even though the law was given as a *gift* to Jews, for wrath is revealed against the whole world (Romans 3:6)—not against one nation or another (and not merely against "the reprobate" whom God has elected to damnation before all time, in contrast to Calvin).

A third misunderstanding is that when "inner" is exalted over "external," this represents Luther's modern discovery that the real issue of justification is inner motivation—that even if the *deed* is not perfect God accepts the right *motive.* Lutherans fell into this misinterpretation under the influence of Pietism (the beginning of the ethical episode) that sought a pure heart instead of pure doctrine. This influence produced the likes of Immanuel Kant and rationalism in the eighteenth century that only appeared to oppose the Pious, but really adopted their premise. Inner motivation is quickly reduced to the matter of what the heart loves, or at best in Kant, what its duty is—despite suffering—and so this case simply returns to Paul's first accusation of unrighteousness (making the "inner" self into the power of motivation to direct desire to its proper end). Reducing law to inner motivation cannot understand why Paul's accusation falls upon the whole world. Sinners always think that someone somewhere must have the potential of getting inner motivation right—why not me!

Keeping the precepts of the law depends upon already being righteous before any deed is done, or any law makes a demand. The righteous do righteous things, and whatever is done by the unrighteous, however worthy it appears, is unrighteous because of its evil origin. The law is useless when a person is not already righteous; it cannot make them so, and when they are already righteous, the law is no longer needed. In the end, all the judges who find fault in the other are correct, and the law will indeed reveal this truth. However, what judges overlook is that the law turns to judge them also and so it is no friend, it is not grace—it neither was nor will be. In the end, when God's wrath comes and the bright light is shone, everyone is pointing the finger at everyone else in a circular firing squad, and they all end up righteously accused. Well, then, shall we sin more that grace may abound? Shall we simply embrace our fate?

Third Accusation: This Repugnant Thought

Paul's third accusation goes beyond reason and law to reveal the depth of human wrath at predestination by preaching and the depth of God's wrath that will not abide such revolt. Luther says, "The law is in the end not able to say anything else to you but: you have not fulfilled, you are not able to fulfill, and yet you should, therefore, you are a man sentenced to eternal death."[23] Wrath was never confined to law, otherwise what is the law doing telling us "you must," and "you cannot" all at once? No one can linger too long at this place without catching "the Stoical madness," but neither can it be ignored.

The law is there so that what it demands cannot be done. Sin is God's withdrawal of the Holy Spirit that hands us over to free will; the giving of the law is the divine act of withdrawal of the "free will." This stands in direct opposition to reason that lives by a mere inference (without a shred of evidence): if there is an "ought" there must be a "can." If God bothers to give a law, it must imply that I have the potential to fulfill it. Instead, Paul reveals that the presence of law does not imply can: *ought reveals cannot.* Luther knew well what happens to people who linger upon this repugnant thought, and wrote his best book, *Bondage of the Will,* about it:

> It is obviously utterly repugnant to common sense, for God
> to be guided by His own will when He abandons man,
> hardens his heart, and damns him. For He seems to take
> pleasure in the sins and in the eternal torment of the
> unfortunate ones, even though preachers praise the great-
> ness of His mercy and loving kindness. It seems that for
> this reason one must look upon God as unfair and brutal,
> as unbearable. This repugnant thought has caused many
> distinguished people of all times to go to pieces. And who
> would not find it repugnant? More than once it hurled me
> down into the deepest abyss of despair and made me wish
> I had never been born—until I learned how salutary this
> despair is and how close it is to grace.[24]

The greatest stories of Scripture are stories of this repugnant thought: God hardening Pharaoh's heart, Abraham commanded to sacrifice his son Isaac, Jacob wrestling with God at the Jabbok, Paul confronted by Christ's "Why do you persecute me?", and the cry of Christ to his Father, "Why have you forsaken me?" Within the second generation of Lutherans, Luther's *Bondage of the Will* largely disappeared from the university teachers,[25] and by the next century the Lutheran scholastics of the allegorical period had attempted to reconciled God's law and God's wrath by reducing wrath to mere "vengeance" against sins. So Johann Gerhard concluded that God's wrath is "the just wrath of a vengeful God," and the term is merely an expression of the way humans feel, rather than God's own universal judgment.[26] The enlightenment and Lutheran moral episode found its creed in Kant's attempt to return religion to the limits of reason (away from the Repugnant Thought) so that every "ought" in life implies a "can." As we have seen, by the nineteenth century God's wrath was removed from the text of Paul altogether, just as Marcion had done, replaced with God's being as love. But at the end of the moral episode two remarkable exceptions to this Lutheran legacy returned to Luther's *Bondage of the Will* and its essential argument regarding the wrath of God: Theodosius Harnack (1817–1889) and Werner Elert (1995–1954).[27] They both argued that wrath was not an eternal structure of existence, but a personal attack by God.

What an offense! God tells you what to do, and gives the law *so that you cannot do it*. Just because you have the sense of "ought" in life does not imply any factual ability to do it. In fact law never implies anything—it confronts. Law reveals that you *do* not, you *will* not, and you *cannot*. On the day when God judges, it is not potential that is judged; it is actual works. Now works do not make anyone good, but a good person does good works, thus what is judged is the *person*—specifically the heart—not works of law.

This accusation from Paul does not say that those people are hypocrites who champion the law. It says God's judgment is universal, it has already arrived, the sentence is destruction, and there is no way out. Then, *despair at Paul's first and second accusations gives way to what Kierkegaard (1813–1855) called *dread*. Paul reveals the truth that there never was any way out of the judgment of the law for anyone. He dedicated his final argument on justification (Romans 9–11) to the matter of divine election where he could safely speak of it to people who have a preacher: "Why then does he still find fault, for who can resist his will" (Romans 9:19 NRS)? Answer: so he can make an unthwartable promise to the ungodly: "No one who believes in him will be put to shame . . . everyone who calls upon the name of the Lord will be saved" (Romans 10:11–12 NRS). With a preacher, divine election is blessed certainty; without a preacher it is *the sickness unto death*. But here in Romans 2 and 3, before the preacher brings the forgiveness of sins in the form of a promise, there is only the blunt reality of life without a preacher: I cannot resist his will; nevertheless his wrath accuses me. What am I to do? To whom can I complain? Where is the way out? For the answer, Luther turned to Psalm 90—*Mossisimus Moses* (Moses at his most "mosaic").

Moses is associated with this single psalm because the demand of the law is so great it could only have come from the man who hid his face, the minister of death (2 Corinthians 3). In this psalm, Luther observed, Moses demands that we transcend or "perfect" ourselves out of time and space and see our life as a "mathematical point"—to see ourselves with the eyes of God. From this vantage point we see the one truth of the human desire for "transcendence," and it is monstrous: everything that humans are and do—even the very best and most noble virtue—is condemned by God, and so his death sentence hangs over us like a cloud. We are treated by God just like grass—here today, gone tomorrow; burned up in the oven. Everyone dies, and worse, God is the one who sees to it: "He causes us to die" (Psalm 90:3 translation from Luther).

Once we have had our fill of God's view, we descend again to our normal place in life and see things through our own eyes, and say that this is Repugnant! Reason rushes to our defense and says that this should perhaps happen to an immoral, wicked person, but not one like us, "moral persons" (more or less), who take God's law seriously and assume that some exception should be made for responsible people. We return to our fairly ordered lives, until we can no longer keep "this Repugnant Thought" at bay, and suddenly are somehow confronted again with the grave when even "distinguished people" from every time and place go to pieces. Death ceases being a distant thought or unseen power, and utterly claims a person: "This is it, your time has come." Suddenly, God becomes personal; the law ceases to be a buffer between you and him and there is no more hope of more time—fate ceases being a distant idea or feeling of inevitability for a person, and becomes abject fear when death breaks into a person's life as Werner Elert memorably recounted it: "when in the night two demonic eyes stare at him—eyes which paralyze into immobility and fill one with the certainty that these are the eyes of him who will kill you in this very hour."[28]

Paul knew how to anticipate the two sides of the same question, one from determinism, the other from liberalism: "But if through my falsehood God's truthfulness abounds to his glory, why am I still being condemned as a sinner? And why not say (as some people slander us by saying that we say), 'Let us do evil so that good may come'"? (Romans 3:7–8 NRS).

How does God answer this? God does not say. There we meet a stony wall of silence before the hidden God outside his words. Paul ends the case against us all with a dreadful litany, an elegy for the cosmos summing up the whole psalms and prophets (using chiefly Psalm 14:1 and Psalm 53:1) and universal history itself: "None is righteous, not one . . . there is no fear." So Paul concludes his first great argument in the letter to the Romans with the dreadful verdict: "Now we know that whatever the law says, it speaks to those who are under the law, so that every mouth may be silenced, and the whole world may be held accountable to God" (Romans 3:19).

No fear means no faith, and no faith means being handed over to our desires that cannot stop making idols. This is the life without a preacher, and so sin is to be without a preacher when we awake one night with "This Repugnant Thought," and from this "There is no excuse" (Romans 2:1), and no escape.

Chapter 4

God Preached

Romans 3:21–31

Though he will shed my precious blood,
Of life me thus bereaving
All this I suffer for your good
Be steadfast and believing
Life will from death the victory win
My innocence shall bear your sin
And you are blest for ever.

Luther, *Dear Christians, One and All Rejoice*

There is a Rhubarb

Paul turns suddenly from the torrent of God's wrath without a preacher to the bestowal of God's righteousness through faith in Jesus Christ. At these words, "But now" (Romans 3:21), the preacher enters into this old world with a new word, so that Käsemann is right to call it "the eschatological turn."[1] The word is Christ in which God wants to be justified—a most preached God who commences a new Aeon. Faith that justifies this God in his words confesses to have "no other God than this man, Jesus." Medieval medicine used the exotic Chinese plant rhubarb (more expensive than cinnamon, saffron, and opium) as a consummate laxative. Accordingly, Luther preached, "Do not despair, there is a rhubarb that is by far the best, namely Christ; lay hold of him and you will live."[2] There is a rhubarb for what ails you under the wrath of God, and he is Christ. To Christ faith clings by taking leave of itself and listening only to his word of promise: "the foe shall not divide us" (Romans 8:35 "Who shall separate us from the love of Christ?"). Such faith is reckoned as righteousness. Preaching gives God in Christ, just as Adam once was given God in the peach, but Christ first arrives as a purgative, ridding us of the idolatrous dream of the legal scheme.

Paul's "Now" gives the Gospel in the present, which is its proper verbal tense. It is not just the tone or subject that has changed in Paul's preaching, the Aeon has changed, so that we hear an entirely different, eschatological word:

> Him God set forth as a Mercy Seat [propitiator] by faith
> in his blood. This was to declare his righteousness through
> the passing over of former sins in the forbearance of God,
> to declare in the present time the righteousness that stands
> before him that he alone might be righteous by making
> him righteous who believes in Jesus, a mercy seat for the
> forgiveness of sins by his blood (Romans 3:24–5 translation
> altered).

Not that this word had never been heard before; the law and the prophets (meaning all of Scripture) bear witness to it, but it is new because what was promised has finally arrived (Romans 3:21b). The Old Testament said: "He is coming," the New Testament says, "Here he is," but it is the same word, Christ, to which both testify. Unlike law with its voluminous books lining a lawyer's shelves, the Gospel is a short word: "I forgive you." Forgiveness turns a statement of fact, like "Jesus Christ is Lord," into a personal confession of faith: "Jesus Christ is *my* Lord," and that makes all the difference between theology and proclamation.

The legal scheme cannot stand this simple gospel: "Jesus, a Mercy Seat for the forgiveness of sins by his blood." Consequently, two basic Christological problems constantly surface with forgiveness. The first is the problem with the "person" of Christ, because the law requires that the holy be segregated from the sinner. The justifying God, and the sinner do not "fit," otherwise God loses his holiness according to the law—or what is equally abhorrent—the sinner never ceases being sinful. This has created a theological fault-line between "two natures" in Christ that awaited Luther and the second generation of Lutherans to resolve in their radical teaching of the *communicatio idiomatum* (the communication of attributes). Secondly, the legal scheme limited what Paul meant when forgiveness came "by his blood." It forced a series of unsuccessful theories of atonement that brought Christ's "work" on the cross under the confines of the law. Christ the rhubarb, or "mercy seat," was not allowed to take, possess, own, and kill the sins of the world because the law's premise is to separate sinners and God on the basis of ownership of the sins. Luther broke out of those confines by teaching that Christ materially, eschatologically took the sins "by his blood" even while the law (as pure spirit) considers this impossible. In the end, the law tells us that sinners and justifying God do not belong together, but the gospel says the exact opposite.

Christ the Preacher and the Preached

Christ's work, his vocation on earth, was preacher, and what he preached was the forgiveness of sin. It was his forgiving that mediated between the wrathful God and sinful creatures, not as a legal theory or proposal to human will, but as an accomplished fact in the form of a promise. The promise of forgiveness given outright is untamed and unlimited, and thereby poses a threat to the legal scheme. To those who are seeking righteousness through the law, there is a constant fear that too much mercy leads to sinners getting worse, not better, as Paul anticipated: "Should we continue in sin in order that grace may abound?" (Romans 6:1 NRS). If forgiveness is the gospel, then it seems to give the green light to every sin. The legal scheme cannot grasp the extent of Christ's forgiveness, which is the point of all Jesus' parables. His forgiveness not only fulfills the law, but breaks it open like new wine in old wineskins, spilling out onto new ground without any law to guide or limit its effluence.

Each time sins are forgiven it is experienced as a breakthrough, a miracle, a new and unheard of redemption that sets a person free—body and spirit—from an oppressive force. In the Gospels, healings and forgiveness go hand in hand, as with the paralytic let down through the roof by his friends. Jesus asked: "Which is easier, to say to the paralytic, 'Your sins are forgiven,' or to say, 'Stand up and take your mat and walk'?" (Mark 2:9). To those who vicariously witness such an act, especially those responsible for the law, Jesus' forgiveness appears like an assault against morality, religion,

God's good creation and free will. If forgiveness is given by Jesus to a sinner merely by speaking, then it presumes the power of *God* to give it in a *man* (blasphemy); worse yet, it gives God's holy mercy to the wrong sort of people. Christ gives forgiveness outright to the ungodly—while they are yet ungodly (immorality). Excessive forgiveness destroys the basis of faith in the legal scheme, and appears to rebel against God's own law. But Christ breaks out of this shell; he loves the unlovely; he forgives actual sinners. How does he dare do this?

Forgiveness first negates—by violently removing trust put in a false place. Then it puts faith in the proper place, which creates something new out of nothing; it takes faith from something in the legal scheme and places it in a particular promise (*promissio*) of Christ. The crux of the issue in forgiveness is what happens to a sin which was real, actual, and loaded with consequences in many peoples' lives. What happens if we let those who have harmed us off the hook? Naturally, the victims of sin are frightened by forgiveness, yet at the same time those who have committed the sin are often the least credulous of its power, since they suspect that it is too good to be true. Forgiveness is doubted all the way around, and because the legality of the act is in question. Sin is deep in the flesh; it is material, and it does not go away by wishing it so. It is not an idea that can be thought away, it is not a feeling that can be gotten over through great effort, it is a thing that corrodes life's goods like debt; sin infects healthy life like a virus and it must be disposed of. However, the law demands to know what happens to the factual sin: who rightfully possesses it and how do we know the virus will not return?

As preacher of forgiveness, Christ (not the law) is the mediator between God's wrath and sinners who have made a mess of life. He stands in contrast to a different kind of mediation which we are accustomed to in our daily lives that depends upon a compromise between quarreling parties. Typically disagreement is negotiated in a give-and-take settlement seeking a middle ground that shares the pain accrued through sin. Nonetheless, when Christ forgives, it happens suddenly, unexpectedly, without preparation, and with little post-therapy, but for a simple, "go home," or "go and sin no more." Forgiveness happens merely by Christ speaking.

What he speaks is a divine word unlike common, human words. Our words are merely signs pointing to some pre-existing reality, but God's words create out of nothing. Christ's kind of forgiveness happens as an assault on material things which own peoples' hearts: death, guilt, and the legal scheme itself. Legally, forgiveness is possible, but always suspect, because if it is to be applied at all it must be done within reasonable bounds; the person must deserve it going in and continue to deserve it going out. "Deserving" means that the law has to be paid, and those who have the law on their side must receive recompense. Utter mercy is a threat to law since mercy seems to ignore the cause of the law and invite chaos and illegality.[3] According to the legal scheme, mercy may accompany legal justice, but cannot overrule it. The fear on the one hand is that too little mercy discourages improvement, and fatalism sets in. On the other hand, too much mercy unleashes lawlessness and recidivism. So the legal scheme requires forgiveness, it needs mercy, but it requires that forgiveness stay within tight, rational limits. Giving a young man "community service" instead of incarceration for destroying property is meant to be a merciful penalty, so that forgiveness means reduction of the full weight of the law. The logarithm says that mercy must compensate law for whatever excuse it gives to a person being forgiven. What is forgiven in one moment or location must be made up for in another.

According to the legal scheme, sin is either a lack (debt) that must be compensated before the law can be satisfied (fulfilled), or sin is crime that must be punished. When Christ himself is pushed into the legal scheme its practitioners demand Christ make a payment for *debt*, absorb *punishment*, or provide *compensation* to those deprived of their goods (like the devil, the law, or even God himself) if he is going to serve as a true mediator between God and sinners. Theories of atonement developed as a means of making the cross of Christ fit into this legal scheme. It is true that Christ pays debt, suffers punishment, and pays ransom to the old lords of this world, but not to let the legal scheme rule. Christ's blood empties and silences them all, creates an entirely new kingdom where the law has no service to render, no claim to make, and no more accusations against sinners.

When Christ preaches forgiveness, he makes a promise in which God seeks to be justified in his words. The justification of God that takes place is for faith to cling to Christ's promise as truly belonging to itself (Jesus Christ is *my* Lord) despite any claims to the contrary. For a sinner, this is difficult because many will maintain that the sin clearly remains upon you. The victims of your sin will claim this, the legal authorities will claim it (whether Pharisee or local judge), the law at least implies it, the conscience chimes in and agrees, and in the end, the Devil comes parading sin in front of you forcing you to agree that your sin is still there. Since sin is so deep in the flesh that nothing seems to belong to a sinner more than this, Christ goes deeper into the flesh than sin itself. He mediates by taking the sin. This is what we mean when we use the term "communication of attributes" (*communicatio idiomatum*). Christ must enter into the flesh more deeply than sin and legally take those sins in order to fulfill the law so that it cannot make any further claim on the sinner. Then, and only then, Christ goes beyond the law and makes a new creation which marks the end of all law.

Forgiveness cannot merely be a repair of the temporary breach of law, bringing the fallen sinner back into the fold of the legal scheme. How deep God goes into the flesh is unfathomable until Christ alone (the sole mediator), personally—not the law—stands between God's wrath and sinners. Incarnation and cross, Christ's person and work, always remain together so that Christ, the "mercy seat," ends the otherwise endless zero-sum game between God's mercy in the form of patience and God's legal requirements that you become righteous by works. Mercy is merely delay of punishment in the legal scheme—but finally the piper must be paid. "But now," Paul says, apart from this struggle between distributive justice of law and mercy there is—Jesus Christ! (Romans 3:25–6) Like two bookends, Paul has Christ's propitiation at the beginning, "through the redemption which is in Christ Jesus, whom God put forward as a mercy seat by his blood . . ." (Romans 3:21), and at the end of his presentation of the gospel: "Put to death for our trespasses and raised for our justification" (Romans 4:25). In the cross the *communicatio idiomatum* extends into the greatest struggle of the cosmos, ending in God's death under the curse of law and of God himself.

Christ the Mercy Seat

Paul wrote, "They are justified without cost in his grace, through the redemption which is in Christ Jesus. Him God set forth as a Mercy Seat (propitiator) by faith in his blood" (Romans 3:24–5, translation altered). Most modern interpreters reject the crucial issue by identifying Paul's reference to the mercy seat (ἱλαστήριον) and blood as "cultic," and therefore not originally from Paul—and in any case they assume it is superfluous to Paul's point that grace is a gift received by faith. It was Nygren who recognized that resistance to translating Christ as "mercy seat," which the word straightforwardly means, comes from likening Christ to Jewish temple furniture.[4] But removing Christ from the temple furniture created an even greater temptation, which was to take Christ's death merely as another sacrifice according to the law. But for Paul "without cost" (or to put it positively the "free gift") is some-*thing*, not just an idea like atonement, and what the gift gives is Christ as the mercy seat by his blood on account of whom there is redemption from the enemy and reconciliation with the Father. Like the ark of the covenant, God's presence is *now* promised in Christ's cross: "There I will meet with you" (Exodus 25:22 NRS), however hiddenly, and the blood sprinkled on the mercy seat that was to turn away God's wrath has now become eschatological—a new world. Unlike the ark, however, Christ is set forth for all sinners, Jew and Gentile, to hear and see; the blood is not a token but a great cost —"redeemed me ... not with silver and gold," says Luther in the *Small Catechism* "but with his holy and precious blood and his innocent suffering and death." It is faith that receives this blood (not the Father in heaven, or the law, or the devil), thus reversing and bringing to a halt all sacrifice that proceeds from sinners to God. Christ's mercy seat comes down from God to sinners. The purpose clause follows immediately, "in order to present his righteousness ... to declare at the present time that he himself is righteous." That means "that thou mayest be justified in thy words" (Psalm 51 and Romans 3:4 *deum justificare*). Just as Paul said to the Corinthians: "God was in Christ reconciling the world to himself, not counting their trespasses against them, and entrusting to us the message of reconciliation" (2 Cor. 5:19).

Two things happen for redemption and reconciliation of sinners. First, Christ became flesh and died once and for all on the cross, never to be repeated. Second, the preacher delivers the benefit of the cross by declaring the promise of forgiveness to sinners on account of that cross—repeatedly. With this cross and its preaching, redemption comes by *not hearing* your sin (because Christ has taken it), and reconciliation by *hearing* only Christ in faith who gives you his forgiveness. Thus the justification of sinners depends upon a scandalous exchange effected through incarnation, cross, and preaching: Christ *takes* your sin so it cannot accuse you and *gives* forgiveness so that you have his righteousness to boast in, not your own. There is a communication that occurred first in Christ's own person between Creator and creature, divine and human, that reverberates through the preacher to communicate God-in-flesh to his forgiven sinners, including them in the new, free, life of God's favor.

Redemption is first a terrible, struggling battle Christ wages against his enemies in order to take away what belongs to you, the sinner. It is called various things in Scripture and theology, like "payment of debt," sacrifice, buying a slave, pillaging the strong man's house and the like. Yet all these boil down to Christ taking away that thing which identifies you as lost, bound, accused, that controls your life—which is sin and its sting: "The sting of death is sin, and the power of sin is the law" (1 Corinthians 15:56 NRS).

Repeatedly, Luther announced in his sermons on John, that if redemption were to be done, whoever does it must have the power of God to save, and at the same time must have the sinner who needs to be saved. This sort of observation inspired the original doctrine of the communion of attributes among the Cappadocian Fathers which went through the fires of the Nestorian and Apollinarian controversies, and by means of the Tome of Leo was received as a settled confession of faith in the Chalcedonian formula (451): "one and the same Christ, Son, Lord, Only-begotten, in two natures, unconfusedly, unchangeably, indivisibly, inseparably, the distinction of natures by no means being taken away by the union, but rather the property of each nature being preserved and concurring in one Person and one hypostasis . . . ."

However, there was a fault in this doctrine because it was a compromise and so erratic. With the confusion surrounding the various meetings and anathematizing (of either Cyril or Nestorius) in Ephesus thirty years before Chalcedon, there was bound to be a need to settle the Christological battles about how to preach Christ as human and divine, and Chalcedon attempted to do that diplomatically in a true, but limited expression of the Gospel.[5] Chalcedon's compromise creed was based on the Tome of St. Leo (449 AD). In it Pope Leo opposed Eutyches for mixing and blending the natures of Christ. But a problem lurked in Leo's concern (as it did in Nestorius') that Christ not be contaminated by sinners or sin: "For we could not have overcome the author of sin and of death unless he who should neither be contaminated by sin, nor detained by death, had taken upon himself our nature, and made it his own."[6] The Tome nevertheless established the Chalcedonian principle: One Person (*prosopon*), two natures (*en duo physein*) each having a distinct *mode of action* (active in its own way)—which always devolved into something like a free will. The perfectly passive righteousness which Luther would later reclaim was abhorred because it established complete intercourse between the justifying God and sinners instead of segregating them.

The difficulties with Leo's Tome were seen from both sides of the Christological schools at the time. The Antiochians were concerned that the human not be subsumed and destroyed by the divine, but from Cyril's Alexandrian view Leo gave weak statements like: "this birth in time *in no way detracted from, in no way added to,* that divine and everlasting birth," and "Accordingly, while the distinctness of both natures and substances was preserved, and both *met in one person,* lowliness was assumed by majesty . . . ."[7] What Cyril was looking for was the *hypostatic union* which spoke not merely about "meeting" or "nothing changing about the divine," or "indwelling," and the like, but that this Logos-in-flesh did something new as one Person in order to accomplish salvation—that is, the gospel is truly *new* for the justifying God and sinners. The incarnation, with its hypostatic union of the person, could not merely be "preserving" things, or "in no way detracting" from previous natures; something new had to happen in Christ, or sinners would never be saved. The divine and the sinner had—in some strange way—to belong together. Instead of Chalcedon and Leo's *Tome*, the Cyrilians wisely wanted a reaffirmation of Nicea with no further creed, but at Chalcedon the bishops plowed ahead to try another confession of faith. The compromise formula worked to some extent, but there was a long crisis of substance categories that came to a head in the nineteenth century, as formulated by Friedrich Schleiermacher in his *Glaubenslehre* (1821/2):

> For how can divine and human be so subsumed under any single concept [like natures] as if both could be mutually coordinated as more precise specifications of one and the same universal; as, for example, even divine Spirit and human spirit cannot be compared in this way without confusion.[8]

Two "natures" implied that some greater category than God exists: "Nature" should be applied only to "a limited being existing in opposition to another." "Nature" was being used as something bigger than God which could then divide up all of the cosmos into a divine type of nature and a human, like two unequal balls of clay. Worse yet, these two natures were presumed to be "in opposition to another." This effort was doomed to failure; incarnation does not mean that "human nature" was added to divine nature—or that Christ assumed "humanity" as a category. The result has been a widespread abandonment of such basic teachings as the two natures of Christ in the church. Yet the problem was even deeper than this "substance" issue; it was the inability to sense how a communication could occur between God and sinner outside the law, the two being opposed in a cosmic battle to the death. God, the justifier, and the sinner are united, but the unity is not original creation—but getting this communication done required the death of God and a new creation.

Communicatio Idiomatum: Christ Deep in the Flesh

Luther suspected the problem when he ran into the strange phenomenon of Zwingli (1484–1531), who wanted to be a Reformer in the wake of Luther, but rejected the *deum justificare* in which God is justified in his specific words given to sinners, especially in the Lord's Supper. To understand this folly, Luther took up a full scale review of the Christological teachings in the Councils of the first Christian centuries called *On the Councils and the Churches* (1539), and found that the problem went back to the partial communication of attributes at Chalcedon and the unfinished disputes with Nestorius and Eutyches. The *communicatio idiomatum* holds that there are characteristics or identifying features of the essence of a human creature on one hand (like being born, sleeping, crying, sinning, and dying), and of God's essence on the other (like having no beginning, not sleeping, not crying, not sinning, not dying). Accordingly, Creatures are segregated from their Creator by these opposite "attributes," and sin refuses to receive God in his chosen things (like the peach) since we do not want to find our God in his word alone, weak and even liable to death. But in Christ incarnate, there is a new communication that effects exchange between creatures and Creator—expressed verbally in the scandalous language in which Luther luxuriated, such as: "*God* was born of Mary and lay in a manger," and "the *human* Jesus created the world, and rules as Lord of the new kingdom." What the legal scheme could only express in terms of opposites (God/human, infinite/finite, eternal/temporal, holy/sinful) has engaged complete intercourse in Jesus Christ between the greatest opposites—justifying God and sinners.

Luther then applied the significance of this language to what preachers should preach. God and sinners belong together most intimately on account of Christ. Words like "This is My body" are a *promise* which only Christ can make to actual sinners. Zwingli reasoned that Christ's body could not be in many places at once, and so "This is my Body" must be a "trope" (a type of metaphorical expression called *Alleosis*). This marked the infamous attempt among Protestants (and Scholastics) to replace the distinction of law and gospel with a way of reading Scripture against Christ's communication of attributes. *Alleosis* is a hermeneutic that divides all references to Christ according to what is deemed the legally appropriate "nature," either human or divine. Rationally this appeared to solve many riddles in Scripture, including eating Christ's body, the weeping of Christ, the miracles—and especially

Christ's death. Luke said, "Was it not necessary that the Christ should suffer and so enter into his glory?" (Luke 24:26). To Zwingli the rational puzzle in that passage was how anything divine could suffer. The solution was to substitute the phrase "the human nature of Christ" for the personal noun "Christ" in the sentence, according to the rhetorical principle that allows a part to substitute for the whole (and the whole for a part). *Alleosis* allowed a person to say, "The king's son is wounded," when actually only his leg was wounded. Therefore, a person could say rhetorically (not factually) that *Christ* suffered on the cross, when in reality it was only his *human nature*. But Luther saw that the *Alleosis* is "damned" because it refused to hand over the heart of the gospel. It is not the human nature that dies on the cross, but the whole person, Christ, who in his communication of attributes was able to take our sins upon him and kill them. Luther argued that if you followed Zwingli's logic it makes Christ merely an "ordinary saint" or holy man to follow as we are able. That is, his human nature would be available for imitation, and his divine nature would then be spiritualized as the way to participate directly in divinity—without dying.

But as Luther pointed out in his *Confession Concerning Christ's Supper* (1528), "The Holy Spirit knows quite well how to teach us that manner in which we should speak, and we need no trope-makers." So, in Hebrews 6:6, for example, "They crucify the *Son of God* on their own account," they do not crucify *one nature*. Therefore, Luther concluded: "For the Son of God truly is cruci-fied for us, that is, this *person* who is God."[9] If this were somehow a "trope," because reason cannot accept it, then we lose Christ, his incarnation, cross, resurrection, the bestowing of the Spirit through the preaching office, the sacraments, and we end up left for dead in our sins. That is why Zwingli "betrays the poor peo-ple," making Christ slip from us as our righteousness and leaving us only with the damned *Alleosis*—wherein we must become righteous in ourselves but cannot. Zwingli's *Alleosis* assumes that the law is the bridge between an angry God and sinners, and Christ must step aside.

Luther found the source of this problem in fear of the com-munion of attributes. As long as the law remained the true mediator between God and sinner, any attempt to preach Christ incarnate and crucified floundered because theology segregated God and sinners in order to keep God pure from sin (death and decay) on the one side, and on the other it sought to leave room for sinners to become righteous by fulfilling the law in themselves. Consequently, the communication of Christ had to be blunted, and his true communion limited so that *God was never allowed to die*, and *sinners were never put to death*; Christ was never allowed to become sin, and sinners were never allowed communion with the holy God whose purity is kept by the law. This insight was not limited to Luther; the generation following him excelled at describing the implications of this communion, including the "oral eating" of Christ's body and blood by sinners in the Lord's Supper, and the ubiquity of the body of Christ at the resurrection, most prominently at the ascension—and so in communion. The work on the radical *communicatio idiomatum* by Andreae, Brenz, Chemnitz, Amsdorf, and Flacius is displayed in the two articles of the *Book of Concord* on the Lord's Supper (VII) and the Person of Christ (VIII).

The two natures of Christ were a way of saying what Paul said at the beginning of his letter: "the gospel concerning his Son, who was descended from David according to the flesh and was declared to be Son of God with power according to the Spirit of holiness by resurrection from the dead, Jesus Christ our Lord" (Romans 1:3–4). Christ according to the flesh and according to the spirit is laid out in three aspects, as the encyclopedist of the second generation of Lutherans, Martin Chemnitz (1522–1586), put it, "These are the headings under which we customarily divide the explanation of the doctrine of the person of Christ, namely, the two natures, their hypostatic union and the communication of attributes."[10] The Lutherans were aware of how neat their fit was with the "ancient orthodox church," and that their disagreements with Rome did not separate them from the church's catholicity— quite the opposite. Much of Chemnitz' compendium of Lutheran Christology is testimony from the fathers like Athanasius, Nazianzus, and especially Cyril, that recognizes the Lutherans are orthodox at their most radical.

Luther determined to take the communication of the two natures to its ultimate goal, to preach Christ so as to bestow his benefits to sinners while they are sinners. Christ, not the law, is the one Mediator. Christ communes with sinners, who remain so in themselves, but now in Christ have no sin *imputed*. Luther began delighting in what Nestorius feared, and so not only called Mary *Theotokos (bearer of God)*, but Christ a "pants-shitter God"— which makes Luther the supreme teacher of the incarnation and led famously to Rist's hymn (1628) "O darkest woe" that awakened Hegel (1770–1831) from his dogmatic slumbers:

> O great dread
> God himself is dead!
> He died upon the cross ... (v.2)

Hegel confessed in fear and trembling, "God has died, God is dead—this is the most frightful of all thoughts that everything eternal and true is *not*, that negation itself is found in God. The deepest anguish, the feeling of complete irretrievability, the annulling of everything that is elevated, are bound up with this thought."[11] But it was much worse (and better) than Hegel could have imagined, since negation is not simply "in God" and the death upon the cross was done "to gain heaven for us, out of love," as the hymn concludes.

Heaven depends upon Christ taking your sin (indeed "becoming sin") because in the end, either that sin will be on you or Christ. This is Paul's argument by "sufficient division," as Luther calls it: If *Christ* "is innocent and does not carry our sins, then *we* carry them and shall die and be damned in them." So, "in short, our sin must be Christ's own sin, or we shall perish eternally."[12] The Gospel concludes the opposite of the law: the predicate "sin" really belongs to the subject "Christ" in such a way that Christ became sin for you. There is no other way; redemption requires the exchange of Christ's innocence for your sin. God does not require it, nor does the law, or Satan—but 'I,' the sinner, require it. In fact, as Christ himself learned, every "I" will do whatever is necessary to make Christ into a sinner, including crucifying him precisely for preaching the forgiveness of sin: "Why does this fellow speak in this way? It is blasphemy! Who can forgive sins but God alone" (Mark 2:7)?

100

Christ Became Sin

How does Christ's blood, as mercy seat, save? To answer this, Luther built an argument in his Galatians lectures from the necessity of salvation instead of a legal necessity, in what is a most remarkable theological exposition. It lies underneath Luther's Catechism confession, "Jesus Christ is *my* Lord," explaining how it is that sinners can possibly ignore their own sin without creating a disaster, and it describes the Lutheran understanding of the work of Christ on the cross, or "atonement."[13]

How do my sins really become Christ's and what does he do with them? First, my sins become Christ's because, contrary to all Gnostic suspicion, he actually, historically, physically took them in his body (*in corpore suo*): "He himself bore our sins in his body on the cross, so that, free from sins, we might live for righteousness; by his wounds you have been healed" (1 Peter 2.24).[14] What does this mean? Sins are not "ideas," or abstract generalities, or "debts" recorded in some spiritual accounting book. Sins are routinely borne in the body, sometimes in our own bodies, and often by another. If anyone has happened to harm another person, perhaps in a car accident, they know what it means to see their sins borne in another's body. Parents and grandparents also can see their sin in the bodies of their own children carried by DNA and ranging from inherited diseases to repeated lapses in judgment.

When Thomas saw the resurrected Lord, he saw him bearing his sins in the form of marks in his hands, feet and side which had become "touchable." Why would Christ take these sins corporally? Why is it so important for preachers to preach *the blood*, and not just an idea of atonement? Sins are taken by Christ bodily in order to catch you in the act of betraying him, and literally to take the sin from your own body. Self-knowledge is only possible when you know Christ "wrapped in your sin," says Luther. Such self-knowledge is not a result of inward reflection; it must happen externally—*bodily*, and so *in Christ* before one recognizes them. Otherwise you simply will bear them (often with a great deal of denial), and the body eventually succumbs to the attacks of sin in the form of something like cancer, or perhaps even a gunshot wound. Jesus knew why the resurrection was hard to believe. It is not that people do not believe in miracles, it is that resurrection is a *person* ("I am the resurrection" John 11:25), not an abstract miracle or idea, and we do not want to face what our disbelief of his promises did to that very person. The resurrected Christ is still the crucified Christ, but as Thomas learned, the sins that were his have somehow ended up in Christ's own body; yet when they are on Christ, instead of festering unto death, they are *defeated* sin (not *defeating sins*). They are "governed sins," because Christ is now their Lord, instead of the sins governing us. For this reason, as Willie Marxsen (1919–1993) noted, the Gospel stories of Christ are passion narratives with extended introductions. The passion narratives dwell minutely on the bodily suffering of Christ. Paul says this briefly, "the blood"—but even proceeds to give evidence in his own body of the preacher bearing the sins of others (just like Christ): "From now on, let no one make trouble for me; for I carry the marks of Jesus branded on my body" (Galatians 6:17 NRS).

Second, if in fact the sins that once belonged to you really do now belong bodily to Christ, then somehow they must be the product of Christ's own, specific, incarnate, deep-in-the flesh *will*. Christ was not forced by the Father (or some law or inner necessity of divine being) to be born of the Virgin Mary, under the law: "No one takes it from me, but I lay it down willfully" (John 10:18 translation altered). The will is the cause of sin, which is not proof of its "freedom" to choose good or evil; it is proof of bondage and hatred of God. Christ's taking of sin could not have happened by accident, as if being in the world he happened to catch a cold, or perhaps as a scapegoat was sent out with the ritual sins of the people—the goat received the *sign* "by accident." Christ did not end up on the cross "by accident" nor were the sins he bore "signs." This is crucial, since a primary way for people to refuse to forgive and be forgiven is to dismiss sin as merely "an accident"— thus you are not to worry. Have you ever attempted to apologize, and the victim says—"Never mind, it was an accident."? Christ will never say to you, "The cross? No need to worry, it was an accident; you could not have done anything in any case." Christ took your sin *sponte* (willingly), which Luther called, "a most delightful comfort." Christ chose to do this in order to fulfill the Scriptures, specifically to come get sinners and take their sin. This is why he did not resist, but like a sheep before the shearers is dumb, "so the Son of man lays down his life for the sheep" (John 10:15). If Christ were obedient to the law, rather than obedient to the Father, then doing what the law required would not be free, willing, and so *sponte*. Christ's obedience is outside the law, since the Father is not the law.

Third, arguing backward from the truth of the crucifixion, Luther recognized that Jesus must have willfully incriminated himself under the law by associating with sinners (*socius peccatorum*). Christ was a notorious associate of sinners just as Isaiah prophesied: "he was numbered among the thieves," (Is 53:12)—which is guilt by association. Recall that the law always required separation of the clean and unclean. So Luther reversed the old church doctrine called "assumption"—whatever is not assumed by Christ in the incarnation is not saved. In that patristic doctrine what was assumed by Christ was either what remained good about humans after sin, or at least what could be made good. For Luther what Christ assumes from sinners is their sin. Likewise Luther's sense of *kenosis*, divine self-emptying (Philippians 2) is more brutal than reason could imagine. Christ did not humble himself (entering what the orthodox Lutherans called a state of humility) merely by being born of Mary; he humbled himself by eating with sinners, which he made a pointed practice as in his visit to Zacchaeus. *Kenosis* is not merely a God in human clothing, hiding his divine powers for a limited time, it is breaking the limit of segregation drawn by the law between sinful creatures and the God of Creation.[15] So Luther said: "the sophists deprive us when they segregate Christ from sins and from sinners and set him forth to us only as an example to be imitated." What do they deprive us of?—Christ deep in the flesh. The law demands an example from Christ and an imitation by sinners. But Christ acts in such a way that to imitate him would destroy the world (vs. Kant's transcendental moral principle that demands you act only as you would have all other people in similar circumstances act). One cannot imitate Christ's assumption of our sins, and indeed Christ does not want that. He wants to take your sins and leave it to no one else; so he sins against the Golden Rule. He does not want you ever to take the sins from him after he has assumed them from you. In this act of Christ's, it is not just morality that is killed, but

103

morality's source in *duty*. When Christ eats with sinners he exclusively violates the segregation of sinner and God, he does not want to introduce a mere revaluation of all values (Nietzsche 1844–1900); he does not treat people as he wants to be treated, or introduce a new moral value. Christ is not merely counter-cultural when he does this; he is the one, sole mediator coming to take sin by associating with it (which the God of wrath cannot do) and so destroying the fabric of this old society of law. That is why the Father is not incarnate, only the Son is; the Father does not die on the cross, only the Son does.

When Christ so took sin by association, he not only transgressed the law, but placed himself "under an evil lord." What links all of us together as sinners is not just that we are misbehaving in similar ways according to the law, or that we are conspiring, aiding and abetting to commit such sins, but that we have a common, tyrannical, demonic *lord*, so that whatever we try to do, even the world's very best and noblest things, is used for evil purpose: "whatever is in this age is subject to the evil of the devil, who rules the entire world."[16] You cannot morally be a "good" pilot in Hitler's army. Now when the law does its work, and sees that Christ has associated with sinners, it takes Christ to be no different than you or me. Here Paul's point is exact: the law is no respecter of persons, it does not identify Christ among the sinners as an exception to the rule. Law as "blind lady justice" executes its judgment regardless of race, color, creed—or divinity. This entire world is under the divine curse, and Christ determined to enter this with us, born of woman, born under the law. "Therefore when the law found him among thieves, it condemned and executed him as a thief," said Luther. This reveals Christ's real temptation by Satan. Satan wanted Jesus to segregate himself from sinners and be righteous all by himself. The devil wished that Christ would perfectly fulfill the law as a true, sinless human being, and return to his Father undefiled—with the law's accusation now made eternal. Christ refused it whenever the devil tempted him, because he loves sinners. Unlike Satan, Christ had no interest in making the law the eternal mediator between Creator and creatures.

Fourth, Christ goes deeper yet into flesh to take our sin. Although he did not commit a sin, he not only ate with sinners, but *acknowledged* sins as his own, that is, he confessed (*confessio*) them. This is like a man whose son has committed a crime, and out of selfless love the father steps in to take the punishment, but then goes too far—he irrationally comes to confess this crime so vehemently that he believes he has committed it—and as Luther famously said, "as you believe, so it is." Christ comes to believe he was guilty. The heart and its faith do indeed determine reality "for me." The most famous theological assertion of the last two centuries came from Ludwig Feuerbach (1804–1872), who knew Luther was correct, that faith makes god, and with this principle effected a Copernican revolution from theology to anthropology that made of God a projection of human needs. Unfortunately, Christ suffered on the cross the cost of anthropological projection of the heart's faith, where he came to believe that his Father was not pleased with him, thus multiplying sin in himself just like any other original sinner who does not trust a promise from God. *i.e. Adam* Christ's own confession of the heart came clear in the Garden of Gethsemane—praying fervently for the cup of suffering to pass him by. Then finally in the words on the cross, "My God, my God . . ." he made the public confession of a sinner, "why have you forsaken me?" (Mark 15:35 NRS). Confessing made it so, and thus Christ committed his own, personal sin—not only an actual sin, but the original sin. He felt God's wrath and took that experience as something truer than God's own word of promise to him ("This is My Son, with whom I am well pleased"). He looked upon himself on the cross and believed in his own belief!

Fifth, Jesus could not seem to stop himself once this sin began rolling downhill, not only did he confess our sin as his own (and believed it), but he proceeded to take on every single sin ever committed in the world: "I have committed the sins *of the world*" ("*Ego commisi peccata mundi*") as the fulfillment of the prophetic word of Isaiah 53:6: "God has laid on Him the iniquity of us *all*," and of John's final prophesy: he bears "the sin of the *world*" (John 1:29). To Luther this was not an abstract universal in the sense that "table" stands for all four-legged, flat-topped furniture. Nor is it just taking the penalty for sin, though Christ surely did that. Luther meant that it was exhaustive of every actual sinner and sin in history: "the sins of the entire world, past, present, and future . . ." so that Christ says, "I have committed the sins that all men have committed . . . the sin of Paul, the former blasphemer . . . of Peter, who denied Christ, of David . . . an adulterer and murderer . . . ." If you have a problem with your own credulity at this point, it is not because Luther had fallen into mythical language, nor can it be excused as "Christ merely *thinking* he had committed the sins of the whole world . . . ." The problem with believing this is the proximity Jesus reached to get you as a sinner and your own sin. Christ herewith began invading "your own space," and taking things that belong to you personally, raising the question, Where will he stop? Distributive justice demands that you distinguish what belongs to whom in this world. So we reason, "If Jesus starts demanding your very own sin where will it stop?" What boundary will he refuse to trespass? After all, when it comes to God's wrath the real issue is not how much righteousness you have compared to the volume of sin; it is the revelation that everything you have and possess is *sin*. Therefore, Christ is determined not to stop until he has taken everything of yours. He comes as a thief in the night, and thieves not only surprise us with their untimely arrival, but they actually rob us of our possessions. Jesus robs us of our best stuff—our righteous deeds by the law, our hopes that things will work out (with a little grace), and the belief that God will find us pleasing on our own account—but he also robs us of the worst. This is possible since human identity is relational, not substantial. We are determined by what others say and do with us. In the cross, Jesus is relationally determining us to be without anything worthy of exchange or negotiation in the eyes of God, nevertheless Jesus exchanges his priceless worth for our filth. When he does this, he is not assuming abstract, bookkeeping, non-historical, or impersonal sins. When Scripture says he takes the sin of the world, it means that eventually he gets around to taking your own personal sins. The universal moves to the concrete, to the particular, material, and personal—but not without great opposition. So Luther noted:

> It is easy for you to say and believe that Christ, the Son of God, was given for the sins of Peter, Paul, and other saints, who seem to us to have been worthy of this grace. But it is very hard for you, who regards yourself either as unworthy of this grace, or too worthy to need it, to say and believe

from your heart that Christ was given for your many
great sins.[17]

Both humility and pride in this matter become disdain for
Christ—as if to say that your sins are so small and slight you need
not bother Christ with them, or they are so onerous a burden that
he would never take them. The pharisaical (fake) sinner, who
thinks his or her sin is not great enough to need Christ, is one
kind of problem; Luther calls such a person "an imitation and
counterfeit sinner." The other is the person burdened with guilt,
but Christ did not come for little, sham sins, but for huge sins, in
fact for all sins, "and unless you say you are part of the company
of those who say 'our sins,' . . . there is no salvation for you."
This is the source of Luther's phrase: "when you are a sinner then
it is that you are not; when you refuse to be a sinner then you are
one." So here is the logic of the cross: Christ is "the one who took
away the sins of the *world*; if the sin of the world is taken away, then
it is taken away also from *me* . . . ."

Sixth, Christ not only became a sinner, he became the *greatest*
of all sinners (*omnium maximus peccator*). Such is the meaning of the
incarnation from Christ's point of view, sent by the Father to
come down to us; not only did he become a sinner, or the one
who bears the sin of the world, but he became the greatest of all
sinners having come so deep in the flesh that "his skin smokes."
Such is the "solemn" or struggling part of the exchange he makes
with us. This does not change the fact that the Son was obedient
to the Father; it only confirms the fact that obedience to his Father
is not the same thing as obedience to the law, nor does it shake the
truth of Christ's innocence in himself. But Christ was incarnate to
be collective, communicative, and defined socially by the "for
you"—which he will not abandon. His obedience ceased to be
legal in nature, and became entirely personal, since the Father sent
Christ to become the greatest of sinners. The Father willed his
Son to go under the law, and thus come under his Father's own
wrath—so much so that Christ is the biggest sinner of them all.

Seventh, Christ was not only the greatest of all sinners, Christ
became a curse (*factum maledictum*) and so became *sin itself* (*fit plane
ipsum peccatum*). Our sins are so much his own that by acknowl-
edging them, not only do the sins become his, but the bearer,

Christ, ceases merely being "a person who has sins" and becomes a sin and a curse—*substantively*. Luther noticed that Paul used "curse" in its substantive rather than its adjectival sense—he is not just accursed (one more person cursed by the Father), he is *a* curse (Galatians 3:13). Sometimes a person is so associated with something that we stop using an adjective and use the substantive. A body builder can, at a certain point, cease "having muscles" and we call him "all muscle." Christ becomes so exclusively associated with sin that it loses any sense for anyone else, and we say of him not only that he is *a* sinner, but *the* Sinner. Here Luther closed one of the great loopholes for sinners—that God "loves the sinner, but hates the sin." Luther recognized that this neat distinction is not possible in reality: "A man who feels these things in earnest really becomes sin, death and the curse itself—not only . . . adjectivally but . . . substantively." That is, we reach a point when we cannot separate ourselves from our sin. Luther then threw caution to the wind and attributed this situation exclusively to Christ.

> All our evils . . . overwhelmed him once, for a brief time, and flooded in over his head, as in Psalm 88:7 and 16 the prophet laments in Christ's name when he says: 'Thy wrath lies heavy upon me and thou dost overwhelm me with all thy waves,' and: 'Thy wrath has swept over me, thy dread assaults destroy me.'

It is as if Christ breaks the reality of his own person, in a kind of self-alleosis—Christ sins against Christ: "He is not acting in his own person now; now he is not the Son of God, born of the virgin, but he is a sinner . . . ." The law accuses Christ of "blasphemy and sedition" so Luther tells us to witness his "bloody sweat, the comfort of the angel, his solemn prayer in the garden, and finally . . . that cry of misery on the cross, 'My God, my God, why hast Thou forsaken me?'" Luther's discussion of the sinner with Erasmus in *The Bondage of the Will* made the same point. When a person knows himself as a sinner, he becomes in that knowledge a sinner all the more. This is because in that moment I know I anger God. If I anger God, then I know I am not pleasing God. To know I am not pleasing is not to trust, and then to fear God not as creator, but as destroyer. God is not pleased with this situation, however confused such a person may be. To the contrary, belief is precisely to know that, despite God's anger, I believe I please him. But, this is an impossibility for ourselves, so sin is "magnified," as Matthew has it in the parable of the talents, "For to those who have, more will be given, and they will have an abundance; but from those who have nothing, even what they have will be taken away" (Matt. 13:12). This means that Christ, in each of the Psalms declared or implied at his crucifixion, was *confessing* sin—and doing so out of love. Thus even Psalm 22, with its "My God, my God, why have you forsaken me?" belongs in a preeminent sense to Christ, not to David, and not to sufferers in general. Christ takes even the Psalms away from us—in order to give them in a new way.

Luther concludes this unparalleled argument by noting what happens to the law at the cross. The law's primary work is to condemn sin. At the moment when Christ took our sin upon himself—confessed it out loud—the law had no choice but to make him guilty of sin then and there (*sub lege, ergo peccator*). The law did as it must, blindfolded and equitable (spiritual) as it is, and attacked Christ—but the law could have no reason to do so (since it cannot act illegally) unless the sins were actually there. Luther learned from Paul to argue backward from the cross, not forward from a pre-conceived notion of what sins are according to the legal scheme. The law that put Christ on trial, and finally got into his own conscience, is the clear evidence that Christ (who was ontologically without sin), in fact *became* the sinner of all sinners; he *accomplished* sin, to speak strangely, thus arriving at the goal of the incarnation. Luther refused to weaken either sin or curse in Paul's use of Scripture by merely concluding that Christ took our *punishment*, but not our sins. That would refuse the clear meaning of the text. Isaiah says: "God has laid on him the *iniquity* of us all," not merely the punishment or penalty. Of course such testimony includes bearing punishment, but Christ is punished because he "has sin and bears sins," as Luther concludes. The law does not punish for no reason and continues to be God's good order in this old world, and the law is certainly pure, holy, and without sin. The law says, "Let every *sinner* die." But to Christ it says, "Christ, if you want to reply that you are guilty and that you bear the punishment, you must bear the sin and the curse as well." This must be the case, or Paul could not have given Deuteronomy 21 over to Christ. Christ became a curse, but he did it not for his own sake, but ours. Once the law accused Christ, it looked around and found no other sin anywhere in the world and suddenly, unexpectedly, when Christ was crucified, its proper work came to a halt.

The Astonishing Duel

Luther concluded this argument with the *coup de grace*, arguing "backward" from the cross. When the law attacked sin on Jesus Christ it also attacked *God* since the incarnation allows no separation between this God and this man. Becoming a sinner, sin itself, did not make Jesus Christ any less God. The battle over sin and death was fought on the ground of Jesus Christ's own Person, but exactly *this* very human (born of woman, born under the law, eating with sinners, confessing himself as sinner, the greatest sinner, and sin itself) was at the same time God's divine will of mercy apart from the law. Christ's will to forgive sins is both the *human* will that fulfilled the law (and is found guilty by the law), and at the same time the invincible will of *God* that gave the law and stands outside it. Yet, Jesus Christ does not have two wills, but one. There the two "natures" of Christ in the one "person" reach their unthinkable depth in communicating attributes. The question is not which wins—God or human—the question is whether the law will win in its condemnation, or if forgiveness of sins apart from the law will win. The struggle that took place on the cross is between the God who gave the law and the God who is attacked by the law: Law vs. Gospel—God outside Christ vs. God in Christ.

Who will win? God, of course, but the God in his *words*—who is Christ—wins by *losing*, coming under the accusation of the law (and the humans who employ its judgment for their own sakes), and finally there bearing God's publicly published curse for any who are raised upon the tree (Deuteronomy 21). When humans have set up their false righteousness according to the law and their imaginary free will, the only means left for God is to interrupt the wild sinners' search by humbling himself under the law and suffering its attack—despite his own, personal innocence. This is why Luther was so careful to draw out Paul's insistence that Christ's death was a curse *according to the law*. Jesus' death was not a case of mistaken identity. Neither was it merely a temporary setback on the road to greater discipleship for those following him. Nor was the law simply misused by the Sanhedrin in a miscarriage of justice, since they appealed to blasphemy, the highest of laws. Nor can it be said that the Romans were naively trying to keep the lid on a revolutionary situation with Pilate's hand washing and the freeing of Barabbas. The Romans joined the Sanhedrin in a higher law that says that one man must be sacrificed for the greater good.

The law was used against Christ in its most holy and high form of justice, at the height of its power (just as death, devil, curse, wrath, and sin were also in play at the height of their powers). The legal scheme was taken on at its best and defeated—by God *losing* to it, and starting with a new creation outside the law. This is the great secret of the battle between curse and blessing on the cross, between law and gospel. The law says: "do this," and nothing is done. Gospel [who is Christ] says, "believe in this," and everything is done already. We call this the *mirabile duellum*—the "great and dreadful duel," that nevertheless becomes the *iucundissimum duellum* (delightful, happy duel). The sins of the world were laid on Christ; we communicated them to Christ by means of rejection of his words; what he communicates in return to sinners is unlike anything we have known: it is grace that is free and that *creates* a new world out of nothing—the law and sin are left behind forever because they have created nothing. This is why sinners confess that we have no other God than this man, Jesus Christ—since any other God is without the cross, without our sins taken and conquered, without the preached word of forgiveness, and so a God that remains unpreached. But God's righteousness and our own are now tied together in simple trust that Christ has forgiven our sin: "Moses, the old settler, has to yield and emigrate somewhere else when Christ, the new guest, comes into the new house to live there alone."[18]

Paul concludes his gospel with the question he knew would be on everyone's mind: "Do we then overthrow the law by this faith? By no means!" (Romans 3:31a NRS). The law was never meant for justifying sinners—or God. Law is not what faith trusts. When the law is freed from coerced labor as Messiah, it has its proper work in driving everyone to Christ, and it has its alien work in preserving life in the old world while waiting for a preacher. Yet only those who live beyond law's limits can properly be said to "establish it" (Romans 3:31b translation altered), in the same way that a baseball player knows that the rules of baseball apply only within the confines of the ballpark, but life is lived outside.

The communion of attributes in the cross ceases the old segregation of the wrathful God and sinners. Paul anticipated that his fellow Jews would immediately grasp the result. For the first time in history the door to reconciliation with the Creator was opened to the ungodly Gentiles. But the thought immediately arose—perhaps *faith* is only for the Gentiles, and the Jews carry on seeking righteousness through Moses and the law? Paul closed this door in order to open another. The *shema*, or praise of the oneness of God, means this opening for Gentiles is also for Jews: "God is one, and he will justify the circumcised by faith, and the uncircumcised by faith" (Romans 3:30). Indeed, faith alone was given to the Jews before it was ever given to the Gentiles.

The law (Torah) has always borne witness against the law itself, and declared instead the righteousness of faith. Righteousness by law *thinks* it holds law in high esteem, and that faith denigrates law, but the reverse is true. Righteousness by law produces boasters in themselves—which the law never intended. Righteousness by faith *establishes* the law, whose purpose has always been to stop such boasting.

Grace is freedom from the old life (Romans 3:24), and Paul's letter now proceeds to describe the extent of this freedom first from God's wrath (Romans 5), then freedom from sin in baptism (Romans 6), freedom from the law (Romans 7), and even freedom from death (Romans 8) in the Spirit who creates a new kingdom. Christian freedom comes entirely from the outside in the form of a promise. The promise is unthwartable and irresistible because of God's faithfulness, so that it never fails for its predestined and elected—Gentile or Jew (Romans 9–11). Finally, there is freedom to extend Christ's *communicatio idiomatum* to others without fear of loss of one's self, because the new life of the

Christian is lived simultaneously with the old sinner's life—until heaven arrives and the Spirit has completed the fulfillment of the law even in us—that is to love without the need of any law (Romans 12–15).

Chapter 5

Faith and Promise

Romans 4

Hope therefore in my God will I,
On my deserts not founding;
Upon him shall my heart rely,
And on his goodness grounding.
What his true Word doth promise me,
My comfort shall and refuge be;
That will I always be awaiting.

Martin Luther, *Out of the Depths I Cry to You*

Christ's Benefits and Their Distribution

The Gospel has now been distinguished from the law in Paul's argument: "for we hold that a man is justified by faith alone apart from works of the law" (Romans 3:28). Luther translated Paul correctly—faith *alone* (*sola fide*)—which is not a Lutheran codicil, but has always been the church's translation from Origen onward, until it became inconvenient for scholastic and Protestant theologies that wanted to add love to faith as the perfection of righteousness. Even Pelagius translated Paul according to the clear meaning—"faith alone"—and when Luther and Pelagius can agree on a translation it is truly catholic. Faith alone is righteousness, with nothing added to complete it, especially not love. Faith thus emerged as "the new locus" which philosophy does not know, on which the entirety of evangelical teaching converges.

Paul has also argued that faith does not obliterate the law from having something to do, but rather faith establishes it by taking law entirely away from righteousness before God. The law witnesses *against* the law; faith alone witnesses *for* the law so law can consign everything under sin in order to stop all boasting. The law has always wanted you to do the things of the law—but without the law having to say it, because "what the law requires is freedom from the law!"[1] Faith does not overthrow law by removing its proper work; it upholds it, establishing the proper place of the law (Romans 3:31). Law's proper place is not righteousness but in stopping every mouth so that what remains of the person is nothing but the perfectly passive ears. The proof of this pudding is Abraham, and the fourth chapter of Romans.

What is faith and how can it accomplish such great things that the law is unable to do? Faith is a sure and certain trust in Christ's promise of the forgiveness of sins given to you, despite contrary experience. Faith's certainty rests not on a power or ability in the believer, but in Christ's faithfulness to deliver what the promise promises. Christ's faithfulness depends upon his two natures and their principle *idiomata*: the unthwartable power of God over all other forces and the merciful love of the ungodly. The communication of divine and human in the cross overcomes the long segregation of the justifying God and me, the sinner.

Three words are needed to understand how the justifying God overcomes the segregation between creator and sinner: *Christ* (whose redemption in the cross we have recited), *faith*, and *imputation* (which Paul now proceeds to recite).[2] Once these three are present, sinners are reconciled with God so that God's wrath ends and his mercy begins. So, as in Paul's *Romans*, we first have the story of Christ—however briefly or at length that story is told; then we have the story of Abraham upon whom all of the questions of faith and imputation converge.

Regarding the word "Christ," two historical events come into play; first comes the *blood* (cross) of Christ, then the *preaching* of the blood in the form of a specific promise of the forgiveness of sins: first the redemption, then the reconciliation. Christ first gains or "wins" his benefits; then these benefits are distributed. Christ first must have the power to forgive, and then he must have the sins themselves that need forgiving. If Christ did not take my sins, then the sins are still upon me—and I die. This is Paul's relentless logic. The redemption which is in Christ Jesus (Romans 3:24) is the communication of attributes by which Christ accomplished the astounding exchange which took the world's sin. If nothing more was done, however, this enormous struggle and cost would

115

mean nothing, except for Christ; he would not be the firstfruits of many (1 Cor. 15). Grace without faith is a gift undelivered, and that would leave Christ as Lord of a new kingdom without any citizens; he would be covered with the sin of the world, and yet live alone without his sinners gathered about him. This Christ refuses to do. Theology has routinely remained at the level of redemption with no preaching, and thus abstracted Christ's exchange in the form of atonement theories which no sinner can quite manage to "believe"—though it appears to them that Paul is demanding that they do something when he says "believe"! If one is to be a Christian, Christ's cross is left as exotic doctrine that must be accepted, contrary to reason, and so preaching is exchanged for teaching a theory, and faith is exchanged for knowledge.

But Paul does not say that faith is belief in an atonement theory—what later Lutheran Orthodoxy, following Melanchthon's lead, mistook for *notitia assensus fiducia* (faith giving its consent to an idea). Instead, the redemption is to be preached, and the benefits that Christ won distributed so that God is no longer righteous only in himself—but comes to be justified by you in his words. To *Christ* belongs *faith*, the two fit like Siamese twins, and to faith belongs what Lutherans have called (from the old theology) *imputation*: Faith is *reckoned* (imputed) as righteous by the preacher applying Christ's promise of forgiveness to a sinner. This means that the communication of attributes now extends beyond Christ's own person. Not only does Christ take the world's sin, but he then turns as the resurrected Christ to forgive those sins; specifically he forgives the whole sum of sin in the crime of his own crucifixion. The first exchange was for Christ to take your sin; the second is for him to bestow all of his *idiomata* upon you, which is forgiveness of sin, life, and salvation (heaven, or the joyous part of the exchange). So Luther preached on Isaiah 52–3 the Saturday before Easter, 1531:

> How does he justify mankind? By taking their sins upon
> himself, as John the Baptist says of him, 'Behold the Lamb
> of God that taketh away the sins of the world.' Those who
> confess him to be that, and believe that he carries their sin,
> know him rightly. Justification in the Christian sense, is not

my work, my merit, my obedience of the Law, but rather that I firmly believe that Christ has borne my sins.[3]

Faith

If faith is reckoned as righteousness, entirely apart from the legal scheme, then all attention converges upon Abraham and the way that he is our father. Certainly, as for Paul and the Jews, Abraham is "father according to the flesh" (Romans 4:1). But the fatherhood that is spiritual, that is the kind that counts in front of God, cannot focus on the particular flesh of the circumcision, and it cannot be an imitation of Abraham justifying himself by works of the law. Neither circumcision nor law is the form of spiritual descent from Abraham that was called for by the prophets: "for all the nations are uncircumcised and all the house of Israel is uncircumcised in the heart" (Jeremiah 9:26). Paul has hereby entered into a struggle with his fellow Jews over what Scripture actually says about Abraham, in contradiction to the legal scheme's makeover of this father. What does the Scripture actually say about *father* Abraham? "Abraham believed God, and it was reckoned to him as righteousness" (Romans 4:3, Galatians 3:6 and Genesis 15:6). Just as Habakkuk 2:4 had been used earlier as the key to Scripture against those claiming righteousness by law (even if with grace), so now Paul took the slogan "Abraham's children" from the law and placed it with faith. Abraham's fatherhood, which is the key to all Scripture, is not the story of justice by law—but its exact opposite; his is the story of justification by faith alone, apart from law. There is currently a cottage industry of philosophies of religion that hold out hope for Abraham as father of Jews, Christians and Muslims, but the hope of reconciliation is doomed as long as there is no distinction of law and gospel.

Paul had earlier come across the misuse of Abraham by the infiltrating preachers in the Galatians churches, when Abraham—unlike Moses—was used as the unifying figure of election for both Jews and Gentiles in the new apostolic mission. Jews had Abraham as father according to the flesh, and when they entered the covenant of law by circumcision they therefore shared also in his spiritual inheritance of righteousness (election). Yet, circumcision is not a uniting act of election, it is a distinguishing and separating act; it is, after all, *the* distinction between Jew and Gentile according to the law. However, the infiltrating preachers in Galatia presented Abraham as the first proselyte—not born Jew, yet chosen out of the mass of the world by God in order to enter the covenant of law by circumcision, so that if Gentile-Christians likewise want to enter into God's righteousness they had to do so by adopting circumcision in imitation of Abraham. This would make Abraham father of both Jews and Gentiles—but only by means of the circumcision, and thereby Abraham's story served as the model for entrance into the covenant of the *law*. Consequently, the gospel of Christ was taken to mean extending this same righteousness by law to the ungodly Gentiles, a controversial position to be sure, but one that could plausibly be sold as the new thing Christ brought—"the gospel." Imagine this confusion for the churches in Galatia: the "gospel" unifies the world by extending the covenant law to those previously excluded. This confusion had then, and continues today, to have a power of persuasion, but it is the direct opposite of the gospel; therefore, Paul set out to correct this subterranean problem that equates grace with the universal extension of covenant law. Scripture does not say that Abraham was reckoned righteous by circumcision, nor by entering a covenant of law, nor does it ever say that grace is law—it uses two words exclusively: *faith*, and *reckoned*. Abraham is indeed the uniting spiritual father of Jews and Gentiles, but not by circumcision, and not by the possession of God's law. The law and prophets all agree, Paul argued, Abraham's story is not law—but faith. Abraham may have much to boast of in front of his wife and nephew, but he has nothing to boast of before God. One cannot take Genesis 17 and the command of the covenant, "As for you, you shall keep my covenant, you and your offspring after you throughout their generations," or the day when Abraham turned ninety nine years old and "was circumcised in the flesh of his foreskin" (along with Ishmael), and read it without Genesis 15—without the promise, faith, and reckoning as righteous. Faith, not circumcision and not law, made Abraham into *father*, and his spiritual descendants are those with that same faith.

Faith is not a quality or characteristic in a person such as a habit of character, or an *idiomatum* of the essence of human nature. Faith is created by a promise that comes externally, as an alien word; it is not generated internally as is an idea, but materially through the ears by hearing. That word is very particularly a promise so that it must be said—no promise, no faith: "For if the inheritance is by the law, it is no longer by promise; but God gave it to Abraham by a promise" (Galatians 3:18). Faith is in something, it needs some-*thing* to believe; specifically it lives from an incarnate and crucified promise, who is none other than Christ, the promised Messiah.

The Promise is Not Like the Law

The Gospel is the promise of the forgiveness of sin, and so of God's goodwill toward us, and it is Christ who is the "yes," or pledge of all Scripture's promises. Melanchthon asserted: "Therefore all Scripture's promises are to be related to him."[4] Promises are different than commands. A command tells us what we are to do; a promise says what its maker is going to do. So the Gospel is a narrative of these promises, which means that history is none other than the history of God making promises and keeping them—against all who would seek to destroy them as lies. The promises are the key to Scripture, as the originator of modern hermeneutics, Matthias Flacius Illyricus (1520–1575), found in his *Clavis Scripturae Sacrae*. With this same discovery, Flacius revived church history in his *Magdeburg Centuries*, the first comprehensive church history written since Eusebius of Caesarea (323 AD).[5] The history of such promises is not quite a "salvation history" (*Heilsgeschichte*) at the core of world history, as someone like J. C. K. von Hofmann (1810–1877) surmised, which held Jesus Christ to be the realization of the divine will to love mankind.[6] The promise is not love—it is Christ, and Christ is none other than the end of the law, the destruction of the old world, and the creation of the new world that is given to faith alone. The history of God's promises is usually overlooked, since the promises seem insignificant in the greater narrative of the world's events told in terms of conquest and tragedy. What difference does Abraham make in the great scheme of things? Is he as important as Caesar or Napoleon? Scripture's promises also stand in opposition to the desires of sinners to be found just in themselves—the "old, pious wish," as Luther put it. Who cares about such little tokens as a promise made to Abraham?

When promise/gospel is distinguished from law properly, then Scripture and history open up differently than in the legal scheme. Scripture is the location of the promises which came to be written so that preachers could be given authorized words to preach. It is not a law book at its heart, but the book of divine promises. A preacher searches Scripture for the promises that apply to sinners—ones that can be given freely to the ungodly. In the same vein, history is not properly the story of humans vainly attempting to overcome fate, but is the story of God's wrath interrupted permanently by unexpected promises. Promises from God stand outside law, and so outside the laws of history. Just so, Abraham was overlooked, even by the Jews, who told his story as that of the covenant sign of circumcision rather than the promise given 430 years before the law.

The first promise of history is given in Genesis 3:15: "I will put enmity between you and the woman, and between your seed and her seed . . . He shall crush your head." Then Abraham was plucked out of obscurity and unrighteousness, and given the central promise of all Scripture; therefore he, rather than Moses, came to the fore in Scripture. But Melanchthon warned his students that even the story of Abraham can be told two opposite ways: one by saying that the covenant of circumcision is what makes him our Father (thus he represents the law prior to Moses), or the story goes as Paul tells it—that Abraham is our Father not because of the law of circumcision, but because he received a promise from God that had its "yes" (or arrival) in Christ. Indeed, Paul told the story as it was actually written. Abraham received a very particular promise—that his "offspring" or seed should inherit the world. In his letter to the Galatians, Paul makes the point quickly, and in Romans draws it out: "It does not say, 'and to offsprings (seeds)' referring to many, but, referring to One, 'And to your Offspring,' (Seed) which is Christ" (Galatians 3:16).

Now a promise like this does not form a *covenant*; it forms a *testament*, indeed a "*new*" testament," so Paul uses a homely analogy.

Just as you would not dare to annul a person's last will and testament, or make any addition to it once it has been ratified—neither can anyone attempt to add circumcision or law to this promise made by God to Abraham some 430 years before Moses (and a good while, even by the Rabbis' count, before Abraham received the sign of circumcision). The election of Abraham was made by an external word—out of the blue—in the form of a promise that forms a testament having nothing to do with any law. A testament is a witness dependent entirely upon the faithfulness of the one making a promise: "upon my death I hereby give to my children my estate . . ." Promises are not like facts that remain inert, they "perform," or accomplish something in a relationship that links testator (will maker) and inheritor in a new way, and thereby Abram became Abraham—the father of many nations—because the promise made to him created faith, and this faith made Abraham the spiritual father of any who share that particular faith in the one Seed.[7] These three necessarily go together: Christ, promise, and faith.

The content of the promise, which is Christ, comes in the form of his *communicatio idiomatum*, meaning that it comes in the form of the forgiveness of sins. This makes the promise given to Abraham unique in comparison with all human promises like those we make or receive on earth. The promise is *reckoned* to Abraham as righteousness, meaning that it is an unthwartable promise based entirely on its giver's faithfulness—despite the ungodliness of the recipient. There is the second key to Abraham's story. Not only is it faith and not circumcision (or law), it is also faith *reckoned* as righteous, and so we have our final word for the way God makes sinners just: "imputation." This word is where the meat—and all the trouble—of Lutheran theology resides.

Reckoning or Imputation

Paul identifies the heart of Scripture in the story of Abraham—told not as a story of the covenant of circumcision, but as the bestowal of the promise of a Seed that Abraham trusted. The promised Seed was Christ, much to everyone's surprise (especially Paul's), and the faith of Abraham in that promise was for that reason reckoned by God as just. For the Lutherans, "reckon" was often summarized by an Augustinian word as in the Augsburg Confession, article 4: "This faith God *imputes* for righteousness in his sight" (Roman 3:4).

How is faith taken as righteousness before God? If it is not a legal arrangement, then what is it? Faith is not a power of the human, even though it is a gift—like an I.O.U. It is not a possession or a quality of the heart, as the Scholastics described it. Faith is always in something. Luther is even willing to use the Aristotelian term "formal" for faith to make this point, although with caution. Faith does not stand by itself as a substance that God counts as worthy; what makes faith justifying rests in the *object* it grasps. Faith as a human quality can grasp almost anything—by itself it is surprisingly profligate so that it has a very special problem that harkens back to the original sin itself—faith can curiously turn back into itself and seek to establish its own self, so that faith can strangely take itself as its own object. That is the special problem of Protestants as they began to break away from Luther; they increasingly made faith into a self-reference separable as an experience from the objective promise of the preacher.

Faith is never without a thing in which it trusts; but when faith's "thing" is a promise from God whose "yes" is Christ, then it has something that "counts" before God. Christ counts before God—not as a token of law, but quite apart from the law since the Father gives everything to the Son, and the Son gives everything back freely. When faith (like Abraham's) gets a promise (like Christ) the whole world changes. Faith finally grasps the object it was made for, and in so doing takes leave of itself and clings only to Christ. Christ then becomes the sole mediator between the sinner and God's wrath. Luther is even willing to say that this faith, given as a gift, makes a new God—who is none other than Christ, the man who takes the sin of the world upon him. When trust is in the right thing, then Abraham's sin is no longer counted; it is ignored because it belongs to Christ, and the very righteousness that belongs to Christ is bestowed upon Abraham with the result that when God looks upon Abraham, he sees only Christ and he is pleased with this Abraham/Christ. That is, Abraham is united with Christ in faith itself. "Imputation" means that your faith is reckoned as righteousness when Christ is its object because your sins are imputed to Christ and Christ's righteousness is imputed to you.

Luther relished Christian life as the union with Christ in faith itself.[8] When God gave a promise to Abraham, God created faith by giving Abraham something to believe in. God is verbal, and when he communicates his word he communes with the hearer—he gives himself to the unrighteous, ungodly. In the end this unites Abraham with Christ; faith clings to that promise, and God imputes (reckons) it as righteous *propter Christum* (on account of Christ), so that when God addresses Abraham he addresses him as none other than his only begotten Son, who pours himself out for sinners.

Imputation means Abraham has righteousness not of his own, but of Christ. This does not mean Christ legally substituted for Abraham so that the law could be maintained as the true measurement of God's justice. It means that life is possible without any law—but only for Christ and to whomever Christ gave himself. God's righteousness is to make sinners righteous by giving them Christ's righteousness. What happened to Abraham in this act was that Abraham got a new God, and he was destroyed as an old sinner in order to be created anew. Paul occupies Romans 6 with this anthropological situation, but here in the fourth chapter the central matter is that Christ's righteousness comes

- As a gift
- Freely, without condition or merit
- Externally, outside myself, and so an alien righteousness
- By means of a preached word, which is the promise of the forgiveness of sin
- Daily, repeatedly, since faith does not merely begin—but encompasses the whole life.
- The only one who can make and keep such a promise is the one who has the power to forgive, God himself, and the one who actually has taken on the sin of the world himself, bodily, who is the true man without sin, crucified for our sakes.
- Imputation is union not in the Platonic sense of participation in the higher good, or by desire finding its true goal, but in

a strange double union. First, a union with Christ in a death like his—so that, second, we might be united with him in a resurrection like his (Romans 6).

- God creates faith in order to receive the word—by means of that very word. Promises do that; commands do not. Once created, faith clings to that word alone even while sin, suffering, and death are all that is seen and felt. Thus, faith takes leave of the old self and flees to Christ, listening only to him and to no one else—especially not one's own self.

To people operating in the scheme of the law it always seems that two options are possible when it comes to how God reckons or imputes righteousness to faith. One is to say that sinners must *become righteous* in themselves—as judged by the law—before God can rightly declare them just. This could either be done straightway by works, or by a mystical participation in that which is "above" the sinner; that is, in God's own being. The other is to say that sinners can be *declared righteous*, forensically as in a court of law—though they are not actually righteous in themselves. A debtor deserves punishment, but if a generous patron paid the debt it may be right for a judge to let a criminal go free. In either case, the key is that the law remains the form of righteousness.

Perhaps Luther, and a handful of others, are the only theologians ever to reject both of these options. In any case, Lutheran theology had problems with the term "imputation" that are usually traced back to Melanchthon. Luther is depicted as holding imputation to be *union with Christ* and therefore the sinner somehow is ontologically changed by participating in God's own being. Melanchthon is depicted as holding a "fictional," *forensic* sense in which a person is counted righteous because of a legal transaction between the Father and Son whose beneficiaries certain sinners have become. The favorite slogan used for this purpose is Melanchthon's opening statement in his *Loci*: "we know Christ only by his benefits." That slogan became the banner of the popular versions of Lutheran theology in the nineteenth and twentieth centuries, strangely employed as a way to have Luther and Immanuel Kant agree that true, trustworthy knowledge comes only through sense experience! The champion of that attempt was Albrecht Ritschl, and it was repeated by Rudolph Bultmann and his progeny. That argument does a disservice to Melanchthon.

The solution to this fault line among Lutheran theologians is not to choose between union with Christ and forensic declaration. A key problem may well exist in Melanchthon's teaching of justification, but not in this place. Lutheran theologians habitually discard or displace imputation from the article of justification proper, where we are now discussing it, and place it in a subsequent discussion called "sanctification," because it would appear that imputation must imply *actually becoming righteous in the self.* That is, Lutheran theology has a habit—like any scholasticism—of taking justification away from what makes a good tree good, and placing it in the discussion of the fruit a good tree produces. This happens when imputation is drawn back under the law—the very opposite of Luther's breakthrough—which is the pious dream that Abraham would be able to stand before God as a righteous man because he somehow managed to "believe" when others could not. Then, of course, people would attempt to use this mock-Abraham as a model for how they too can "believe" their way to heaven.

Lutherans throughout their history have fallen into this problem of making faith into a work, attempting various definitions of "faith" that knit together human response and God's grace in what is called "synergism"—or some type of "compatibilism" (the cooperation of the believer with grace—created or uncreated). Faith then becomes a decision for Christ, an earnest personal relationship in which one remains active or the relationship dies, or faith is made into acceptance of our unacceptability, or "clinging to our being clung to"—and a whole assortment of ways to reduce synergism to an acceptably minor level. This attempt was fought out among Lutherans after the imposition of the Augsburg Interim (1548) in which a specifically anti-Lutheran confession was demanded of what really made Abraham righteous: "Since the human soul was so well constituted (original righteousness), God left him free to make his own decisions (Eccles. 15:14), so that he had no less power to choose good than to choose evil."[9] Even Melanchthon's own attempted compromise in the Leipzig Interim said, "the merciful God *does not deal with human creatures as with a block of wood*, but draws them in such a manner that their will cooperates . . . ."[10] This kind of imposed creed forced Lutherans to reject all compromise with Roman or Lutheran synergism in their Second article of the Formula of Concord, as in an upside-down Pelagian pyramid of pleas from a dying old sinner: perfection in this life is possible; if not in this life, then the next; do your best, God does the rest; at least try to improve, and if not then simply "accept" the gift of grace, and in the end, if you cannot accept at least do not reject it. Even the last cry of the synergist is then silenced: "I'm not wood, am I?"

But the true understanding of how God's righteousness is applied to a sinner lies in the fact that God's justice fits with faith—not works and law. But the way it fits with faith is crucial. Faith needs a Word, and the Word creates faith. These two are inseparable, otherwise one simply returns faith to the legal scheme and ends up describing it as a tiny little work (like a decision, or acceptance, or at least not rejecting the gift), or as an "attitude," as Luther calls it, coming out of the human capacity to think or feel—assenting to a proposition, or expressing one's inner conviction to the outside world. Justification by faith does not refer to some *general* notion of faith, such as "you have to believe the sun will come up in the morning." Faith has a very *special*, particular, theological sense. It is faith in Christ in the form of a promise made by Christ, and conveyed to you by a preacher. Faith is not a work, like a virtue or habit that a person has, nor is it an attitude (or feeling)—such as learning to look on the bright side of things—nor is it assenting to a proposition such as, "I guess I can come to believe Christ performed miracles." Faith that justifies entirely gains its worth from its object, Christ. Christ is present in faith, but in a hidden way, that is by means of a simple word. Christ is heard, not seen; even when the disciples had him in plain sight. The word is also not general, it is the concrete promise of Christ, and that promise is always the same: it is the forgiveness of sins to sinners who have no other hope of being right before God. That promise—in order to be believed—must come with a person's own name on it through preaching. Faith is in this particular word of Christ delivered by a preacher *for you*.

126

Grace is God's Favor

Early on, in his first *Loci*, Melanchthon taught precisely how to understand the kind of reckoning or imputation that keeps faith from being another human characteristic, virtue or work. He said grace is *Favor Dei*—God's favor, or reckoning. The Scholastics misused grace, as if it were a "quality in the nature of the soul." So, faith, hope, and love (1 Corinthians 13) became "theological virtues" added to Aristotle's moral virtues, and thus all three were mistaken as powers of the soul.[11] Melanchthon suggested that it would have been better to translate *hen* (in Hebrew) and *charis* in Greek not by the Latin *gratia*, but *favor*. This means grace is in God (not you), but by it he favors you as in "Julius favors Curio," meaning Julius is the favor with which he has befriended Curio, so Melanchthon suggested we should turn to Scripture and find that when it says "grace" it means the "favor in God with which he has befriended the saints." But Melanchthon added quickly, "Those Aristotelian figments about qualities are tiresome." Aristotle wanted everything to be a quality so that we could know for sure who owns what according to the law. But Melanchthon knew (at this early point in his teaching) that God's mercy operated differently than the legal scheme.

This means that the early Lutherans carefully distinguished *favor* (grace as God's reckoning) and *donum* (the gifts of grace) as Paul did in Romans 5:15. Favor is Father and Son (the Father sending the Son, and the Son becoming a curse for us), and what they give is the Holy Spirit (*donum*). Lombard was closer to the truth than the bulk of the scholastics since for him the gift of grace is the Holy Spirit *himself*, not a *quality* given to us. Though it was not typical for medieval theologians to follow Lombard on this matter, the Lutherans knew they were not saying anything new—except for the crucial specification that this gift of the Holy Spirit is the preached word of the forgiveness of sins—entirely outside the law. That was the great point of Paul's argument concerning Abraham. Grace is the favor of God with which he embraced Christ (and because of Christ all the saints). When God favors someone, he cannot help but pour out his gifts, sharing what he has, which is the Holy Spirit himself (not a possession of a substance in the soul).

The key problem with mixing up grace and some capacity of the soul, as Aquinas and later Protestants did, is that we fail to understand how the Gospel justifies by faith alone. Martin Bucer (1491–1551) argued against this Lutheran position in the Schwabach Articles (predecessor to the Augsburg Confession) saying "that it is not enough to be *reckoned*, but one must actually *become* righteous."[12] For Protestants like Bucer, righteousness must really be possessed to be real, but Melanchthon countered: "we are justified when, put to death by the law, we are made alive again by the word of grace promised in Christ." Possession is nullified utterly by law in death, and does not return when we are made alive again. Instead, what faith grasps is a promise, but a promise is not legal property; it is a word that engenders hope because its veracity depends upon another. Our justification happens by a Christ who is not simply a new Moses, but a Christ who himself went through death for our trespasses, and was raised for our justification. So sinners like Abraham will be made exactly like Christ—put to death and only then raised from the dead—not by any process of moral improvement that seeks in the end to be just in itself.

The righteousness is Christ's, and always will be; sinners never possess it as a piece of distributed justice by which we can stand before God's eternal wrath and be exonerated. Therefore, justification is not a single event upon which sanctification is then built. We return again and again to justification by Christ's favor, and therefore there is no salvation without a preacher—whom we need daily. Melanchthon observed that papal theologians made faith into "the assent" to what is in Scripture. They assumed there is in all souls a neutral quality that could choose to go toward the good or the evil, assenting to Scripture's command or not. Or worse, they inferred a nature created by grace that has within it the capacity for divinization in the supernatural life. Consequently scholastics like Biel (1420–1495) divided faith into "incomplete" (unformed faith needing love to complete it) and "complete" (or "acquired") faith that is loaned from the church on the principle that the church can be collectively trusted when individuals cannot; thus, to believe Christ you must first believe the church.

There is no neutral, natural quality of soul waiting to be taught how to make the right choices in life, or how to orient desire to its proper goal. God's wrath is total, and unrelenting, and no one escapes. There is no neutral territory for this imaginary "faith" as a virtue or act of humans. For the Lutherans, Christ is the only righteousness, and his righteousness is preached by a word of promise that says, "Your sins are forgiven." How? "On my account (*propter Christum*)." Hearing this word makes faith, and this faith is reckoned or imputed as righteous, though there is no righteousness there by any measure of law—including the presence of love as *caritas*. To call divine imputation (as a declared word) a "fiction" is to say that the only truth in life is law, and in turn that is to blaspheme the Gospel—to make Christ into a Moses and to make of Abraham the father by circumcision, not by faith.

The difficulty with holding Christ, faith, and imputation together is taken up in the next two chapters. The first problem is that sin is without repair, since it is all original—which remains even after justification, or baptism. The second is that justification of the ungodly begins with killing the ungodly—and this no one "believes." Salvation goes through death, not around it. Promises of Christ like those given to Abraham are routinely rejected by unfaith because they are too good to be true for people in the legal scheme, and furthermore, they mean death before any resurrection is ever felt. The only possible response to this conundrum is preaching that overthrows the voice of a troubled conscience, so Melanchthon concluded his argument with a word of comfort for those who say, "I believe that salvation was promised, but that it will come to others . . . But listen! These promises are made to you also, are they not?"[13] Only the Holy Spirit can overcome this bound will that fears the promise because it destroys the old person—and he does so by creating an entirely new will.

It was the second article of the Formula of Concord in which Lutherans distanced themselves from Melanchthon's later experiments of returning to the term "assent" as a proper description of Abraham's (or Peter's or David's or Paul's) conversions from law to gospel. That term "assent," and the attempts to find something salvageable in the natural human (like a "spark" or image of God that remains after wrath), were all identified as disasters for preaching that could not accept the radical nature of the conversion. Conversion is not a change of mind, or feelings, or religions, or even behavior; it is the most radical change possible—to die and be created new. To express this, the second generation Lutherans agreed that instead of saying that faith was "assent" to anything, one must stay with the story of Abraham to say "reckon" (or if need be, "impute")—just as Luther and Paul had taught:

> We are not, as Aristotle believed, made righteous by the doing of just deeds . . . but rather, if I may say so, in becoming and being righteous people we do just deeds. First it is necessary that the person be changed, then the deeds will follow . . . the righteousness of Scripture depends upon the imputation of God more than on the essence of the thing itself . . . he alone is righteous . . . whom God wills to be considered righteous before him. Therefore . . . we are righteous only by the imputation of a merciful God through faith in his Word.[14]

Faith has nothing to do with free will—except that faith is given only after death and the annihilation of a free will's desire. Faith is entirely the work of the Holy Spirit. The Spirit does not make new demands, but gives his own self. Thus "reckon" and "impute" have as their subject the Holy Spirit—not only once, but always so that faith never becomes the active possession of a Christian. Reckoning means that an either/or has been reached (an argument by sufficient division) as to how sinners become justified: either it is works, or it is faith. Since reckoning is God's grace, and grace is God's favor (*favor dei*), then one has to agree with Paul that to one who works, her wages are simply *due* her, "But to one who without works trusts him who justifies the ungodly, such faith is reckoned as righteousness" (Romans 4:5 NRS). Reckoning is God's act, given as a gift. But because gifts can be deserved (as at an award banquet), God's gift is specifically made to justify the *ungodly*. Abraham was elected out of ungodliness, and given the promise *gratis* so that he is not only perfectly passive in receiving this, but perfectly undeserving, which is to say that he deserves nothing but death. This means, further, that the only kind of gift justification could possibly be is the forgiveness of sins, since no gift to the ungodly means anything other than this single matter of the forgiveness of sins. What good is reckoning to one who lives? But to a dead person, the only thing that matters is getting a new life.

Reckoning, as the forgiveness of sins, has two "parts" or moments. One is *reckoning* (bestowing) faith to Abraham. Abraham is not given an inner power, instead his faith is finally given the right thing to believe in—the promise of Christ. With this he has everything that belongs to Christ—including the New Testament. The other part is shown by David, where forgiveness of sin is given as *not reckoning* sin. David, the greatest of sinners and yet the man "after God's own heart" (1 Sam 13:14), is taken up by Paul in addition to Abraham because the same word applies in the sinful king's case: "Blessed is the man against whom the Lord will not reckon his sin . . . who imputes no iniquity" (Psalm 32:1–2, translation altered).

For Paul, the whole law and prophets (Abraham and David) witness that no other righteousness exists before God than faith. The law was given later than Abraham's promise, but not to make anyone righteous. This *reckoning* and *not reckoning* is precisely the application of the *communicatio idiomatum* of Christ's two natures, in which Christ takes your sin upon himself, and in its place puts his forgiveness—which is life now and eternal life to come. When Christ takes sin he no longer "imputes" it; indeed, he takes it out of you (exputes it). Then he reckons, or creates faith as righteousness since that faith trusts his promise of forgiveness just as Abraham trusted God's promise to him of the Seed—and this trust in the promise is reckoned as righteousness by God, period.

Faith's Certainty

Faith, and only faith, makes Abraham the spiritual father of those with the same faith. Jew and Gentile are united by this faith in the promise—outside the law, not in it. All family squabbles and tribal division end with faith, including the dividing lines made necessary by the law: male and female, slave and free, Jew and Gentile. Faith is known by how it frees—from circumcision, law, wrath, death, and the Devil.

Now faith is a *locus* which no other philosophy or religion has, Luther liked to say, because all others fall under the legal scheme.

The world does not consider faith to amount to much. Even when a philosophy deigns to considers the phenomenon, it cannot help but seek to replace it with something more substantial, because in the world's eyes faith is the most uncertain thing there is. Kierkegaard (1813–1885) attacked Hegel (1770–1831) on this count because, though faith was treated in the idealistic system, it was made infantile while reason was given the ultimate place. It was no coincidence that Kierkegaard returned to the story of Abraham to create the "knight of faith," whose struggle is greater even than reason thinking of the highest good.[15] Faith is not a thought, although thinking follows it; it is not a feeling, though the feeling of comfort emerges from it; neither is faith a virtue nor a moral act. Faith is not glory; it gives no power in the world, it guarantees no success or relief from suffering—indeed suffering increases with faith. What faith does, however, is give unshakeable certainty, the very kind that human works fruitlessly seek, since they place trust in something other than Christ's promise of the forgiveness of sins. All else in life fails to bring peace or release from anxiety and uncertainty because everything beside Christ's promise is in the process of being destroyed by God. Melanchthon especially liked to call faith's certainty "comfort to the conscience," and so it is, as long as the psychological implications are not divorced from the preacher's external word to which faith clings. Humanism perceived the advantage of Luther's teaching on faith's certainty, and so it became the entrance into the teaching of the Reformation for young Melanchthon.

Melanchthon had conceived and titled his *Loci* ("commonplaces," or "topic") after the rhetorical tradition of Cicero. Within this term lay the story of an ancient battle between Aristotle and Isocrates on the matter of human certainty according to the legal scheme.[16] Between Aristotle and Isocrates' "New Academy" two different views of education, knowledge, and human being emerged. Aristotle placed thought in separate categories of that which could be certainly known (Analytics or logic) and that which was probable—composed of opinion or "points of view" (dialectic). In that way Aristotle set out the basic distinction between certainty and probability. Science was possible on the basis of deductions from true starting premises. Knowledge could thus be an end in itself, since humans were thought to be rational animals whose fulfillment of desires comes by private contemplation of the truth in imitation of a God (whose own being is certainty in self-contemplation). Nevertheless, even though certainty is not available in most matters, at least some order could be given to the work of convincing others of an opinion so that the better opinions would be adopted. Aristotle attempted just that in his book on Topics (*Topica*) that take up *loci* as the way of organizing opinions in the direction of the pure sciences.

In contrast, Isocrates held that nothing known by humans is certain, mankind is social and fluid in essence, and knowledge is used as an instrument, not an end. The highest human achievement is thus speech, and education should be organized toward that end—producing orators, not scientists, whose goal is to produce clear, agreeable, and persuasive speech. Aristotle's *certainty* soon gave way to Isocrates' *persuasion*. Dialectic orders speech to these instrumental purposes, and the tool used for organizing was none other than the topics, or *loci*. The *loci* went out into the buzzing, blooming multiplicity of the world to find those "things" that ought to be discussed so that orators could in turn find (*inventio*) words that were persuasive, agreeable, and clear for a rhetorician.

Although Aristotle remained the great philosopher, it was only his *Topica* that was used by Cicero's day, and even it was conveyed according to the tradition of Isocrates so that Cicero (106–43BC) and later Quintilian (35–100 AD) held that truth could only be approximated; *probability* was the goal, since no such thing as certainty existed. Meanwhile, on the wings of Augustine's (354–430) subsequent rejection of the New Academy, the scholastics—starting with Anselm (1033–1109) and proceeding through Thomas Aquinas (1225–1274)—considered the body of dogma given through the church (the rule of faith in the form of revelation) to be the one, certain thing in life. Faith could not be left to mere opinion or probability. Therefore, it was determined that the articles of faith preserved by the church (from God's own revelation) must be expressible in propositions that are necessarily (logically) true. New scholastics (Nominalists), and the old like Thomas, disagreed on how far natural reason could go in knowing the highest good (God as the goal of human knowledge)—but they did not disagree on reclaiming a ground for *certainty* in the human knowledge called theology and its doctrine. How much of this scholasticism entered back into Lutheran theology among the Lutheran orthodox of the seventeenth and eighteenth centuries has long been a matter of debate, but the idea of a *corpus doctrina* revealed by God in the form of a rule of faith has long tempted theology to put certainty in *human reason*, and remove it from the one necessary place—the communication of divine attributes in Christ that pours itself out in *preaching*. It was Luther and Melanchthon who together moved away from the Aristotelian/ scholastic idea of a revealed body of doctrine that is preserved by the church (and to which faith must then assent). Instead, they found the Ciceronian, rhetorical legacy fruitful because it could comprehend something of the importance of preaching—but yet certainty was missing from this tradition.

Lutheran theology could adopt neither of these schools (Aristotle or Isocrates), and yet accomplishes the goal of each. The most important thing that happens in this world is speech, but the particular speech that makes for proclamation does not give mere opinion—it is the single source of absolute certainty. Melanchthon named his Lutheran theology textbook *Loci* after the Ciceronian tradition of oratory that rejected human certainty, but he proceeded to advance the *loci* from mere opinion (Aristotle) to the *sedes argumentorum*—the veins running through theology (and any discipline) that allowed one to investigate the rhetorical, pumping heart of any matter. This was part and parcel of the rejection of both Nominalism and early scholasticism for the Lutherans. Melanchthon made theology into a dialectical instrument of preaching (homiletics), and thus all theology is for proclamation. Theology is instrumental, not an object of contemplation or an end in itself. Melanchthon was always a rhetorician like this at heart, especially when he was organizing Lutheran theology in his classic works—the *Loci (1521)* and the *Apology of the Augsburg Confession* (1530). But there was something the rhetoricians did not give Melanchthon either—that he found only in Luther.

Luther did not approximate the heart of theology by means of the veins (*loci sedes argumentorum*)—dallying with various "topics" which then led back to the real argument of Christ. He went right to the heart, which is the particular kind of communication found in Jesus Christ's attributes. Christ's communication created preaching that was not merely persuasion or approximation of truth—nor was it merely a body of doctrine revealed by God and preserved by the church. Certainty is had on earth in one place and moment, which is the certainty of *faith*, based neither on contemplation, nor the power of the oratory—but only on the faithfulness of Christ to his promise. Faith is certain when it hears the voice of its Shepherd who speaks in the form of a promise—whose content is forgiveness. Luther often said that when he thought back about his days in the Seminary, he was taught the Augustinian high-wire balancing act between pride and despair in the form of managed doubt. If one *never* doubted it was pride; if one *only* doubted it was despair, and so a *via media* (middle way) was sought. But faith like Abraham's is never commingled with doubt; it is always absolutely certain. Even the great insights of Kierkegaard on Abraham could not quite grasp this point. Faith is certain because it takes leave of itself—its subjectivity—and clings to a promise from the only one who can keep a promise beyond the law and beyond death.

The world is shocked by this kind of unwavering firmness of conviction, especially when its source is revealed—for it is not something that is certain because it was decided *before* all time in the mind of God (a false predestination). Christ's promise was decided *in* time by the accident of preaching that takes place between a preacher and a sinner at a particular moment that could never have been logically anticipated—but after the fact is the most necessary truth of one's life. Luther brought certainty back to faith, but not as Aristotle and the scholastics had attempted. The certainty of faith is not a *scientific body* of certain knowledge, revealed specially to the church and vouchsafed there. Instead, it is a *person* who has spoken a single promise. So faithful was Christ at his hour of trial that he became not only a sinner, but sin itself and thus a curse for us (Galatians 3:13). Then Christ underwent something the world knows nothing of—he was raised on the third day and so is able to forgive the very sinners who killed him. His communication of attributes is like new wine in old wine skins, breaking out and pouring its contents upon sinners in the words: "I absolve you." Abraham received the very same promise that is given to any sinner today—the certainty of Christ, who forgives sin. According to the Lutherans, heresy no longer resides in those that think that the body of received, churchly doctrine is uncertain, but in those who think the preacher's promise from Christ is uncertain.

The Proper Application of the Pronoun

Any promise that comes through law, like circumcision, remains uncertain because it awaits some doing of your own. Paul thus makes the distinction: "For the promise that he would inherit the world did not come to Abraham or to his descendants through the law, but through the righteousness of faith" (Romans 4:13NRS). Law voids the promise; but faith learns to ignore the law, and depend only upon this promise. Faith does not stand upon what it feels or sees; it is only an ear, and the ear listens solely to Christ. That is the nature of faith, so that Abraham believed "in hope [in Christ] against hope [that he sees] that he would become the father of many nations" (Genesis 15:5 and Romans 4:18 NRS). When he looked down at his own body—or that of Sarah—he did not "weaken," and "no distrust made him waver concerning the promise of God . . . fully convinced that God was able to do what he had promised" (Romans 4:19–21 NRS).

So Paul says: "the words 'it was reckoned to him,' were written not for his sake alone, but for ours also" (Romans 4:23–4 NRS). Paul then began to preach outright to his hearers: "It will be reckoned to us who believe in him who raised from the dead Jesus our Lord, who was handed over to death for our trespasses and was raised for our justification" (Romans 4:25 NRS). In this little sermon one finds the true art of preaching that Luther called the "proper application of the pronoun." Preachers do not create new gospels; the promises of Christ are given in Scripture where God intended to make them available for public consumption, but what the preacher does is apply the pronoun "for you" to the promise of Christ, thus making the word a *living* word of direct address in the present. Faith not only knows and trusts the story of Abraham; it not only knows the history of Christ which Melanchthon called "historical faith," (that even the devil believes). Instead, *justifying* faith is a different animal. It not only knows Christ made some general promise, but it knows for certain that the promise is made "for you." Between a public promise and your faith is a great chasm that cannot be leapt by human power, but is delivered as the gift of the Holy Spirit. Therefore, to receive a promise from Christ with the pronoun "for you" attached is imputation.

Only when this belief is created—out of nothing (*creatio ex nihilo*)—"giving life to the dead and calling into existence the things that do not exist" (Romans 4:17)—do we have justifying faith that imputes the *favor Dei*. When the faith that trusts God's favor has been given to me, then I can confess in all circumstances: "God is pleased with me—on account of Christ's cross." The soul (or conscience) that can do that is then perfectly comforted—and certain.

Freedom from Wrath

Romans 5
And yet the Law fulfilled must be,
Or we were lost forever;
Therefore God sent his Son that he
Might us from death deliver.
He all the Law for us fulfilled,
And thus his Father's anger stilled
Which over us impended

Paul Speratus, *Salvation unto Us Has Come*

Access

There is no freedom for anyone until God's wrath ends, and the end of wrath comes only through preaching Abraham's promise "guaranteed to all his descendents" (Romans 4:16 NRS). Once the promise is communicated, Paul can say: "Therefore, since we are justified by faith we have peace with God through our Lord Jesus Christ. Through him we have obtained access to this grace in which we stand . . ." (Romans 5:1 translation altered). Access to grace came at a great price for Christ, and was given freely to us. Christ is the mercy seat, whose first communication with his sinners is a struggling, agonizing exchange by which Christ takes our sins and becomes a curse for us. Theologically this exchange is usually called "redemption." Simultaneously, Christ makes a second exchange which Luther called the "joyous" communication in which Christ gives all that belongs to him: in the place of sin he gives forgiveness, for death he gives life, and in the place of Satan's lordship of this world he gives his own kingdom of heaven. "Reconciliation" is Paul's word for the free gift: "For if while we were enemies, we were reconciled to God through the death of

138

his Son, much more surely, having been reconciled, will we be saved by his life" (Romans 5:10 NRS). Reconciliation means access because sinners belong to their Creator again.

Access to God begins in Christ's own person, where the struggling and joyous exchanges are first made, and then pours out to sinners: "But more than that we . . . we [!] have now received reconciliation" (Romans 5:11 NRS). God's communication in Christ is now announced—boasted—publicly in the preaching that makes three communications of the *idiomata* of Christ. By his death he took our sin upon him and put it to death on the cross; by his resurrection he conquered this sin once and for all, being raised as Lord of a new kingdom without law, wrath, death, or devil; the third communicates Christ's benefits to us in preaching, "pouring them into our hearts through the Holy Spirit who has been given to us" (Romans 5:5 translation altered).

At this point we can pick up Luther's argument in the parallel passages of Paul's letter to the Galatians and Luther's Christological lectures. The bestowal of the benefits of Christ provides us with a new kind of language that Luther called "delicious": Christ has become the death of death, as Hosea sings (13:14), "O death, I shall be your death!" This language makes reconciliation the story of a great, cosmic battle. The destructive powers of the curse of sin, death, devil, and law that we could not overcome now receives "bitter conflict" in Christ's own person. In him curse (destruction) contended with blessing (creation) to see which would win. The battle's apex occurred at the cross where the law, the most salutary doctrine of life, contended against the gospel (Christ's forgiveness of sins) because law and gospel do not work hand in hand to make anyone righteous, but are mortal enemies:

> Therefore the curse clashes with the blessing and wants to damn it and annihilate it. But it cannot. For the blessing is divine and eternal, and therefore the curse must yield to it. For if the blessing in Christ could be conquered, then God Himself would be conquered.

But, Luther assured, "this is impossible."[1] God wants to be justified in his words, incarnate in Christ, crucified on the cross, having taken our sins and become a curse. The last question left on earth was whether death is stronger than Christ's own, particular life—but not even death could bind him. On the third day his Father, with the Spirit, raised Christ from the dead. After that, nothing could conquer this God and keep him from his purpose. Yet, what is God's purpose or goal? It is the strangest thing imaginable: he wants to pour out his love on sinners and free them by killing them and then create them new—a strange desire and love indeed.

Nothing on earth could have served as the scene of battle between curse and blessing, law and gospel, other than the incarnate person of the Son of God. As human, born under the law, Christ was "able" to become a curse; and as divine he was nothing other than pure blessing himself. The reason Arius (c.250–336) was the greatest heretic of all is that he disallowed this great Duel from taking place: if Christ were not truly human he could not become a curse or die, and if he were not fully God Christ could not be raised as Lord of a new kingdom—who rules only the forgiven.[2]

Reconciliation comes not through the law, but Christ—no other access to God's grace exists, and so the legal scheme is overthrown. The battle that took place in Christ's person at the cross was not mythological, though it has that ring in our ears. It did not take place "once upon a time," or in that time "that never really occurs and always occurs." The death of Christ on the cross took place in time and space, and so is historical. But the "once" of this cross is also "for all." If the sins of the world really were on him, and he became a curse, then when he died they died, and when he was raised there was nothing less than a new creation, a new time or Aeon and Christ reigns over a wholly new kingdom: "So if anyone is in Christ, there is a new creation. Behold, in Christ all things have become new" (2 Corinthians 5:17 NRS). The awaited new kingdom of heaven has arrived in this man, Jesus Christ—through whom we have obtained access to God's grace, the hope of sharing in God's glory—but, where is this glory?

On Being a Theologian of the Cross

"We boast in our hope of sharing the glory of God. And not only that, we boast in our sufferings . . ." (Romans 5:2–3 NRS). Jews seek a sign; Greeks seek wisdom, but we preach the folly of the cross. From the jaws of glory Paul pulls us into the cross and suffering, not away from it. In faith we do not see glory; instead we see suffering, and if that were not enough, by the seventh chapter of Romans, Paul says we feel and see in our own flesh the very sin that Christ is promised to have taken and defeated. Everything promised to faith seems to be taken away immediately in experience: glory turns to suffering; seeing turns to hearing; resurrection to dying; sin that has been taken away is nevertheless felt, seen, and the devil wags his finger at the sin still residing in the old flesh, forcing us to account for it. What has happened in this faith? The Adam that was condemned under God's wrath is still there. Paul tells us that glory waits in hope; meanwhile "we boast in our sufferings." The irony of having Paul put suffering where Aristotle put virtue is transfixing. Suffering rather than practice in moral virtues produces endurance, and as any athlete knows, it is endurance that produces character—but how can perfect passivity or suffering do that? Moreover, character is to produce *eudaimonia* (happiness), not Paul's "hope, and hope is not to disappoint us because God's love is poured into our hearts." Paul answers that the true suffering, or perfect passivity (receiving everything and producing nothing), both come "through the Holy Spirit which has been given to us" (Romans 5:5 NRS). The gift of the Holy Spirit is suffering and death.

To be made a theologian of the cross rather than glory is always a shock. Faith that receives the communicated blessings of Christ's victory does not see or feel those benefits. Faith therefore teaches us to believe against our feelings, and only in the promise. Promises are "already and not yet," meaning fulfilled and present—yet both in faith itself and alone. Luther recognized how suffering operates in Christian life when he observed that there really are three parts to the basic catechism of Christian life. First is the Law with its impossible command: Do this! Second is the Creed with God's promise: Behold what I have done! The third is the Lord's Prayer, which means that Christians are not removed from this world at baptism, but kept in it and made into theologians of the cross. The Lord's Prayer is not made to complete justification, or test it to see if it is valid, but rather is the act of suffering the divine work of God as a perfectly passive receiver whose old life still clings. Every power of the old Aeon fights against this divine work to the bitter end. The old Adam fights it, convinced that there is no new person of faith, but only the old being trying to believe the impossible. The law fights against it, attempting to take the place of Christ in the conscience so that it can demand righteousness in the self. Death tries to frighten faith into appearing weak and useless against the sorrow of losing this life. The devil especially fights faith, claiming that Christ is an obvious liar, since the sins of the world are not on him and not defeated, but still hang around the neck of a sinner who is therefore responsible for them himself.

Glory theologians have a simple rule: if Christ's kingdom has come there will be visible, experiential glory; if it has not come, then there will be suffering. For them, the two Aeons of the old world and new creation are separated forever. Faith is then correlated with success, victory and power—if one has true faith, then one succeeds and feels glory. In this scenario, the faithful themselves are the litmus test of the truth of Christ's promise, and therein lies the root of our problem. Sin looks for an authority outside the promise, and it thinks it finds it in its own power to believe. This is why Paul finally took up the meaning of sin so late in his letter. "Sin came into the world through one man and death through sin, and so death spread to all because all sinned . . ." (Romans 5:12 NRS). Original sin is glory theology that uses itself as the litmus test for God's blessing. It takes its eye off the prize, who is Christ, and listens to an inner voice rather than the external, preached word of promise. Glory does not like promise; instead it likes what it thinks of as "fact"—visible, tangible, experiential glory in the form of power in the self to stand before God and be just, or glory looks for a power of a community that can change the injustice of the world.

To the contrary, Christ's victory is sure and his promise is communicated fully by a preacher, but yet Christian lives are hidden. "Hidden" does not mean obscured so that our lives are meant to be tested for strength and depth; it means hidden under the opposite of glory so that they can never be found by inquiring minds. "Hidden" means hidden under suffering just as Christ's victory is hidden under the "sign of its opposite" which is the cross. Nothing could be more opposite the glory of God than the humiliating death of Christ under the eternal curse. Likewise, the mark of the Christian life is the cross. Luther put this in three famous theses in the Heidelberg Disputation (1518) that awakened so many of his fellow Augustinian friars to the gospel:

19. That person does not deserve to be called a theologian who looks upon the invisible things of God as though they were clearly perceptible in those things which have actually happened [Rom. 1:20].
20. He deserves to be called a theologian, however, who comprehends the visible and manifest things of God seen through suffering and the cross.
21. A theologian of glory calls evil good and good evil. A theologian of the cross calls the thing what it actually is.[3]

The eyes of the sinner delude a person about God, world, and self; the ears of the faithful can finally say what "a thing is." Glory theologians think they know a good work when they see one, but they fail to grasp that everything a person does under the wrath of God is evil and worthy of death. Glory thinks not only that good works are possible, but that the free will is what has the power to do them. But if that were case, why was Christ hung on the cross? Theologians of glory think the law implies freedom of will, and therefore the law must be the way to gain access to God's grace—but nothing could be further from the truth. They think their sin is *suffering*, and the way to defeat it is through moral virtue that produces endurance; endurance would then produce good character, and character must be acceptable to God on the basis of the law—no doubt with a good deal of grace. In that case, boasting in suffering would be rejoicing in the very sin that obscures a person's vision of God as the greatest object of love. Boasting in suffering would be perverse, since visions of glory are needed to motivate human desires to pursue the higher objects like the good, true, and beautiful.

The legal scheme cannot find a proper place for suffering in its system that relates sinner to God. It either rejects it as the opposite of faith—a sign of disbelief—or it tries to make suffering into a preparation for grace along the monastic line. Because suffering has no proper place, the frustration eventually turns to God, and thus *theodicy* is born that takes all of history and theology to be a justification of God for causing suffering, allowing it, or being unable to overcome it. Yet God does not want to be justified by means of universal history, he wants to be justified in his words. At its root, suffering is not merely the bodily, animal flight from pain; it is the sinner's struggle with the problem of divine election or predestination. Suffering means to suffer God's almighty power while completely passive. Complete passivity is the horror of sinners who see it as a fate worse than death, because they imagine that even in death they will have some free will. It is true that when God is not preached, and his wrath goes out over everything, there is no rejoicing in his power and glory. However, when that almighty power is exercised in the cross of Christ—as weakness in the world—and we have access through Him to God's grace, then an entirely new face of suffering shows itself. Suffering leads to rejoicing when it is no longer my active production of good works that justifies, but Christ's promise alone. When I *suffer a divine promise*, then God's almighty power leaves nothing to me; he does all—death, devil, and even my own opposition to God matter not at all. That is why suffering means passion, and passion means passivity; passivity is the joy of saying to the accusation of the law: "Do you then do nothing for your justification?" I answer, "Nothing at all." I rejoice in suffering when I suffer the loss of the law, my good works, and my hope in moral improvement—and ultimately suffer Christ's unthwartable promise as my ultimate destiny.

The theologian of the cross has the legal scheme removed, and so all of the obstacles to calling a thing what it really is are also removed. Denial is the result of obstacles to the myth of free will. The first obstacle is that I do not want to see that I myself am a sinner, and the second is that God delights only in justifying sinners—apart from the law—and we do not want to lose the law in the form of human "potential." Luther cut to the core of the real question of the glory theologian: if my sin is truly taken and defeated by Christ, and if there is a new kingdom, then why do I still feel, see, and do sin? What do you make of that? Luther's most offensive observation now follows: "This [righteousness by faith alone] does not mean that there is no sin in us." "Sin is always present, and the godly *feel* it," Luther says. But what happens to it?

Did Christ's communicating exchange fail? Did he take the world's sin—except my own? Hardly! Yet, what does Christ do with the kind of sin that I plainly see in myself? Answer: "It is ignored."[4] Is it ignored because God does not truly care about it? No! God is angry at it. But why does he then ignore it? Your sin is ignored by God because he put it on Christ. God's view of things—not your own—matters here; especially you cannot depend upon your "sense experience." Luther says, "But it [our sin] is ignored and hidden in the sight of God, because Christ the mediator stands between; because we take hold of Him by faith, all our sins are sins no longer." Where Christ is not, sin is imputed, reckoned, applied, and attributed; but where Christ is, sin is not applied. The Christian is "above the law and sin."

Faith finds itself in an active struggle with the devil over the veracity of faith, and faith is a struggling conflict—a duel—with Satan over the issue of ownership of sins. If Satan comes and shows you your sin saying, "but what of this sin here?", the Christian learns how to respond: "You are mistaken, those sins you see upon me now belong to Christ." And if the devil persists: "but I see it, and you feel it! How much more real can you get?" You respond: "But it is not what is seen and felt, but what is heard that makes the difference; because you do not know faith you call the good evil and the evil good—but I have learned to call a thing what it really is." Luther taught his own students that they may no longer hold onto sin, nurse it, use it, and otherwise live by it. Sin now belongs to Christ, and no one can rob him of what rightfully belongs to him, so Luther coached the pugilist: "you let Christ be the cross-Lord," (the curse for you)—refer the Devil to Christ, who has promised that the world's sins (including your own) are truly His own.

The theologian of glory looks at sin upon himself, forgets all about Christ, and goes back to the law as the means of ridding himself of the thing. The theologian of the cross looks at sin upon himself—and ignores it, referring all judging to Christ. He denies ownership and refuses to look at them while listening only to Christ's promise of forgiveness. Christ did not die for us *because* we rid ourselves of sin; he died for sin because we could not be rid of it, and did not even know that sin was all that bad: "while we were yet helpless . . . while we were yet sinners Christ died for us . . . while we were enemies . . ." (Romans 5:6,8,10). The proof that justification is not by law is that it happened to us while we were sinners—helpless and dead. This is called the justification *of the ungodly*—not of the *formerly ungodly*. The law theoretically allows for the latter, but not the former, yet Christ operates outside the law and without the litmus test of glory.

God's Love vs. Human Love

One of the perpetual theological debates takes place over Paul's conclusion to the logic of rejoicing in suffering in which he describes God's love: "God's love has been poured out in our hearts through the Holy Spirit who has been given to us" (Romans 5:5 translation altered). Lutherans like Johann Agricola (1494–1566), Andreas Osiander (1498–1552), Albrecht Ritschl, Paul Tillich—so different in many ways—have attempted a common project, following the model of Augustine, to make God's love fit human love. The many schools of Roman theology followed this line as well, seeking to match desire (*eros*) to its proper object (*caritas*), so that theology became "educating desires" to strive for the higher, spiritual goals more willingly than the lower, animalic ones. Often this project is expressed ontologically—as a return to the original, "natural" fit between Creator and creatures. The theory is that an unfortunate break due to sin occurred in this natural arrangement, and Christ is used to mend and restore the primitive arrangement. It is primitivism that uses ontology to fit God and sinners—not the cross, and it does this by laying out being in a hierarchy of loves. The modern Lutheran classic on this theme was Anders Nygren's *Agape and Eros* (1953) in which he observed that Augustine misused Romans 5:5 'ἡ ἀγάπη τοῦ θεου' as an objective genitive (love for God) that forced love back into the legal scheme.[5] Humans are by created nature lovers, Augustine argued, but what they love will either elevate humans or cause them to fall in relation to God. When God gives the Holy Spirit, it means that he infuses the love of higher things—charity—in man, and so the real import of Paul's argument was taken to be how the human boat of love becomes "righted," or righteous amid troubled waters. This interpretation dominated Christendom because it fit into the deepest desire of sinners, which is to be righteous in the self by law. Augustine went so far as to replace Paul's verb "poured out," for his ontologically correct verb "poured in," thus completing the transfer of God's love to humans.

Ever more subtle versions of this reversal of love were tried, including the most important among Lutherans that was attempted by Osiander, one of Luther's students, who ignited one of the great Lutheran controversies over his theory of "divine indwelling." Christ's divine essence of love was poured into the Christians so as to overwhelm the lower, human love with its righteousness as a drop of water is overwhelmed by the sea. Osiander thought he could then rid faith of all the forensic talk of "reckoning or imputing" (and even rid the church of the public declaration of absolution—since there was no limit to such profligate forgiveness) by declaring that what mattered in the Christian life was an ontological indwelling of Christ. That indwelling was imagined to displace all that is not Christ (and so evil)—by the sheer power of his divinity, on the principle that where Christ's divinity is, no sin can reside. This mysticism of Christ's indwelling by the divine nature was merely a theory of justification *by love*. It was repudiated by every type of Lutheran—those who followed Melanchthon (Philippists) and those who sought to follow Luther (Gnesio-Lutherans)—eventuating in the third article of the Formula of Concord (1580). The problem that they all saw was that Osiander bypassed the forgiveness of sins in the preached promise of Christ. Many are the attempts to establish justification apart from a preacher, and the biggest temptation is to create a theology of love that displaces lower loves of bodily desires (*eros*) with higher loves of the spiritual kind (*caritas*).

Nygren pointed out that Paul was not interested in the reclamation of *human* love of God. He was interested in *God's* love, for which he uses the special term *agape* alone with the verb "poured out" because this was exactly unlike human love—and remains ever opposed to human love. Nygren emphasized the difference between divine and human love so that there is a break between these, a fracture, that will never be healed because it is not love, but Christ himself, who mediates between creature and Creator. God is not true love's goal; God is the one who acts—alone—to make the unjust just. What Nygren was not as clear about is how this phrase in Paul is the fulfillment of Joel 3:1, and the pouring out of the Holy Spirit. For this we need to know precisely what kind of love God's love is. Nygren noted that human love is always directed to some other object, but ends up lodged in the ego or self—whereas God's love is *sui generis*; it does not have an external object that draws it, but rather it is entirely based in God's own self. This is not quite correct. God's love is free, that much is true, and no object, law or nature outside God draws it out without his free choice. However, what God chooses to love is precisely, and inexplicably, his direct opponent—his enemy—the unjust sinner. God loves not just from himself, but he loves shit. There is hardly an elegant way of putting this, as Luther often found in his preaching, but the principle is announced without crudities in his Heidelberg Disputation's final thesis 28: "The love of God does not first discover but creates what is pleasing to it. The love of man comes into being through attraction to what pleases it." This sentence marks the break with Augustine, neo-Platonism, the various schools of Roman Scholastic thought, and therefore the end of the legal scheme when it comes to love. To Nygren's argument, we simply add that God loves not because of desire, but because he is the one who creates out of nothing, that is, who raises the dead. His love, strangely, kills the object before it creates it. Reconciliation is not just between Creator and creatures; it is exactly between Creator and sinners—while they are sinners, ungodly, and enemies. This happens by Christ's cross, not by an adjustment to the human love mechanism. Paul has in mind the arrival of the promise of the outpouring of the Holy Spirit (Joel 3:1) by which a new heart would be given (Jeremiah 31:31).

It is a common mistake to think that the heart needs only a better object to love, or more encouragement to actually do it. However, what is truly needed is a completely new heart, created by the love of God because God is pleased to do so on account of his Son—not because there is anything of enduring value in the heart of the sinner. Boasting in a hope that is not yet seen is exercising a freedom of speech that the world does not know by means of suffering God's love—not being attracted to it—and that rejoicing is none other than "we even boast in God through our Lord Jesus Christ, through whom we have now received reconciliation" (Romans 5:11 NRS). Our justification is an alien righteousness—belonging always to Christ—from start to finish. Our justification is outside us in the form of a preached promise, and is never a legal possession of the heart. Therefore the Holy Spirit is not given as an experience of power to be used in this old world, but is in the form of a down-payment (Romans 8:23, 2 Cor 1:22)—it remains an objective pledge that our hope will not shame us, even when we look at ourselves and constantly are ashamed. The free gift is not like the trespass (Romans 5:15) because it is not possessed, or "in" the old creature—Christ's unity with the sinner is not available by ontological or mystical means like those attempted by Augustine, Osiander, and this neo-platonic line in theology. When Paul says that the gift is not like the trespass, he is exorcising the legal scheme, which wants to make any *gift* from God equal to a *trespass* so that Christian life is simply wiping the slate clean, and starting over with the hope that a free will might choose the right thing to love the next time. It is too slight a change to think of orienting the desires to their proper goal; God's love destroys desire and in its place is the sole, active God doing what a creator does. Luther once tried to express this eschatological shift from the legal scheme's depiction of love to God's creative power in the sixth stanza of his hymn on the Lord's Supper (*Jesus Christ our Savior*): "God is not enlarged by consecration, nor used up in the change, nor divided in the fraction, but fully God standing at full stature." God is not the one who is changed in the bread and wine, the sinner is, and the change is more radical than sinners could possibly want, since it puts you to death.

Original Sin

Two false teachings always go hand in hand: The rejection of God's wrath in favor of love, and the rejection of the teaching on original sin. While God's wrath is underway, whenever the subject of sin comes up it is skewed by denial. In our daily lives we do not feel this wrath, nor do we have any trust in those who claim that there is some "original" sin that binds us through no fault of our own. With Christ's reconciliation, and so the wrath of God behind us, Paul can finally lay sin bare. Therefore, he announces that all sin came through one man, Adam (Romans 5:18). This has seemed absurd to anyone in the legal scheme where distributive justice teaches that you keep your own possessions and do not take those of another. Christ violently transgressed this law in the cross, but those who cling to this principle say it makes no sense for God to punish sin that we never committed, so they reject original sin as a myth. Consequently, they also must make death into a myth, saying death is not God's condemnation, but is rather a natural process that all creatures ineluctably undergo like the change of seasons. Typically, sin is then taken to be a substance, like a virus that infects the otherwise healthy patient (entering through intercourse), or it is taken as "missing the mark," or "straying from the path" (the latter from the picture of humans as desiring subjects using the law to direct their love to a proper object). This is a ruse used by sinners to limit their guilt and seek escape from wrath that ends, inevitably, in death.

Paul then concluded a series of things about sin in light of God's wrath—in opposition to human feeling and reason. First, "*all*, both Jews and Greeks, are under the power of sin," (Romans 3:9 NRS) whose mark is that "There is no fear of God before their eyes" (Romans 3:18 NRS). Sin is *no fear*, not because of nobility of human desire, but because of deception. All are under a power that deceives them into denial of God's wrath. Secondly, "no human being will be justified in his sight by works of the law, since through the law comes knowledge of sin" (Romans 3:20 NRS). The law demands faith: you have not done it, must do it, and yet cannot. Sin is having *no faith*. Worse yet, this faith is not a human power and cannot be manufactured, so the knowledge of sin means there is no escape, including by way of the law. Then, thirdly, sin is God handing us over to our desires, thus *concupiscent*, and in this way lies death under the rule of Satan. Hence the Lutheran definition of sin in the Augsburg Confession article II, "without fear, without faith, concupiscent."

For this reason, once sin was revealed from the ground of God's wrath, and not only from comparison with the law, Lutherans recognized that they had to teach *original* sin to people who were in the act of denying it. The first thing they note is that there is no reason to categorize types of sin, especially venial and mortal, since all sin is a version of the original sin. This utterly confuses anyone trying to make the law into a means of righteousness, since any description of original sin is patently unfair. Why would infants be born in sin that they did not commit? Even if children could be burdened with their ancestors' sins, what kind of a good God counts like that? Of course, the way original sin is taught directly relates to how baptism is taught, and why it is that infants are also baptized among Lutherans.

Original sin is a power over humans by which they are deceived about God's wrath, and place their faith in images that are used to placate wrath through sacrifice. Yet even this is not a free choice of will, for God has handed them over to idolatry. Sin is called original because it came into the world through one man, Adam (Romans 4:12), and because through this one man death reigns over all as a power—death does not wait for actual sins to be committed before it comes to rule our lives. Heidegger observed that we are born "leaning toward death." By the same token, Luther recognized that there really is only one sin—the original kind—that is repeated in variations of a single theme. What is that original sin of Adam, since for most of Christian history it was attributed to sexual intercourse, or the misplaced desire for an apple? There is no doubt that sin is transmitted in every possible way among creatures on earth, including biologically, and so enters into the very DNA of our lives. Intercourse is one of its *instruments*, but the sin itself is that of Adam and Eve's *trust*. They were given God's words in things of creation. Nevertheless, through the temptation of the serpent, they refused to justify God in his words, and sought to find the "hidden" God behind words by peering through creatures. They made images where only a word was, and sought to justify God without (or behind) words, rather than in them. Sin wants God in the self in order to avoid the preacher.

Luther expressed this in a classic way in the Smalcald Articles (1537) by calling original sin the only sin, whose nature is *enthusiasm*—seeking God within the self rather than in his words. No one wants God "clothed" in his words—instead we all imagine that if we could find God "naked" in majesty we would be able to justify him and his strange, verbal ways. Luther thought this original sin was *imagination* running wild, and this imagination has the sense of an "inner eye" that infers that spiritual things lay hidden above or behind the created things—not in them.

Adam and Eve stopped listening to the words of their Creator and sought a vision of the holy that would prove them to be holy, and thus "like God." Therefore, original sin is unbelief—a lack of trust in the words where God wants to be justified, and a superfluity of trust in the wrong things that are merely figments of imagination. Original sin always works the same way. It is to receive a word from God in the form of a promise, and then to accuse God of withholding something of himself—calling God a liar. Luther called it *disputare de deo*—arguing with God, in his lectures on Genesis, which fits Paul's conclusion: "for whatever does not proceed from faith is sin" (Romans 14:23).[6]

Sinners do not want God by means of a preacher; they want God in themselves, by themselves, as themselves—without words. Beneath this lies the lurking desire to be God, rather than to have a God, because we reject being merely a creature of the Creator. At this theological point of bottoming out, Luther gave his famous advice to Erasmus: "Let God be God." There is no worship outside God's words/things except to run away from the unpreached God. Sin means to be left in the world without a preacher, seeking to be God yourself, and consequently one is always on the run from the Creator's wrath. This sin entered through one man, Adam; it is also removed by one man, Jesus Christ: "Then as by one man's trespass condemnation came upon all, so by one man's righteousness comes justification and life for all" (Romans 5:18 translation altered). There is no "third" between Adam and Christ, especially not the law. Freedom is to trust the promise that in Christ the wrath is over—even if we feel the opposite.[7]

Chapter 7

Baptism's Freedom from Sin

Romans 6

> *To me he said: 'Stay close to me,*
> *I am your rock and castle.*
> *Your ransom I myself will be;*
> *For you I strive and wrestle;*
> *For I am yours, and you are mine*
> *And where I am you may remain;*
> *The foe shall not divide us.'*

Luther, *Dear Christians, one and all rejoice*

Death and the Two Aeons

Once the gospel has arrived your first question for the preacher is, "Shall I sin more?" Paul's answer is astounding: "You cannot, you are baptized." Baptism has already done something the law could never accomplish—it makes it impossible to sin. If that were not eccentric enough, the reason Paul gives for the impossibility of sin is that you are dead; then to top it off, Paul says not to worry, since death is freedom: "For whoever has died is freed from sin" (Romans 6:7 NRS). Some freedom, death! It hardly seems worth the prize in the end.

The moral theologians following the Enlightenment tried to create a broad chasm in *Romans* between the first five chapters that spoke of a doctrine of justification and the sixth that strangely slipped into "Christ-mysticism," or the unity with Christ by baptism. They were revolted by baptism, as with all the sacraments, and were also revolted by unity with Christ which seemed to leave out room for the will to exercise Christ's moral teachings. Union with Christ could neither be "physical," nor could it be "eschatological"; the one was too much in this old world, the other too much in the next. Such "mystical" unity would ruin the moral unity of will that they hoped would take place when the legal scheme once again slipped into the doctrine of justification. So for centuries Lutherans taught that Paul defined his doctrine of justification by faith in the first five chapters, and when he got to the sixth he began laying out the "ethical complement" of the teaching of faith: "Do not let sin exercise dominion . . ." (Romans 6:12 NRS). Therefore, among Lutherans of the seventeenth and eighteenth centuries (tropologists) union with Christ went back to the pre-Reformation form of a union of wills—all the way back to the Chalcedonian disputes over Christ's two natures.

However, baptism is not ethical, and union with Christ has nothing to do with the law. It was not until Hermann Lüdemann and Otto Fleiderer (1872–1873) that this division of Paul between a forensic justification and a mystical union was questioned among academics simply because the words in Paul's letter wouldn't allow it (though all seemed to agree it was intellectually preferable for the legal scheme if Paul had not said freedom was death). Albert Schweitzer claimed in his book *The Mysticism of St. Paul* (1911) that Paul was, alas, a mystic: "Now, however, it had to be admitted that the ethical was not present in a pure form, but was intermingled with physical conceptions." Indeed, Schweitzer concluded, Paul was a sacramental mystic, "But the plain fact is that we must resign ourselves to all the Pauline sayings to retain their plain meaning. Treating it in a way incomprehensible to us (as a self-evident thing) he speaks of living men as having already died and risen again in Christ."[1] What else could Paul be but a mystic who claims that living people are dead, and dead ones are living in direct contradiction to plain fact? At least Schweitzer realized that Paul had a "realistic" understanding of the sacraments, meaning that baptism and the Lord's Supper united sinners bodily with Christ. Moreover, Schweitzer took as his task to prove that Paul's mysticism was not quite the same as the Greek mystery cults with their baptism of initiation into unity with the god for the sake of gaining power for life. But Schweitzer could never integrate what he considered Paul's ambulation between three spheres of thought: one the eschatological anticipation of the Last Judgment, the other the Rabbinic world struggling over the meaning of the law, and the last this "united-with-Christ" mysticism.

Baptism does somehow relate to the Last Judgment, to the law and justification, and also to unity with Christ, but not quite as Schweitzer assumed was true for a mystic—transcendence of feeling from this earthly realm to an unseen, eternal one. Paul is actually not a mystic, nor was Luther, because mystics seek to transcend death, not suffer it. They seek either positively to preserve the ego, the "I", and so leap over death, or they seek negatively to make death into merely the loss of ego (the "I") like a drop of water falling into the ocean, and so not dying but expanding many fold. Baptism does none of that.

What is this baptism, then? Baptism is not a religious act of the free will that fulfills a law by undergoing a required ritual; it is an attack on sinners by God. That is what Paul means when he says, "where sin increased, grace abounded all the more" (Romans 5:20 NRS). There are two dominions, kingdoms or Aeons. In the one, sin rules by using death: "sin exercised dominion in death," and in the other grace "rules by using justification leading to eternal life through Jesus Christ our Lord" (Romans 5:21 translation altered). Admittedly, this is a good deal to swallow if you are a free will; there are two worlds or Aeons, not one, and the way to enter the Aeon of Christ is not the law, it is baptism. Moralists also think of two "times," or Aeons, one in the present made up of all your past deeds, and the other in the future when those deeds will be judged. But they divide up the ages "teleologically," whereby eternal life is a goal to be reached, and this life is a pilgrim's journey whose compass is the law. But baptism is not a human act of obedience to a law, it is God's attack on sin by attacking the actual sinner; it is death. Once done, all that can be said is that you "have died" in the only way that matters—you have died to the ruler of the old Aeon, which is sin. That also means, as Paul explains in the seventh chapter, dead *to the law*. The two Aeons of sin and grace have no point of connection. It is not the case that in the first age one chalks up merits and in the second the judgment is finally made. Nor was Paul in the old age one day and the next in the new, like turning the page of a book. In those cases the difference of Aeons would be a life prior to judgment vs. a life after judgment, and the similarity between the Aeons would be the law—in the old world the law tells you what you must do, and in the new the law tells you whether or not you have done it.

Paul's point is that the law does not constitute either Aeon, and so law, strangely enough, does not seem to have a place of its own, especially not in any *ordo salutis* (ordering of the steps creatures must take toward judgment or salvation). Moses is a father (or collective person) neither in the way Adam was, nor in the way Christ is—nor even as Abraham is father through his Seed, Christ. The law and Moses, Paul observed, came 430 years after the promise to Abraham, and yet between Adam and Moses sin reigned, even if sin was not reckoned to the kind of faith Abraham had (Romans 5:13). Paul tells us that law not only does not rule in the New Aeon of faith, but neither did it ever rule in the Old Aeon. From Adam to Moses, and from Moses to Christ, *sin* ruled; Moses never ruled anything.

Then exactly how are the two Aeons related? We may say they are "eschatologically" related as new to old, but this too can be misinterpreted in the old legal scheme as a goal relates to a pilgrim. The key to understanding the two Aeons is *baptism*, and surprisingly baptism separates the two Aeons as far as the East is from the West—it does not join them with a bridge. This frightens sinners in the old Aeon who are depending upon the law as their gift from God, and so anyone hearing that baptism now stands where the law once was thought to stand attempts to shut up the preacher by reducing his gospel to absurdity: "If there is no law in the new Aeon, shall we increase sin in order to increase grace?" The first attempt to shut the mouth of the preacher is by demonstrating his perversity with the specter of moral laxity: life without the law—by your "baptism"—will unleash the beast of desire which the law keeps caged. A second attempt to silence the preacher is not perverse, but pathetic: If I can do nothing for my righteousness, as your baptism suggests, am I then an unfortunate prisoner of fate, doomed to be a passive sinner while God works his mighty works of grace? With the law I did something and God's grace was added. With your baptism, do I remain bound and fated in sin for grace to abound? What kind of life is that? Who wants to live in a world established upon an accident of history like a preacher arriving and a baptism bestowed? Are we reduced to doing nothing but sinning so that Christ can forgive, and forgive, and forgive *ad naseum*? But Paul is implacable:

Sinner: "Why am I unable to do anything to cause grace?"
Preacher: "Because you are dead"
Sinner: "Shall I go on sinning then to increase the grace?"
Preacher: "How can you? It is too late."

Death is Freedom from Sin

Death to sin is what we have all been waiting for; heaven is just as Augustine defined it: not being able to sin—yet being dead seems to deflate the purpose. Death stands between the old and new Aeons, but who can cross that passage? None but Christ, and him crucified. Baptism's power for salvation is union of the sinner with Christ precisely in his death. Why is baptism given the exalted place that used to belong to law in the old scheme? Since Christ's death, baptism is the first and primary word given by God in which He may be justified by a sinner (*deum justificare*). It fulfills David's promise "That thou mayest be justified in thy words." This is the moment in which God ceases being just only in himself and becomes justified in his words for me. Yet now we see why baptism's promise is so difficult; it is not assenting to a proposition, it is the personal attack of God on sin (the eschatological in-breaking) which has now arrived to me as the sinner of his own claim, so that baptism puts to death my old Adam living under the rule of sin—and to this death I cannot consent. In order to justify God in this act, I must lose my "I" and be given a new heart just as David prayed: "Create in me a clean heart, O God" (Psalm 51). The law cannot create. This is the reason why baptism is placed in the crux between the two Aeons, removing the sinner's attempt to make law into a bridge to the Justifying God.

Baptism teaches a crucial truth about justification. It is not exoneration, improvement, alteration, or cleaning off the old Adam. David's new heart is not a *change* of heart, but a new creation *ex nihilo*. Baptism is therefore death and new life, which reverses the sort of living anticipated in the legal scheme. Without baptism we live with death looming in front of us; with baptism we live ecstatically, death lies behind us and life blooms like an opening flower ahead. Fear of death covered life like a cloud in the Old Aeon of Adam; the Christian lives from death to life and so all of existence is now not regret for the past but "tense hoping," as Luther says.

Schweitzer warned that this is the way Paul talks, speaking as if the living are dead and the dead are living. You are dead. When the dative clause "to sin," is added, it does not make death metaphorical, or less true; it increases death far beyond the normal definition of the cessation of bodily organs. The legal scheme assumes that it knows what death is because it imagines that the free will once stood as a master of sin, "able to sin and able not to sin" (*posse peccare et posse non peccare*) at its own discretion. In that scheme, death is terrible because it is the end of potential. Even after the Fall, as Augustine taught, when humans are "not able not to sin" (*non posse non peccare*) one imagines salvation as regaining mastery over sin by free will. Accordingly, death means the loss of all hope of returning to the original state of mastery over sin. However, Paul speaks of death not as *loss of potential*, but as *freedom*. Life is not realizing potential, as the Scholastics taught. True life is release from the power of sin to accuse you of retaining sins that Christ allegedly failed to remove. The old Adam—with all of its desires of heart, idolatry and unfaith, its "many trespasses" (Romans 5:16)—is baptized unto death. Death is, after all, not being able to do anything more to fulfill the law and rid one's self of sin in the sight of almighty God, and this point is reached suddenly and completely in baptism because there God is applying his final judgment to an original sinner. However, this death loses its terror when one is planted into death with Christ, because in Him sin died, or better—*I* have died to sin: "Do you not know as many of us who have been baptized into Christ Jesus have been baptized into his death?" (Romans 6:3).

Union with Christ's Death

Baptism into Christ's death is an even more offensive claim than "you have died." It says your baptism is unity with Christ, and that that unity is first a *unity with his death*. Baptism is not a mystical unity with the god in a being that transcends this visible world (preserving my life eternally); it is to be planted with Christ, buried in the ground, and judged by God as "short of his glory" because Christ was hanged upon the tree. What is this unity in His death? It is not participation of the lower being in the higher, as the Platonists teach, but the communication of Christ's attributes which now have a powerful effect on the sinner. Christ takes the sinner's sin, but the exchange that takes place does not leave the recipient as she was—only without sin. The sins were not just possessions of mine, but they were *me*. They were not appendages, but my very heart. So, Christ first takes my sin, then he attacks me, the sinner. For this reason the first exchange with Christ is death. Christ does not offer an escape from sin and death, like the Gnostics dreamed about, but he came down from heaven into sinners, under them, and suffered to take the sins—and with them he took "me"—or my heart. This unity is not simply a unity of wills or ideas, it is patently material. Christ took the world's sin, including my own, even in his own body, and became a curse on the cross. I cannot reclaim as my property those old sins by the old theory of distributive justice—though strangely this is precisely what sinners *desire*. Sin is a matter of the heart, and when sins are removed from a sinner the heart just manufactures more like the government mint printing money. The value of money, it is said, depends upon trust in the government that stands behind it. For this reason an unfaithful heart cannot merely be cleaned off in the way soap removes dirt from the hands. Luther said in his Romans Lectures that it was not so much that sins were being taken away from a human subject, but that the person must be taken away from sin. Sin is a power, a power has a territory, the territory has a kingdom, and the kingdom has citizens. To remove sin, the person must be removed from sin. Christ gave this description when he said in Mark 3:27, that the Strong Man must be bound before his house can be pillaged, and Christ had come to do just that. Yet, it is an odd reality, called in the modern world the "Stockholm syndrome," that prisoners identify themselves with their captors, and even desire in their hearts to be imprisoned to them: "Should we continue in sin?" Is that what we do now? No, in fact that is impossible, however strange the desire may be to stay imprisoned.

When the problem is the heart, Christ's unity must go even deeper than the intimate exchange of *sins* as property. There must be a unity in the *death* of Christ. Christ must now put the old Adam (the unbelieving heart) to death in a final judgment for

each person, just as death does not come in general, but in a particular time and place for each of us. Christ's death on the cross
took the sins of the world, but this must now be preached and
given so that a person no longer remains more-or-less intact after
sin is removed—endlessly able to produce false trust in idols. That
heart, and so the entire person to his or her roots, must *die to sin*,
just as Christ did on the cross. A heart, after all, is not simply the
organ of love (as the world supposes) in the form of erotic desire,
it is the source of *faith* and so also of unfaith in the form of
idolatry. To destroy Adam's heart and receive the new heart in
Christ, God uses nothing else but the instruments of his words
preached to a sinner that are first given in baptism.

Once this promise gets through to the heart, death is no longer
a natural function of biological decay, but death is death to sin.
The heart of the old Adam is dead so that it cannot manufacture
any more idols. How does one die to sin? By being removed from
it. Sin's power is to point the finger; death is to *believe* sin: "Yes, you
are right, that sin belongs to me." But to believe sin is to call God
a liar, and negate Christ's cross. Baptism is the only thing that stops
the voice of sin along with its accusing finger once and for all, but
of course, it stops it only for faith by putting another word from
Christ in the ear: "I have taken the sin of the world, including
yours." Faith that trusts this promise cannot sin anymore—it is
impossible.

Baptism and Resurrection

Baptism kills, which is its freedom, "for the one who is dead is
set free from sin" (Romans 6:7), yet freedom without my "self"'
seems a waste. Just so, there is a second, incomparable benefit to
the death of the Old Adam in baptism: "Therefore we have been
buried with him by baptism into death, so that just as Christ was
raised from the dead by the glory of the Father, so too we may
walk in newness of life" (Romans 6:4 NRS). The end of the old
is also the beginning of the new life. Living according to "our old
self," (Romans 6:6) was to live "to sin," which was hardly epicu-
rean freedom to follow one's desires; it was slavery to the Lord of
this world. Following Adam, everything came under sin's dominion,

and so everything was turned to sin's end—no matter how good it seemed according to the letter of the law. The new life, to the contrary, is precisely the one that Christ lives, and the life Christ lives he lives "to God" and not "to sin" any longer (Romans 6:11). The Aeons have changed with Christ's resurrection. The new life given in baptism is not starting over or being cleaned off, like Anselm's pearl that fell into mud, but is the resurrection from the dead. Baptism gives you a death like Christ's, and so also a resurrection like his. He "died to sin once and for all" (Romans 6:10); having been raised from the dead he never dies again, death having no more rule over him.

Paul means that baptism is not reaching back to the past to start again. Christ's world is not like Adam's where one wants to start over, try again, and find a way of regaining lost potential. What kind of life is it then? It is "walking about" in the new life—freely—knowing that you cannot sin because of the new Lord you have (Romans 6:4). Freedom is not being one's own God. If somehow we could get rid of our old Lord by ourselves, we would still need a new one, since we cannot raise ourselves from death, and creatures cannot be their own Creator. Both the death and the new life were accomplished in baptism by a word, and for this reason that word is "I baptize you in the name of the Father, Son and Holy Spirit." Life is not an ontological given; it is not based on itself. Just like death, life is not a self-subsisting essence. Life is to someone, it belongs to someone, and life in Christ is entirely to God, instead of to sin. But God is not a goal toward which you move by fulfilling potential. Life "to God" looks to this God expectantly to provide for every need out of fatherly and divine goodness and mercy. Whether one lives or dies is not the issue, but dying to God and living to God—because then whether one lives or dies, one belongs to God (Romans 14:7–9). Having such a God means that you are free to turn to Him expectantly for everything needful and delightful—even in your own death.

What makes Christ's Aeon "new" is not that in place of humans there is a new species running the kingdom, say of apes or angels, with a new set of laws. What makes this life new is that life to God is like Christ's in the resurrection. When raised he left death behind, along with sin; the devil has no authority over him because the sin is gone, and most importantly, the law is no more—having been eternally established *behind* Christ as a memory of the past. It *has been* fulfilled—it requires nothing more. Christ's new life to the Father is just like his incarnate life on earth, except that there is no law between him and the Father and between him and his sinners. Baptism frees you to belong exclusively to God, the justifier who is Creator-out-of-nothing. Baptism is therefore the life of the Christian from which there is no progress. All life "daily" returns to baptism because of its promise, "if we have died with Christ we believe we shall also live with him" (Romans 6:8 NRS). Baptism's promise is given once and stands against the greatest enemies sin, death, and devil—whose attacks are daily. Sin is then taking leave of this promise in order to fight sin solely on the basis of the law; faith is returning to baptism's promise which it finds always there—unshakeable. This promise's power is not past, it is (as a promise must be), always ahead of us, always accessible to the ungodly—day in and day out—useful to no other creature since sinners are the only ones who need such a thing.

Preaching Baptism

When Lutherans teach baptism (called catechism), they teach people precisely what to believe in. To do this they find the promises of Christ and open them up like a pirate's treasure chest. Luther taught baptism best in his Large Catechism by treating the sacrament as divine rhetoric in the sense of the outpouring of the communication of Christ's exchange of attributes. To grasp that kind of rhetoric one must first identify the *stasis* (state) of the argument: *what* baptism *is*. Baptism is preaching, and because preaching is always sacramental, it is God's word put in a thing of creation. That means it is a promise placed in the setting of water, like a diamond is put in the setting of a ring in order to display it fully. Luther recognized that God's putting of a word in water is the reason baptism is always hated, and had become in the Reformation "the chief cause of our contentions and battles because the world now is full of sects who proclaim that Baptism is an external thing."[2] How does the water of baptism do such great things? It is not water only, but water used together with God's word and by his command, says Luther. The justification of

God is not a justification in general words, formed as "ideas," such as "God is love." They are specific words "for you," which cannot be given in the abstract, but must be delivered in the particular by a preacher: "I baptize you in the name of the Father, Son, and Holy Spirit." To this word faith clings, and by the word of promise God creates a new life where there was only death.

Second, Luther considered the end purpose of the divine rhetoric, that is the *benefits* of baptism—or its reason *why*. An orator has a goal, and God's goal in baptism is simply that sinners "be saved," as the words of Christ say: "He who believes and is baptized shall be saved" (Mark 16:16). Salvation comes to the sinner by the forgiveness of sin. Enthusiasts like Adam do not like this word, or the fact that it is set in the ring of water, because enthusiasts want something inside themselves to be their salvation instead of waiting for a preacher to forgive their sins over and over. So they extricate themselves from the preacher and look inside for salvation. But, Luther contended: "faith must have some-thing to believe."[3]

Third, divine rhetoric then considers the *use* the hearers make of all this, including especially who receives these gifts or benefits of baptism (*for whom*). Since faith alone, not any work, receives these gifts, only faith can make use of what is given there. Routinely people have attempted to re-insert the free will at this point and make faith a deed; but faith is the only thing that can make use of baptism because it alone can use a promise. A promise is used not like a law that provides a model or principle of guid-ance to the will, but by trusting what is given against one's own experience to the contrary—that is faith trusts life even in death: "Whoever believes in me, though he die, yet shall he live" (John 11:25, translation altered). A promise is used by faith in times of need or desperation in order to lament and struggle against sin, death, and the devil. So a promise is leaned upon to yield a new future—and the sooner the better. Recall that the opposition to Paul's argument, "Shall we sin more," or "remain here in sin," anticipated that when the law was removed all struggle against sin would also be removed. But in truth, it is a *promise* that enables struggle against a lord like sin, not a law. Sin points out the kind of sin that belongs to you; its power is to identify you with sin itself. But Luther pointed out that when the voice of sin has gotten into the conscience, a Christian responds with an infallible boast: "But I am baptized!" Just as a marriage promise gives the right to nag the spouse, baptism's promise is the ground on which to pester and bother God for what is needed (lament), and to cut off the voice of any sin that identifies you with itself (to ignore sin). Baptism does not end life's struggle, but begins it in earnest. It does not remove the old world from you, but positions you in that old world so that you are no longer a timid, "obedient slave" of sin, but become a troublemaking rebel against sin. Baptism makes a Christian an eschatological revolutionary—a true fighter. The baptized *fight* sin; those without the promise *obey* sin. Luther calls this the difference between governed sin and governing sin. Without the promise of baptism, sin rules; with baptism, sin is ruled.

Once he has addressed baptism as unity with Christ's death, Paul turns immediately to the struggle of faith that no longer uses law: "Therefore, do not let sin exercise dominion in your mortal bodies, to make you obey their passions" (Romans 6:12 NRS). On account of the promise, not the law, you have the ground to fight sin. Law fought it with a theory of good works, but it could not produce any. Promise fights sin at its root by means of faith and makes for feisty living that knows it is Lord over everything in the old world. Faith says to sin what law cannot: "But I have died! Why are you still pestering me?"

Faith Needs Something to Believe

Belief is material, not ideal. Faith needs a "thing" in which to place its trust. Creatures are made this way, though Adam and all his children have attempted to live as their own Creator rather than as creatures. They want to meet God in the sky, rather than here on earth. It is no surprise that Karl Marx (1818–1883), who became a Lutheran by baptism, corrected Hegel's idealism with persistent materialism. A person is nothing without the product of his or her labor. Now labor does not make free, but a free gift from God will always be *material* since for God a word is always already a "thing of creation." Paul argued that worshipping the creature rather than the creator is original sin, but he was not therefore speaking idealistically, for he immediately said God's power is seen "in the things he has made" (Romans 1:20). Idolaters take things of creation as things-in-themselves, not masks of God (*larvae Dei*); idolatry seeks God *behind* things rather than *in* them. The incarnation was God's attack on idealistic "faith," by which the Creator became (and so is) a creature—*Creator est creatura.* Though it is not the most useful way of saying it, the Lutherans have always held that the finite thing is capable of the Infinite God (*finitum capax infiniti*) in contrast with Reformed theology that developed the incapacity of the infinite as a rejection of the communication of attributes: *finitum non capax infiniti.* Sacraments are God in things given to sinners in the form of a promise that forgives sin—and all of the nouns in the sentence are material. For Lutherans the ubiquity of the body of Christ (discussed in the *Formula of Concord,* Article VIII) is the greatest comfort since it assumes that Christ's incarnation was not only possible, but is now able to reach even sinners like me in their unique time and space. The great teaching of the majestic communication of Christ's body is not that Christ is present to me, but that *I am present to him*—that means that I have been translated from Adam's Aeon to Christ's, which is the theological Copernican revolution. Copernicus saw that law de-centered the earth and places the sun at the center of the solar system, baptism now de-centers the sinner and the accusing law, placing Christ at the center. As long as I, the sinner, determine Christ's presence, Christ will be made absent. But when Christ determines whether or not I am present to him, then Christ becomes abundantly—majestically—always and everywhere present in his ubiquitous body and divine power.

Now, the great temptation of justification by faith apart from works is to confuse faith in Christ's promise (the Lutheran teaching) with faith in faith itself (enthusiasm). That is to reject the materialism of faith for idealism. That basic "slippage" from the object of faith to the subject has dogged Protestantism from the beginning and given faith a bad name. American Protestants are infamous for making faith into a work—admittedly not a very hard one, but a work nevertheless, that decides for Christ or establishes a personal relation with him, or examines itself for evidence of faith. Baptism gives some*thing* to believe in. Faith needs a thing, otherwise it curls back into itself and repeats the sin of Adam.

Yet it is not as if just anything will do. Baptism is God removing the many wrong things people believe in, and giving the one right thing for faith to cling to—a word from God in which God is justified for what he is doing. The promise of baptism relies only on the faithfulness of its giver. The reason God's promise is the right thing for faith is that God keeps his promise—all other promisors in life end up lying because they are slaves to sin and death.

A problem developed immediately with this teaching when it came to the sacraments. In its "crass" form (as seen in Zwingli) it was an attempt to replace promise with *symbol*, so as to avoid the offense of eating Christ's body as justification. More subtle forms developed later that likely began with Melanchthon's experiments with the Pauline word *koinonia* (fellowship in 1 Cor. 10:16), as a way of speaking of Christ's presence "spiritually" without having to make reference to eating bread and wine as communion. In the second generation of Reformers two pictures of salvation developed: for Gnesio Lutherans salvation was like a baby being born after the picture of Christ given to Nicodemus. The Philippist Lutherans began to picture salvation as an adult making a decision.[4] Naturally, the sacraments began to function differently for the two groups of Lutherans as well. For the Gnesio, sacraments give faith by giving a promise put in an object in which we believe, and so when we take and eat, we obey and believe Christ himself by taking him and eating him. For the Philippist, the sacraments increasingly became a seal, or confirmation of growth in a faith already there. A line began to project out of Melanchthon to his students and then to other Reformers that speaks of the sacraments as a "sign" and "assurance" of "grace already bestowed" (*iam donatae*)—which occurred already in Melanchthon's 1521 *Loci*.[5]

Calvin (1509–1564) and Bullinger (1504–1575) took the next decisive step in their *Consensus Tigurinus* (1549) that faith routinely comes *before* the sacrament of baptism. Calvin asserted that the Apostle Paul had already been granted remission of sins and the Gentile Cornelius had already received the Holy Spirit before baptism—so when baptism was added later it only confirmed and increased the amount of faith that was already there. Once sacraments began to be an addition to a faith already there, conversion theories developed that altered the basic doctrine of justification.

For Luther one is justified once and for all in baptism, but returns to it daily, which means one returns to the specific promise given by Christ and clings to that promise despite whatever contrary experience one has. Paul called it daily dying and rising: "I die daily" (1 Corinthians 15:31). Growth in faith is hidden, especially to one's inner experience, but is grasped only in the outward word and sacrament. So we have a split between soteriologies, the Lutheran "external word" and the Protestant "internal conversion."

The crasser forms of conversion in American evangelicalism actually have a subtle, but important origin in something the Reformed orthodox called the "practical syllogism" which rejected Luther's teaching of *promissio*. The practical syllogism was a way for Protestant orthodoxy, following Calvin, to establish the certainty of the divine election, or assurance.[6] A logical syllogism has a major premise that refers to a universal principle. In this case the principle was to be taken from Scripture (as the Protestant version of *sola scriptura*)—as if that were the meaning of "external word." Classically this word of Scripture came to be:

Major Premise: "Whoever truly believes and becomes of
a right spirit is elect."

It is no coincidence that this is an alternation of the baptismal promise in Mark 16:16, and the major premise must have a minor that applies it to a concrete situation:

Minor: "But in fact I believe."

This is understood to be the "internal word," put there by the Spirit and read out from the heart. Thus we have the subtle beginning of the two-stage process that moves from external to internal. The conclusion of the logical syllogism is then without any doubt:

Conclusion: "Therefore, I am elect."

The crucial matter in this logic becomes the minor premise. Everything about faith becomes internal, and rests upon the truth of the statement: "But in fact *I believe*." By the syllogism, faith curves into itself and depends upon the faithfulness of the faithful—that is believing in one's own belief.

Luther warned of this problem in his Smalcald Articles when he witnessed the way Protestant enthusiasm functioned. For purposes of contrast we can set up Luther's kind of "syllogism," which he learned from Paul:

Major:	Christ has said, "I baptize you" (by the preacher)
Minor:	Christ is faithful to his promise despite my unfaithfulness
Conclusion:	I am baptized even in the face of sin (that is, "shall be saved").

Faith is in the word put in the water, and is certain because *Christ is faithful*. Faith does not turn inward, but ecstatically goes out from itself into Christ's death and resurrection, which is always an "alien righteousness" given by an external word. This is a preached soteriology rather than a conversion soteriology. Now conversion soteriology can be "crass" or "subtle" as the Formula of Concord put it. It can obviously reject the sacraments, or subtly reject them relegating them to the status of "seals," or "confirmations," or "analogies" of faith, but a faith nevertheless that belongs in some other place than in the word put into the bread and wine of the Lord's Supper or the word put in the water of baptism. Reformed teachers, whether of the Zwinglian, Calvinistic, Bucer-Bullingerian types, began to think of the sacraments as a parallel, but lesser, liturgical world to that of Christ and the Spirit. Bread and water provided analogies, but faith's concentration moved away from the *things* to what they considered the realities of faith that resided elsewhere, like Christ's cross back in history or Christ's resurrected body residing on a chair in heaven at the Father's right hand. This means that the sacrament was spiritualized.

Lutheran theology holds that the sacraments are not "signs" of a partially absent Christ, but the Person of Jesus Christ—standing there at full stature, who uses created things to break into sinners in the here-and-now-life lived under Sin's dominion in the Aeon of Adam. Sacraments are therefore not windows through which we seek to see divine things residing in the Spiritual world, nor are they "testimonies" to us of God's hidden, internal workings of election prior to the sacraments. They are specific *masks* of God's words in the world (*larva dei*), used by God to make faith by bestowing Christ's benefits—himself. Faith like this makes us truly human, down-to-earth creatures who are no longer running fearfully out of the world, but the kind who can actually trust whatever words God gives because they now have something to believe in.

Chapter 8

Freedom from Law

Romans 7

Sorrowing, Lord, I yield to Thee,
Weary of sin's heavy burden;
Let Thy grace my portion be,
All I crave for is Thy pardon.
This Thy promise, I believe:
'Jesus sinners doth receive.'

Erdmann Neumeister, *Jesus Sinners Doth Receive*

Pugnat Fides

Fresh up from the water and preached word of baptism, united with Christ in his death and by faith in his resurrection, one expects the full glory of God (the Hebrew *tikkun* when all creation is mended and Israel rectified). But instead of glory, the baptized immediately endure a spiritual attack fiercer than before. Who could have anticipated that justification of sinners did not end life's struggle, but started it? What other struggle is left in life once sin is over? The legal schemes' struggle is conceived as a ladder of perfection that sinners seek to climb, but faith's struggle (*pugnat fides*) is to listen only to Christ's promise against contrary experience—and nothing is more contrary than death. Nevertheless, death is the freedom from sin, and now Paul reveals it as the gift that keeps giving: "But now we are fully *freed from the law*, dead to that which held us captive, so that we serve in the new being of Spirit, not the old of letter" (Romans 7:6 translation altered).

Yet, freedom from the law is frightening for people who live in the old, secular Aeon because the end of law is chaos and hell according to the legal scheme. This freedom operates against our feeling or experience; where baptism says, "free," you feel bound;

where baptism says, "Christ is Lord," you see nothing but sin. The promise from God seems to change nothing, and yet the preacher says it has changed everything. The basic attack on baptism's promise is that "nothing has changed." The baptized respond to such an attack by saying, "But I have learned how to ignore sin, since it speaks to my old, dead self and I only listen to the One speaking to my new, living self—as the Psalmist says, 'Sacrifice and offering you did not want, but you made me ears'" (Psalm 40:6–8, translation altered). The new creature of faith is all ears, and the ears belong only to Christ.

This offends the legal scheme whose goal is visible, felt power that we called "the pursuit of happiness," or "love of the greatest good." Being a theologian of the cross means the Christian's life is hid under the sign of its opposite (death, bondage, suffering) so that the prisoner of sin has now become the French underground, the embedded terrorist to the body of sin, and so faith is not the end of struggle, but its beginning. "You must reckon yourselves dead to sin and alive to God in Christ Jesus," says Paul, using the same word "reckon" for what God did with Abraham's faith (Romans 6:11 translation altered). What do freed people do who now have faith reckoned as righteousness? They fight, for the first time—not letting "sin exercise dominion in your mortal bodies to make you obey their passions . . . But thanks be to God that you, having once been slaves to sin, have become obedient from the heart to the (new) form of preaching to which you have been entrusted" (Romans 6:12, 17 translation altered).

The life of the cross means that the old life of Adam (the body of sin) and the new life of Christ (the body of righteousness) overlap for now. Why the cross rather than immediate glory? Such was Christ's death, and yours is identical, since you are being formed into his likeness (*imitatio Christi*). The progress in a Christian's life comes from the outside, and is best thought of not as "a certain movement" of the morally justified person, but the geographical movement of Christ's new Aeon as it impresses itself on the baptized ever more forcefully.[1] The legal scheme always wants the sinner to move toward righteousness, but baptism is the movement of Christ in upon the sinner until he is "closer to me than I am to myself." The new kingdom moves into the space of the baptized, squeezing out the old leaven—the last vestiges of the old kingdom of sin—until no room is left for a "free" will. Two key teachings follow in Romans 7:

1. The eccentric (outside ourselves) teaching of freedom called *simul Justus et peccator* (Just and sinner simultaneously). This is a drastic alteration of the familiar Augustinian description of a whole Christian who is partially just and partially a sinner— two contrary desires wrestling for control of the one person. In Lutheran teaching this becomes a doctrine of two persons separated by death: one person who is entirely sin and dead, and the other a person who is entirely just and alive—each existing "simultaneously" for the time being, and referred to loosely as "I" or "me"—or more precisely "the Christian," or new creature, and "the old Adam," or sinner. We can abbreviate this teaching as "the *Simul*."
2. The doctrine of the law itself, which has its limit set in baptism, and law's alien and proper use established as a result. The proper use of law is to drive sinners away from every hope but for Christ by accusing and killing; the alien use is to preserve and sustain life in the old Aeon until the preacher arrives.

Law Attacks Baptism's Promise

Baptism's promise is no sooner given than it is viciously attacked by all who stand to lose—Old Adam, the old sinful self, the old world, death, and Devil—for the sole purpose of rending the promise from the sinner who received it. It is to be expected that you would hear their sour grapes: "You have not died, see here you clearly live" and "Sin is an addiction; it is not so easy to leave as baptism." But the most potent attack on faith following baptism is made by the law, and so Paul announced his purpose in the seventh chapter: "I am speaking to those who know the law . . ." (Romans 7:1)—both Jew and Greek. To baptism's promise the law is both deaf and blind, it simply points to sin whenever and wherever it sees it. Its attack on the promise is nearly indefensible because it accuses out of spirituality and goodness. The baptized have just been told that their sins are taken by Christ and killed, and yet the law says, "But there—I see a sin remaining on you."

By saying this it does not directly challenge Christ, but the law is spiritual and, as like the angels, is not equipped to grasp the incarnation and communication of attributes. Christ's person and work are not in the law's repertoire, but it does have a job to do, and it does it without fail. Law points out sin like a hunting dog points out a dead duck. In doing so, the law is easily mistaken for a guide to the pathway of righteousness, but it is the direct opposite of that when it is doing its proper work, and realizing this mistake is what Paul calls our human "wretchedness" (7:24).

Wretchedness (Ταλαίπωρος) is the state of delighting in and willing the good to which the law witnesses—nevertheless to have that delightful law accuse and reveal nothing but our sin. It is a shock to be promised that Christ has taken your sins in his body so that you "may bear fruit for God" (Romans 7:4 NRS), and the very next voice you hear is the law's accusation that you retain sins in your own body: "Wretched Man that I am, who will deliver me from this body of death?" (Romans 7:24 NRS). Is the promise void, powerless, a figment of the imagination? To get a direct promise from Christ in baptism that is then contradicted by the law of God accusing us is wretchedness indeed.

Paul is quite clear about his work in the seventh chapter, even though various interpreters fight him and plead ambiguity in order to retain the legal scheme. It is no wonder that this chapter has served as a battlefield of contradictions. The question normally posed is whether Paul is speaking in this chapter about life under the law *prior to baptism*, or of Christian life *after baptism*. Origen and the Eastern Fathers thought it denigrated Christ's work to think Paul was speaking as a Christian of such struggle and sin remaining after baptism—could Christ be of so little account? Augustine attended better to the text when it dawned on him that Paul spoke in Romans 7 *as a Christian*. Paul is very precise about his argument here: "*When we were* in the flesh, the passions of sin, aroused by the law, were at work in our members to bear fruit for death. *But now* we are fully freed from the law . . ." (Romans 7:5–6 translation altered). And again, Paul says, "I was once alive apart from the law . . . However, I died" (Romans 7:9–10). The change in time—the death—is baptism, as he argued at length in the sixth chapter, but what has troubled interpreters is that Paul reveals that the *law* has not died; it is "I"—the perpetually existing subject under the law—who has died, and yet the law goes right on accusing. If baptism worked, shouldn't the law be silent and "I" be without sin? No. The difficulty is that the law is right; sin remains after baptism—and we *feel* it. Does this not put the lie to Christ, or at least to church teaching on baptism? This is the question of Chapter 7, and frankly of the whole Christian life; is Christ of so little account that he could not take the sins as he promised?

What do you, a baptized person, say when the law (correctly) accuses you of sin? You do not claim that the law made a false accusation. Nor do you claim that there appears to be a sin beyond Christ's reach, and therefore you must seek another remedy or rhubarb—like penance. Paul teaches a peculiar defense by which you plead guilty, but claim a remarkable extenuating circumstance: "But I am dead, and you have no jurisdiction over the dead." Death is an unforeseen defense for a sinner that leaves the law speechless because at death the law has reached its outer limit. The baptized says: "Law, your accusation is quite correct, but the 'you' to whom you point is dead, and therefore you are without authority in this case." Paul says: "Do you not know . . . that the law rules over a person only as long as he lives?" (Romans 7:1 translation altered). The law is exactly right—but only about living people. Sin is not reckoned where there is no law, and law cannot reckon sin on dead people—there the judgment has already been made and there is no more work for the law to do, since that would be kicking a dead horse. Death is the limit of law, and so at death, law itself is shown to be limited—not eternal—in terms of its applicable authority or *use*.

Luther appears to have developed this very important termi-nology of "uses of law," perhaps borrowed from Lyra (1270–1340), because he was able to distinguish between God's righteousness and the law.[2] Obedience to the Father and obedience to the law are two different things. When Christ is obedient to the Father it is not merely a synonym of obedience to law. When God and law are distinguished, God is the subject, and the law is his instrument to use. Both Jews and Gentiles have much invested in making law and God synonymous, for then loving law is none other than lov-ing God, and doing the law is none other than becoming united with God. Law is then thought to be the path to righteousness, but it is this precise sin of trusting the law (against the first commandment) that Paul brings to an end, for if law and God were synonymous then there would be no need for unity with Christ, especially not in his death. All who unite their wills to the law would then manage divinization without the need for either Christ or one's own self to die. Christ would then have died to no purpose—but he did not die to no purpose—so the point is mute (Galatians 2:21).

God and the law are not the same; he uses law as a tool with a definite purpose in mind. Now, if the wrong person or power uses law for the wrong purpose, the law steps out of its place and becomes terror, as when a baptized person uses it as a personal test for the promise of Christ: "Is Christ's promise of baptism valid? Let us see if any sin remains upon me after my baptism. If it does, baptism has ceased to function as freedom, and I must seek help in some other place than his empty promise." Luther experienced this problem when the sacrament of penance became the second "plank" of salvation following a baptism that had become functionally useless for "actual" sins committed (paradoxically) by the baptized.

The ongoing disagreement between Roman Catholic and Lutheran teaching on sin after baptism reveals a very different understanding of the role of the law in God's work of justifying the sinner. For Lutherans, sin remains, obviously, after baptism, but it is not reckoned to faith. On what basis? On having been united with Christ's death, which means when law accuses one the proper defense is not penance, it is the return to baptism: "I have died." In the Roman sacramental system baptism gets left behind and ceases to be of service once it has rid a person of original sin. Yet law might logically ask a Christian, "Who then is speaking?" Answer: The "inner man," the "heart" which, "thanks be to God through Jesus Christ our Lord," means that "I serve the law of God with my heart, but with my flesh I serve the law of sin" (Romans 7:25 translation altered). Christ has become law to law, accusing the accuser (Psalm 68, taking captivity captive) and to bring the eternal law to its limit. The limit of the law is at the words: "I died."

The *Simul*: Freedom from Law

Baptism is death; death means you are "fully freed from the law" (Romans 7:6). How does this work, since the law is so eternal and hegemonic that it really seems impossible to reply to it or be done with it? Imagine a convicted felon being told he was headed for the death chamber and his reply was: "Too late, I am already dead." The plea seems just too strange. Paul uses an infamous illustration of a married woman subject to her husband—until the man dies (Romans 7:1–4). How is a person freed from the law? Only by death. If the woman wants to live with another man she is accused as an adulterer. However, if the husband dies, she is free from law and can take another husband without any accusation. The law sees no marriage covenant where there is no spouse, and so it cannot imagine accusing a single woman of adultery.

But as exegetes point out, the problem in the illustration is that the woman does not die—only the husband does, and she is nevertheless free. Why does Paul immediately say: "In the same way . . . you have died to the law through the body of Christ . . ." (Romans 7:4)? The dead husband isn't free to do anything! Many have used Paul's illustration as an allegory, with the woman serving as the model of the continually existing human subject which the legal scheme demands. But of course Paul knows the problem: if I must be dead to be free, who wants it? In that case freedom would be pure passivity which is a fate worse than death—no one desires that kind of freedom. I desire the law as my means of life and righteousness before God so that if freedom is death to the law, I do not want it—What a Wretched Man am I! (Romans 7:24 NRS). My loophole to freedom is offered, yet I find it repugnant.

Teaching the *Simul* is like Jesus teaching Nicodemus. When every word of salvation is translated back into Adam's old Aeon it comes out jumbled. "Born again? Do I crawl back in my mother's womb?" (John 3:4). Paul has the same problem here. What has happened in baptism is that you have died, and you have been raised with Christ. This faith is either a fiction, as it appears in the Old Aeon, or it is truly a new Aeon and life. When E.P. Sanders leveled his modern criticism of Luther's exegesis of Paul, it is precisely at this point: faith in baptism's promise is a fiction—the law is God's form of righteousness for the Jews, and it can become so

176

for Gentiles when elected restrictiveness is finally loosed in Israel and the law is "graciously" extended to the uncircumcised—not only to include them but to keep them in the new people of God.[3] But for Paul, as for Luther, the promise is not the fiction, however hidden it remains.

Part of the problem in grasping the *Simul* is the hangover of the Old Aeon's ontology (the legal scheme). Aristotle taught that the basis for logic was the law that two contradictory things cannot be in one "thing" at the same time. Yet, the baptized "person" is two separate people—the dead and the alive, sinner and just. When the law accuses of sin, it accuses the old, dead Adam, and is doing its job correctly. But the baptized Christian says, "But I am free of your accusation, because that person is dead." The law does not believe this since it is spiritual and knows nothing of faith. Nevertheless, the great freedom of the Christian is to distinguish between an old "self"—unto death and law, and the new being—unto Christ. "You" are now both the dead husband and the free wife: two persons. The problem is that the old person is the one you *feel and see*; the new is *only ear* and so lives by the hearing of the external promise. Paul says this death in baptism was "so you may belong to another, to him who has been raised from the dead that we may bear fruit unto God" (Romans 7:4 translation altered).

Identification of yourself comes by *to* whom you belong. If one belongs to sin, then the law's accusation is accurate; if to Christ, then you are dead to sin and the law has no more power over you. In the modern world we have learned to think of selfhood or identity outside the boundary of self-subsisting entities by thinking of being as socially conditioned, so that "I" am what others call me. One is either what the law calls you, or what Christ calls you, and as long as both voices are heard, you are both at the same time—but one is old and "as good as dead" (like Abram before the promise), and the other is new and belongs entirely to Christ. Everything depends upon to whom you listen. Sin, however, has an opportunity in the commandment (Romans 7:8, 11), which is to have the commandment speak to the heart/mind of the baptized, when its written words really belong to the members only. Like any good teacher, Paul used illustrations like the woman whose first husband dies in order to teach the *Simul,* and in this case

Paul uses an illustration of one person having two dimensions—a mind/heart and hands/feet—inner and outer, or "heart and members" (Romans 7:22–3). The Old Adam and New Creature are not two parts of a whole. They are two distinct wholes, since nothing is more separated than when death stands between them. As I have said, speaking to people who know the law means that everything gets translated and reduced into the secular, old world. The problem in any illustration at this point is the unwillingness of our old creatures to make a distinction as Paul does between old and new—death and life, as two *times* (Aeons) divided at baptism: "while we were in the flesh . . . But now we are fully freed . . ." (Romans 7:5–6 NRS).

The law looks as if it could be the solution to the problem of sin after baptism, since with the promise of Christ and the work of the Holy Spirit "I actually delight in the law of God according to the inner man," (Romans 7:22 translation altered), but the flesh—the old Adam, the "members" (or hands and feet)—actually do not do it, and so I cannot bring these two together in one person: the old flesh and the new spirit. I cannot integrate myself or become "authentic" following baptism by using the law (i.e., make myself one who stands under the law and accomplishes what it says), and if I cannot do that, then the old person concludes, "what good is baptism?"

The law presents a definite problem to those whose sins have been taken by Christ. With its attack on remaining sin, law appears to hold out a "new" opportunity for justification. If a new heart has been given that loves the law, should I not now, finally, be able to get its requirements done? But "I" cannot! Paul keeps saying, "not I but sin which dwells in me . . ." (Romans 7:16, 20) seems to be running the show. There is no "I" left who can get anything done according to the accusation of the law. But while the law is frustrated at every turn, the Spirit is busy getting all the work done—*without any law!* In his *Preface to Romans*, Luther says: "To fulfill the law, we must meet its requirements gladly and lovingly; live virtuous lives without the constraint of the law, and as if neither the law nor its penalties existed."[4] Your job as a Christian is *not* to integrate your alienated person or seek authenticity or use the law to get rid of remaining sin. In fact, your true freedom is that you don't have to worry about that anymore. Let the old die, and trust Christ's promise in opposition to the impotence of flesh—and let freedom ring.

It is this very resistance to the distinction of persons that presents what Paul calls an "opportunity" or foothold in the commandment for sin, since both law and gospel are in fact two words from the one God. The commandment tells us what to do; the promise tells us what God has done in Christ. Yet the opportunity which sin has in the law is that for now the Old, dead Adam clings *simultaneously* to the New Creature. This is not a flaw in the law, it is the weakness of human flesh that wills the good in accord with the law, but cannot do it. So the sinner can still be seen and felt while the faithful creature listens only to Christ. The law does not see this simultaneity as a possibility, because there is no potential for doing the law in the new creature. Therefore, law attacks, and when it does, it accuses what it takes to be the whole and only "you." The law speaks to you without making the proper distinction between new and old because it is spirit, and doesn't know what Christ has done. This is sin's moment—its "opportunity"— and last hurrah. The opportunity lies in God giving himself in an earthly, simple word of promise. What sin does with this opportunity is to *intercede* by injecting its voice between Christ's promise and the hearer.

Knowing this, Paul could then lay out the stark reality. What happens to the baptized is exactly the same thing that happened to Adam and Eve in the Garden of Eden. If the almighty God is going to put himself in a word of promise, then the weak point is the faith of Adam (or the baptized) that hears the word as the promise of life. All sin needs to do is short-circuit the tie between faith and promise with one question: "Did God say?" (Genesis 3:1). By that question, one is turned away from the external promise to examine the self—or as Paul says here, to watch the law "at work in his members." From an ear-animal who *listens*, the righteous is turned into a hand-animal who *fabricates*—who uses an appendage like an opposable thumb, an arm or leg or other dangling part in order to make something for itself. Suddenly, a receiver is turned into a desirer; Gift is turned into "task," and so the promise is given up for a law. As with Adam, so with the baptized—belonging to Christ was given up for belonging to myself, since a self in this old world is nothing other than a relation of the self to the self. But a self relating to itself has by definition ceased getting its identity from outside in the promise. Paul concludes: "For sin, seizing the opportunity in the commandment, deceived me and by it killed me" (Romans 7:11). Luther calls this "the old, pious wish" to be found righteous in myself. Wretched man that I am! That is never going to happen. Christ was my righteousness in my baptism, and will remain ever my righteousness—extrinsic to myself so that only my unity with him in death will ever deliver me from this body of death. I cannot do anything more.

If the Law Killed Me, Is the Law Sin?

The old sinner could ask: "Is it not the law's fault that I sinned, since if it would not have attacked my sin after baptism, I would still believe Christ's promise? If the opportunity for sin was found in the law, is the law not sin?" Paul answers: "God forbid! The *law is good*" (Romans 7:16). The law *is* good—but does nothing to justify; it is good when it kills me.

Lutherans have not often followed Luther here. Liberal theology, part of the tropological episode of Lutheranism, is built on a positive attitude or desire for the law as the very means by which salvation comes. For them, faith means developing an ardent desire for the law. Albrecht Ritschl used "the law is good," to prove his thesis that Paul has two contradictory attitudes to the law. Ritschl thought Paul had a change of heart toward the law as a positive force by the time he wrote Romans because Paul finally realized that the law was "spiritual," divine and therefore extremely desirable. Supposedly, Paul had earlier been too harsh about the law due to the circumcision debacle in Galatia that led him to conclude at that moment that the law was a curse (Gal 3:13). So he distanced God from the law by making Moses its mediator and the angels its deliverers. That is, in Galatians Paul was pictured as thinking of the law as emerging from a lower cosmological order. Ritschl worked this out (as countless theologians did before him beginning with Origen), by dividing the law into lower and higher forms. Ritschl believed that Paul criticized Jewish, ceremonial law in Galatians and Colossians, but in Romans the higher form of moral law, especially in its Christian or "third use," was praised as the eternal goal of the law—love. So Ritschl concluded, Paul tried to get the Romans to fulfill or "satisfy" the moral law, while Christ handled the lesser Jewish ceremonies that could finally be abandoned—thus "freedom from the law" was freedom from Jewish ceremonies. Next Ritschl aligned Paul's positive "Roman" sense of law with the Old Testament generally, in which the law was viewed positively and Torah itself was a gift of grace—as long as the Jewish "ceremony" did not obscure its inner, moral truth.

Ritschl thought Luther was not able to see this distinction in Paul and therefore was unable to properly distinguish ceremonial and moral law. The problem with law, for Ritschl, was only "Pharisaic" misuse, not the Old Testament's positive sense of the law as *love*—and therefore Ritschl argued against what he called the Lutheran "nonsense" about *simul Justus et peccator*.[5] Ritschl's position has been endlessly repeated to the present, but misses the point both for Luther and Paul when they say that the law is *spiritual*. Because law is spiritual—not incarnate Christ—the person under the law is wretched. Spiritual means the law communicates what God wants us to do, but it cannot get us to do it. Much has been made since Ritschl of Paul's "confusion" over the law between Galatians and Romans, but in fact there was no change in Paul regarding the law and the simpler explanation is the best. Freedom is freedom from law. Law provided sin an opportunity—but the law in its place is good.

Where is the law's place? It does not belong in the inner heart, it belongs in the external members like hands and feet—the outer self or old self. Starting with, "Did the good become death to me?" (Romans 7:13), Paul actually smuggled a small sermon on Genesis 3 (and original sin) into his letter, which directly ties the baptized to Adam. The law's accusation replaces the promise with a commandment in the ear of the baptized. Paul picks the lowliest and last of the commandments to show the problem of listening to the law instead of the promise because "coveting" is the very sin the law points out after baptism (Romans 7:7–10). The law cannot very well say after baptism: "Behold you have an idol in Christ," or, "you do not trust God when you believe this promise," that would be a direct attack on the law itself in the first commandment. Nor can the law say: "You are taking the name of the Lord in vain, or you have not observed the Sabbath," because, as Luther taught in his *Small Catechism*, "the Sabbath is remembered and the Lord's name kept whenever His word is honored by gladly hearing and learning it." For that reason, the law does not accuse what is in the newly made heart, but points out what remains in the "members," since that is what God gives the law to do—to have dominion over the appendages of desire, namely, the hands, feet and male member. What does the law find in the members? It finds they are chasing after the neighbor's wife or his goods or his ass—yes, even following baptism. The law accuses you of these desires and can always find evidence of this concupiscence since it clings to the saint as the Old Adam.

The law is doing precisely what God has it do, which is to reveal sin in the Old Adam: "I would not have known sin except through the law. I would not have known to covet if the law had not said, 'Thou shall not covet'" (Romans 7:7 translation altered). The law makes sin huge so that it is shown, as if put under a microscope, for what it is. The law's work is alien to righteousness to be sure, but it is proper and so "good" for the law to do this work. Good is not "whatever contributes to making you right-eous," but is whatever leaves you all alone with faith in Christ. Now sin, seizing the opportunity (space) in the commandment, "produced in me every kind of coveting. Without the law, sin was dead. I was once alive apart from the law, but when the com-mandment came, sin came back to life" (Romans 7:8–9 translation altered). This is the negative version of the *communicatio idiomatum*. When sin was dead, I was alive; but the law entered and "sin awakened." Sin is a power; law becomes its "occasion," (not quite its tool). When law is alive then I am dead—when I am alive the sin is dead. The law is the thing that does the work of killing me—and I don't like it—but this is far from being sin.

Now sermons on Genesis 3 are easily found, but surprisingly Paul's is preached *to the baptized*. Sin, whether it comes before or after baptism, works in the same way. Its power is law, not because the law is sinful, but because of deceit. Adam and Eve were deceived by sin this way (Romans 7:11). Sin finds an opportunity in law to interpose between a creature and a divine promise. The opportunity is deceit, but deceit is not an innocent fiction, it is deadly when it leads away from believing a promise given by God. Life is certainly there in the old Aeon, we are not Gnostics who even question the true existence of Adam and Eve or our own life before baptism, but here is the old, old story: until the law came, sin was dead, but when it came—through Moses to me, or through the Gentiles who are law unto themselves (Romans 2:14), then sin came alive and I went lickity-split the other way to death. Sin took opportunity to turn me away from hearing God's word to looking at my appendages and wondering when the glory would start.

Paul concludes this part of the sermon on original sin (even after baptism) this way: "We know that the law is spiritual, but I am fleshly, sold under sin" (Romans 7:14, translation altered). "Spiritual" means holy (as separate from the unholy), and specifically this means *not incarnate*—not "under sin." Law cannot be born of a Virgin, or under the law, it cannot suffer and die, nor can it rise—and most of all the law cannot forgive sins. It tells us what to do, and is extremely accurate, but it cannot accomplish a single thing because of the weakness of our flesh. Its "fault," if a sinner must look at it that way, is that it gives no path to righteousness because it is *not Christ*. But Paul knows better. The law never was for righteousness. The law is not supposed to be Christ, only Christ is Christ. Law is spiritual, not incarnate. It points out sins, it can't take them from you.

When law entered into the old Aeon it did not decrease sin, but increased it. When law enters after baptism (the new Aeon) it does the exact same thing it always did—for it cannot do anything else. It revives sin, which otherwise was dead. But now Paul is set to describe something that belongs only to one who has a promise apart from the law in Jesus Christ—which faith is reckoned as righteous: whether Abraham, Paul or a baptized Roman in the Church to which Paul wrote: "delight in the law in the inner man." Delight in the law takes place while seeing a great war raging by that same law "in the external members" (7:22–3), all because the baptized have a deliverer from this body of death: "Thanks be to God through Jesus Christ our Lord!" (7:25a RSV). Paul, like Christ, has been raised into new life in the Spirit with a fulfilled law that now lies in the past. The *law of God* is served with the soul, because its delight is in the fact that the law is already fulfilled by Christ, and thus law has no more accusation to make. The delight the baptized take in the law is in fact that law is finally past. Meanwhile, the *law of sin* is simultaneously served by the flesh (7:25b) (that is the law not fulfilled and continually accusing until it puts me to death). Paul serves both "laws," one by faith—the other by obedience to that law even while it is killing him as the old Adam.

Antinomians

Were it not for Christ's new Aeon (and our transference there by baptism), no one could give this God thanks for the death being worked by his good and holy law. Most tropological theologians like Ritschl find it impossible to square these two: the law is good, nevertheless the law does not lead to righteousness—indeed law fights against it. They attempt a compromise, saying law does not lead to righteousness by itself, but that without it the first necessary step would never be taken. Law and grace then are like two mules each pulling in the same direction.

Luther's teaching is clear at this point: law does not aid in making anyone righteous, yet it is necessary for true repentance, or conversion. This teaching is an endless difficulty for theology as long as one tries to synthesize law and gospel within the legal scheme and refuse the *Simul* of Romans 7.

Faith is a struggle because a promise is heard, not seen, and human experience is driven by the eye, so that it contests the promise. The *Simul* is the eschatological way of expressing this struggle that makes the entire life of believers into repentance, just as Luther anticipated in the first of his 95 Theses: "When our Lord and Master Jesus Christ said, 'Repent' (Matt.4:17), he willed the entire life of believers to be one of repentance."[6] This discovery unleashed a deep controversy not only with Rome and the later Protestants, but among Lutherans so that the issue of the *Simul* and Romans 7 was fashioned into a fight over the meaning of repentance after baptism.

Luther fought with Rome's teaching of repentance by shifting the sacrament of penance from the recipient's work of producing sincere remorse and satisfactions for sin to the priest's external

proclamation of the absolution as a promise. Luther discovered the
promise of the Gospel does not demand but gives righteousness
apart from any law.[7] Freedom from the law, however, scared
Lutherans into being either Nomian (aggressively legalist), or
Antinomian (passively legalist). One of Luther's students, John
Agricola (1494–1566), argued against using the office of the law
for the baptized, and in doing so he also made an argument against
the *Simul* and Paul. If Absolution is the main thing in repentance,
he thought, is it not really the *only* thing? Does Paul not say that
faith is freedom from the law (Romans 7:6)? Why then would
Christians continue to have any use of law once they received
Christ and his promises?

Agricola determined that when preachers follow baptism they
should leave law to nature or the civil authorities and do the one
thing the world cannot do—preach the gospel of Christ's cross
alone. So far Antinomianism has a Lutheran ring to it, however, he
then proceeded to make the same argument that Rome had made
against Luther: "Contraries cannot be part of the same" (the phrase
borrowed from Aristotle that served as the foundation of the
whole Antinomian controversy). Said Agricola: "I prove the Major:
It is obvious that contraries cannot be simultaneously and at once
in the same subject." Luther recognized this argument was made
by natural law, and even within that law sin and faith battle in
the person while holding different ranks so that *faith* battles *sin*
and conquers, while *sin* battles *faith* and loses. Contraries routinely
exist in one thing, but if the contraries are total opposites they
battle until the higher routs the lower. This is why it is the crux
of the matter to determine whether a promise is stronger than a
command, then the good resolve routs sorrow and faith conquers
fear.[8]

Yet, the psychologist in Agricola was rather astute. He surmised
that "harping on the law" could not accomplish repentance,
but instead "stimulating people to love" would do it. Agricola
attempted to make the Lutheran theology of *faith* back into a
theology of *love* that ordered desire to its proper *telos* in God's
goodness. Within the catholic church, Lutherans could then serve
as the positive motivators who eschewed guilt because repentance
is elicited better by pity for the crucified Christ than fear of the
wrathful God. Agricola surmised that God's wrath should only be

taught from the gospel where it is immediately coupled with a promise and defeated—otherwise the heart does not turn to God in love but turns away from God in hate. The law was believed to convict of sin—entirely without the Holy Spirit—so that law accomplishes nothing but damnation.

Lutherans are certainly interested in the effect of preaching on the sinner, but Agricola set the pattern of an excessive psychologizing that takes its focus away from the external word and places it on the labyrinth of the inner motivation of the human heart. The effect of Agricola's teaching was to equate the gospel with love and the law with hate, and as any parent knows hate does not motivate.[9] This was an ingenious return to ancient theologies of love, and so also to the legal scheme, with its Aristotelian notion of life oriented to a goal and sin/repentance/forgiveness all premised on the theory of sin as disordered love. Luther always taught that it was not the ordering of desire to its higher goal in God, but the end of desire altogether that mattered. Sinners did not need a better goal for the heart to aim at, they needed a new heart altogether. Antinomians think sinners require only a midcourse correction of their desires in order to be free of the law, and for them a carrot works much better than a stick: preach love, not wrath! But freedom does not come by abolishing law in preaching—it comes by *fulfilling* the law.

Once Agricola gave faith back to love there was no difference between his teaching and Rome's. Antinomianism is 'nomian' (legal scheme) in the end. Love sounds like the gospel, but it is the epitome of law. Love does not save, only faith does that. Contrary to his own expectations, Agricola succeeded in bringing back the legal scheme, not being free of it. So it was that Agricola became the great conciliator with Rome in a series of ecumenical meetings following the Augsburg Confession (1530) in an attempt to bring Lutheran theology back to the church of Rome and "reform" Catholicism from within by means of a preaching that attracted rather than repulsed the repentant. Agricola became notorious to Lutherans for his part in the forced return of Lutherans to the old Roman liturgy, the papacy, and most of its practices in the Augsburg Interim (1548). Melanchthon made a career of disputing the Antinomian position, and quite possibly lost the forest for the trees by defending the role of the law in teaching after baptism by introducing a novelty called "the third use" of the law as a guide to Christians that utterly confused Paul's use of the *Simul* and freedom from the law. Lutherans and antinomians are admittedly agreed in principle on one point—faith means freedom from the law—but Luther recognized that faith was not love, and that "We do not destroy the law by faith but establish it" (Romans 3:31).

The Antinomian is a one-legged enthusiast who thinks that preaching love can attract a faithful person to God. Agricola did not grasp the *simul Justus et peccator*, because he thought of it as a faulty method for getting people to love Christ. He did not know that total, perpetual repentance is to take leave of the self (die) and cling only to Christ (be created new). But sin's remnants remain in the flesh and fight against faith. So the distinction between sinner and saint is not a partial distinction between more or less vice in a person, it is the distinction of belonging or not belonging to Christ—being "in Christ" or "outside of Christ."

Paul concluded the argument about the struggle of faith with a summary: "There is therefore no condemnation in those who are in Christ Jesus" (Romans 8:1 translation altered). Even the remnants of sin in those united with Christ are not imputed, and the Holy Spirit is the seal guaranteeing the sins are put to death. On the other hand, those outside of Christ (and so necessarily confronted by the law), must "pay even the last penny" (Matthew 5:26). There the work of the law is absolutely necessary—to terrify the hardened hearts, and as Luther argued, "to admonish even the pious ones, so that they may remain in repentance once begun until the end of life."[10] You are then making the law necessary for justification, said Agricola, at least by way of consequence! Luther answered, "I respond: No. He who is made contrite by the law is far from reaching grace; he rather goes farther away from it." Peter would have ended up like Judas—as far geographically from Christ as his legs could take him—had the law not done its good work, which is to testify that the "law is simply impossible for justification."[11]

Agricola did not grasp that a preacher preaching to baptized people is addressing two persons, not one, and the great confusion about the law is always over timing: are you dead already? Are you not yet dead? Paul teaches us to speak boldly to the good law and even be willing to stone Moses with it: "But I am dead." This resolves the confusion by Biblical historians over the grammatical changes of person and tense in Romans 7 by recognizing that Paul is speaking about the *Simul*—the old and past life and the new life of faith, which now overlap. Paul shifts rhetorically from the primary preaching mode ("I" to "you," as in "Do *you* not know, brothers—for *I* am speaking to those who know the law . . ." Romans 7:1 translation altered), into the secondary preaching mode ("we") by which the preacher is softly included so that hearers are not offended: "so that *you* may belong to another, to him who has been raised from the dead in order that *we* may bear fruit for God" (Romans 7:4, translation altered). These shifts must happen whenever there is preaching. Then, in order to teach his people how to use faith by trusting the promise, Paul actually moves from preaching into *confessing* language that fights against sin from the heart. So Paul shifts again from "we" as in, "What should we say then?" to "I" who is confessing his sin in repentance and getting ready to hear the preacher himself: "I was once alive apart from the law, but when the commandment came, sin revived and I died" (Romans 7: 9–10).

The cosmic truth (that before the law, sin already ruled but was not reckoned until Moses—so that Adam is the type of all to come) becomes true in every concrete, individual case, so that Paul is speaking about Adam's whole Aeon, and himself as the "old Adam." Collective person and individual confession are precisely united. So the many attempts to slip back into the legal scheme by imagining who is really meant to be the speaker of these words in Romans 7 (e.g., the original Adam, the collective person Adam, Israel, the sinless childhood of a Jewish youth, or all of humanity together) is now easily settled. Paul is making his own confession as the baptized who has been attacked by the law—as all the baptized have and will be. Faith is the struggle that is emboldened by the promise to shout down the law. Luther was especially adept at working with this cosmic (Old Aeon) and individual (my old Adam) relationship in preaching so that Adam remained the father of all transgressors, and yet Luther freely called himself the old Adam and in preaching called *you* the old Adam too. That is what Paul meant when he said Adam was a *type*, "even over those whose sins were not like Adam's transgression . . ." (Romans 5:14 NRS).

Wretched Man That I Am

Perhaps no single misinterpretation has had such an impact in modern Lutheran theology than the secular psychologizing of Paul's final confession as a baptized Christian: "I do not understand what I do, for I do not do what I will, but I do what I hate ...Wretched man that I am!" (Romans 7:15–24). When the two Aeons are not distinguished and the two persons of the *Simul* denied, the distinction must be transferred to a division *within the self*, confining Paul's wretchedness to psychology.

The likes of Wolfhart Pannenberg and Krister Stendahl in recent theology represent one form of the anagogical episode of Lutheran theology following the First World War that had learned from Schweitzer the importance of the *eschaton* both for Christ and Paul, but they turned this against the Two Aeons and into a teleology of history (old world) moving toward its final goal (completion or perfection of the old world). This way of thinking adopted the picture of Lutheran theology painted by the social historian Ernst Troeltsch—that the distinction of law and gospel destroyed morality, making Lutherans both "passive" to government authority and conservative—even Medieval—because it carried over forgiveness of sins as the central matter of the Christian life. Troeltsch imagined that any type of forgiveness simply repeated penance as the central sacrament of the post-baptismal life, and so whenever it appeared among Lutherans was nothing but a Medieval hangover of the "church" (or Roman) type of religion. He then surmised that more perfectly Protestant traditions than Lutherans had freed themselves from papal control of the means of forgiveness to become a "sect" or, if even more free, a mystical religion of personal spiritual quests.[12]

A withering attack on anything that made a person experience "guilt" followed this assertion, and the stereotype of "old Lutheranism" by the nineteenth century was that it could not communicate the doctrine of justification any longer in a world that did not experience guilt. They developed a theory of progress that said sixteenth century people felt guilt (and needed forgiveness as comfort), but forgiveness of sins was meaningless in a modern world that had evolved from servile guilt. Some, like Paul Tillich (1886–1965), determined that the modern problem was

189

Existentialism

not guilt but meaninglessness.[13] Applying old Lutheranism to the new guiltless society set up an artificial imposition of law followed by a useless application of grace as forgiveness—and it all was a house of cards. Law and gospel became an artificial, psychological ruse that the intelligent simply walked away from. Wolfhart Pannenberg's Lectures at Yale on Christian Spirituality (1977) characteristically contrasted two pieties: the first, an old, Protestant guilt consciousness that used a forensic justification as forgiveness of sins without transformation of the sinner, leaving the person a lonely, alienated individual torn from the catholic goal of unity with the good. The second was a newly minted creation of his own called ecumenical or "eucharistic" piety that centers on joy, thanksgiving, and communal experience of a church that is visibly united in one common fellowship (as in the public symbol of the "kingdom of Christ on earth.") To find that church, Pannenberg believed one had to leapfrog backward, bypassing the Reformation and the Scholastic-middle ages to return to a purer source of church in the patristic teachings, the first seven ecumenical councils and early liturgies (but not the earliest, which were legalistic).

Psychology that does not understand the difference between new and old Aeons always makes the same mistake as Troeltsch. It pictures the essential person as a whole, neutral "ego," that mediates or chooses between a moral super-ego (or law in the conscience) and the immoral, lower pull of bodily desires (or even deeper in the unconscious *id*). In this psychology, wretchedness occurs in one of two ways. The first possibility is when two contrary "wills" or "desires" conflict in the one person. It is not a coincidence that this "modern" Lutheran position actually mimics the Roman teaching on *concupiscentia*. Rome taught that sin does not remain in the baptized, but its *passion* does. Concupiscence is "an inclination arising out of sin and driving toward sin," which can "become the entryway for sin" but is not sin itself. Luther specifically rejected this because it does not grasp the *Simul* (that delights in the law in the inner self, and the flesh that clings in which a war remains), nor does it grasp the power of the promise to create a new creature.

The other possibility, picked up by Nietzsche (1844–1900), mimicked the Greeks. In this case, one is not faced so much with the smaller matters of "coveting" (competing desires that are

190

difficult to control), but with the large, cosmic matter of *fate*. Can my will be turned to love God's inevitable movements in history? Followers of Wrede and Schweitzer, like Stendahl, chose this path of the history of religion, asserting that Paul's anxiety is not personally expressed in Romans 7, but belongs to Romans 9: 2: "I have great sorrow and unceasing anguish in my heart." Paul's wretchedness is not over an inner conflict of will (concupiscence and guilt), but over how God can manage to overcome Israel's rejection of Christ's promise and save his own Jewish people. Paul agonizes over the course of history, not inner urges, said Stendhal. Fate appears as imminent destruction for Israel so that Paul, like Moses before him, would be willing to go to hell in their place if he could (Romans 9:3), but instead he must wait for God to work things out in history. This way of thinking also has a long, Lutheran tradition from German idealists that conceive of *history* as the process of God's justification (*Heilsgeschichte*). J. C. K. von Hofmann (1810–1877), an "Erlangen" theologian whose Lutheran faculty became synonymous with Lutheranism in the nineteenth century, had set the foundation for this argument a century earlier.

The anagogical episode (that recognized Christ as an eschatological prophet of some sort) emerged out of the burning ashes of these moral, tropological Lutherans and their theology of love. But the awareness of some truly new, otherworldly kingdom was channeled by no less than Rudolph Bultmann (1884–1976) into an existentialist position that demanded the *Simul* be replaced by a decision of one's whole being that overcomes duality of will in order to live authentically—a decision to believe even when one does not know *what* one believes, but one at least knows *himself as believer*. Authenticity was imagined to be a true life that is not divided from its own desires, and so true life must will one thing—not two:

> The proclamation puts to everyone the question whether he will venture to understand himself in his authenticity from the perspective of the world, or will be silent as a creature before the Creator, that is, will understand himself as creature .... This understanding can only be seized in decision. But the decision would be purely arbitrary if the proclamation did not disclose a real self-understanding, in which one can understand himself.[14]

But Bultmann merely returned to the old problem of faith in faith itself. Preaching became the presentation of a moment of decision by which a preacher finds the way to ask the right question, as a provocation, and then the hearer responds with the answer that is authentic, bringing the will in line with God's. For Bultmann, Paul in Romans 7 must exemplify that moment of decision—a wretchedness of the instant in time, prior to a decision, that pits contrary choices against one another and demands that the single choice finally be made—a *Sophie's Choice*. In that case, Paul could not be used if he were speaking as baptized, for then it would mean that no decision ever brings peace, including the Christian "decision" for Christ.

The legal scheme is pleased to have Lutherans fighting to get back in, to make good will to love into the marker of human authenticity or righteousness. But what Paul actually says is that he has only one will that already loves the good. His problem is that he cannot get what he already wills fulfilled—"done" in his "members" (flesh). This is not the psychological problem of a divided will. The problem is the *Simul*: "So I find it to be a law that when I will to do the good, evil clings to me" (Romans 7:21 translation altered). His problem is not "inner" psychological dissension, but an outer attack by the law that challenges the outer word of promise: "Behold, this is my Son, with whom I am well pleased, listen only to him" (Matthew 17:5b translation altered). Wretched man that I am, who will deliver me? Which is stronger: promise or law?

Chapter 9

Freedom from Death

Romans 8

What can death do to you, or sin?
The true God is for you come in.
Let hell and Satan raging go—
The Son of God's your comrade now.
        Martin Luther, *From Heaven the Angel Troop Came Near*

The Declaration of Independence

Paul's letters are often mistaken for doctrinal treatises with no narrative, yet they not only have a narrative, it is the most dramatic of stories in which God makes faith through a preacher where formerly there was only naked, deicidal mania. It is none other than Israel's story whose rising action is found in the way Israel becomes a blessing to the Nations through Abraham, not Moses. The climax is baptism that ends in death and begins in a new life—a fracture in the middle of the story. After baptism, in the midst of the struggle of faith, the Apostle delivers his dramatic declaration of independence for all to hear in public court: "There is therefore no more death sentence for those who are in Christ Jesus!" (Romans 8:1 translation altered). As an old gospel tune had it: "Jesus dropped the charges." This *actus forensis* was the point of Paul's mission, the preacher acting as God's court bailiff announcing the end of the death sentence which ruled the cosmos from Adam to Christ. Finally the time had come and Paul unleashed the word, "no more death sentence!" Of course, he announced it to those who are already dead, which seems a bit late—were it not for the Holy Spirit. The Gospel always seems to come too late to those in the legal scheme who say, "thanks, but what can I do with this news now?" But with this forensic announcement, the Holy Spirit springs into action in a new way, taking leave of his *alien* work and beginning what properly belongs to him—to create from nothing, hence the Spirit's proper name is *Creator Spiritus*. The Spirit lay deeply hidden while the death sentence hung over humanity, because his work was alien both to himself and us. So repulsive was the Spirit that sinners created myths that replaced him with the unicorn of all theology, the fiction of the free will. "But now," once Paul makes his announcement, the Spirit reveals his joyous work. The Spirit is the one who raises the dead, starting with Jesus Christ who became the first fruits of many (1 Corinthians 15). Therefore what appeared at first blush to be belated good news for dead people has become the gospel itself that raises the dead. We are freed from wrath, sin, and law by death; the last enemy is death and from it Christ has freed us once and for all—becoming death to death and so Christ kills killing once and for all (Psalm 68). The dead always need more than the lifting of the sentence, they need resurrection. So Paul announced it: death is dead! What does it matter if independence was declared to dead people? The Holy Spirit is now at work in this very announcement, and he frees us from our final enemy, death.

Spiritus Exstinctor et Creator

When we left the story in Chapter 7, the newly baptized had encountered the problem of the distinction—and momentary overlap—of two worlds and two persons (the *Simul*). When Spirit is associated only with glory and life, flesh appears as if it wins. One of the great treatises on the *Simul* is found in the *Formula of Concord* article V that summarized the findings of the Torgau group of second generation Lutherans like Andreae, Chemnitz, Selnecker, and Mörlin. They recognized that for sinners the difficulty to trust God's baptism is that "the Spirit of Christ must not only comfort, but through the function of the law must also 'convict the world of sin' [John 16:8]."[1] The Holy Spirit is the comforter, but before he can comfort he must kill. How can these two opposite works come from one divine person? The Formula continues, "thus, in the New Testament the Holy Spirit must perform (as the prophet says [Isaiah 28:21]), an *opus alienum, ut faciat opus proprium*." He must perform an alien work—which is to convict—until he comes to his proper work—which is to comfort and to proclaim grace. In Romans 8, Paul addresses the last enemy, death, and the strange and alien work of the Holy Spirit in relation to death. But he also delivers the Spirit's proper work which is to give himself to sinners so they trust Christ, and not themselves or the law. Baptism is unity with Christ's death, and it is this death—strangely—that frees us (Romans 6 and 7): "But if Christ is in you, the body is dead on account of sin" (Romans 8:10a NRS). So, is that all there is? If it took dying for me to get rid of sin and law, what good is that for me? Is death the last word? No, Paul concludes: "but the Spirit is life on account of righteousness. If the Spirit of him who raised Jesus from the dead dwells in you, he who raised Jesus from the dead will also bring your dead bodies to life on account of the Spirit who dwells in you" (Romans 8:10b–11 translation altered). There are no enemies left to conquer after that.

How does Christ free us from death? The same way he was freed—by the Holy Spirit. When an enemy ensnares us, that enemy must be put to death in order for us to be freed, and so the Holy Spirit must *kill death*: "The last enemy to be destroyed is death" (1 Corinthians 15:26). Of course, the death of death sounds mythical or excruciatingly obscure, especially to descendents of Greeks who think of death as fate. Yet, the death of death is exactly how Paul's great argument (The One who by faith is righteous *shall live*) concludes with a sermon of unparalleled power: "There is no more death sentence!..Who shall bring any charge against God's elect? It is God who justifies" (Romans 8:1, 33–4 translation altered). Paul's purpose in writing his letter was to deliver this sermon. What happened to Christ—put to death and raised from the dead—is exactly what the Holy Spirit is doing with you in order to bring the rule of death to an end.

The evangelical discovery in the teaching of the Holy Spirit is that the Holy Spirit has two works: killing (an alien work), and creating anew, which is the proper work of Spirit—*Exstinctor et Creator*. Only this distinction takes the Holy Spirit out from the legal scheme and makes him a free person—which he truly is. Paul says this directly in 2 Corinthians 3:6: "who has made us proficient to administer the office of the New Testament, not of

195

letter, but of Spirit; for the letter kills, but the Spirit gives life" (translation altered). These two works are accomplished in the two words that make the distinction of law and gospel. It was the confusion of law and gospel that led to a misapprehension of the Spirit in the world and theology. Death is not defeated by having you avert it, but undergo it in the flesh, and then the Spirit raises our dead bodies—because when he sees the baptized dead, he sees only Christ and cannot resist raising him.

Now apart from baptism's promise, the Holy Spirit's two works would be abhorrent, but Luther poked through the legal scheme when he read in Romans 8:3 (translation altered): "For what the *law* could not do in that it was weak through the flesh, *God did by sending His own Son* in the likeness of human flesh, on account of sin: He condemned sin in the flesh." Paul contrasts Spirit with Flesh, but not as we normally do. We separate them by the law so that flesh disobeys law, and spirit obeys it. However, Paul separates them by what gives Christ and what does not. Flesh has a goal, but it is not "the Good," and certainly not God. It is common to think that once Christ comes he frees us to live according to the law—fulfilling the law in ourselves. Is that not what it means to "walk not according to the flesh, but according to the Spirit" (Romans 8:4 NRS)? Luther discovered, to the contrary, that the very highest goal of human desires is to be righteous according to the law before God—but this desire is not spiritual, it is the worst possible flesh. Morality is routinely flesh that fights against the Holy Spirit. The highest goal in life—to be a righteous persons—hates God: "the goal of the flesh is hostility to God; it does not submit to God's law, indeed, it cannot" (Romans 8:7 translation altered). A true hatred of the self knows all of its "goals" or desires, especially the best, are hostile to God because they put free will and law where only the Holy Spirit and Christ belong. Luther makes this astonishing claim in one of his most famous statements about the Holy Spirit when he gives the meaning of the third article of the creed: "I believe in the Holy Spirit . . . What does this mean? I believe that by my own understanding or strength I cannot believe in Jesus Christ my Lord or come to him, but instead the Holy Spirit has called . . . ." If we reduce the sentence to its core it reads: "I believe . . . I cannot believe." What does that mean? It means free will ends at the Holy Spirit, and there is also the end of original sin (believing in one's own belief)—not "I believe I believe," but "I believe I cannot believe."

For Luther there are two Aeons, two masters, and so two "yous" at complete enmity: one is either determined by the flesh, which cannot please God because it is not only impotent (like law) but *hostile* to God (8:9)—or one is determined by the Spirit, in which case you belong to Christ and everything you are and do is pleasing to God. If Christ is in you, the result is quite simply that your body is dead on account of sin, but "if the Spirit of the Father (who raised Jesus from the dead) dwells in you, then he who raised Jesus from the dead will also bring your dead bodies to life on account of the Spirit who dwells in you" (Romans 8:10–11 translation altered).

The Holy Spirit's proper work is *removed from law* altogether. This distinction of alien and proper work allows Christians to say that the Holy Spirit uses the law to kill in an alien work, and the righteous agree that is good even when it happens to them—"in everything God works for good with those who love him" (Romans 8:29, translation altered). This is the exact opposite of "looking on the bright side," because the Holy Spirit's proper work is given a Christological fixation. It is not your human goal that matters any longer, but the Holy Spirit's goal. Your goal is flesh, and flesh is hostile to God; the Spirit's goal is "life and peace" because the Spirit's goal is Christ alone. If Christ is in you, the Spirit raises your dead bodies to life since the Holy Spirit has Christ on the brain. In opposition to this, spiritualism seeks to unlink the Spirit from Christ in order to bypass the cross in its immediate relation to God, but the Spirit's proper work never goes anywhere without Christ, and does nothing apart from resurrecting Christ. The Holy Spirit does not moonlight in another job than to witness, show, and drive everything in the universe to Christ.

In opposition to the free will, the preacher "gives the Holy Spirit who produces faith, where and when he wills . . ." (Augsburg Confession V). The Spirit does not come to enhance, correct or limit human desires or will, but to remove them, thus the Holy Spirit and free will do not mix. As a result, the Holy Spirit is routinely mistaken for an inner feeling, or something called "self-transcendence" that makes one rise above everyday life to a higher goal. Both feeling and self-transcendence attempt to dress up the old Adam in spiritual clothing and present it to God as righteous, so that Luther called these "fanaticism." Lutheran theology, especially in its moral episodes, has reproduced this ageless problem. The typical approach is to think of the Spirit as perfecting our free will so that spirit becomes a union of human and divine wills. We can take the case of the notable Luther scholar Karl Holl (1866–1926), who propagated the "Luther renaissance" of the late nineteenth century that sought to unify Kant and Luther: "Where both (prayer and the Word) are used faithfully, Luther does not doubt that the warm feeling for God and the inner joy because of goodness grow steadily, both of which he designates directly as the Holy Spirit or as the Christ in man."[2] Holl thought Luther simply equated the "warm inner feeling for God" with the Holy Spirit and so likewise with the indwelling of Jesus Christ. Once you decide that, your own insides are where the action of God really is; thus, when you have a warm inner feeling for God, you cannot distinguish whether you have the Spirit, Son or Father in there—since they all feel the same. Worse yet, not only does one lose the person of the Holy Spirit, but the work of the Spirit is utter confusion—it is not the Spirit's work to provide inner joy because of goodness.

To grasp who the Spirit is, and what he does, one must understand the Spirit's relation to *preaching*, not simply to the law. By doing so, Luther was able to overcome the problematic teaching that the Spirit infuses *caritas* (proper love). The old idea of love was to strive to the highest good (to love as God loves), but the new idea of love is: God loves a sinner, like me, and in so doing destroys me in order to make a new creature. When Paul addressed the Romans, he assumed that Christ is already in them, and the Holy Spirit dwells in them ("since the Spirit of God dwells in you" Romans 8:8 NRS) because *the Holy Spirit is given in baptism*. This has been very difficult for theologians to believe because they want the Holy Spirit's presence tied to the law, and thus to some act of infusing love in addition to the mere declaration of forgiveness from the preacher. Instead, the Spirit is received in baptism plainly and simply. Paul makes the same argument in the parallel passage in Galatians 3: "Let me ask you only this: Did you receive the Spirit by works of the law, or by hearing with faith? . . .

198

Thus Abraham 'believed God, and it was reckoned to him as righteousness' . . . for in Christ Jesus you are all sons of God, through faith. For as many of you as were baptized into Christ have put on Christ" (translation altered). The Spirit dwells in bodies where he has been put by the preacher through the promise. Once done, the Spirit works strangely by killing the old creature, and only then raises the dead body that now belongs exclusively to Christ, driven (8:14), determined (8:9), and subjected (8:20) to Christ by the Spirit as an entirely new creature. Such verbs do not sound like freedom, but when Christ rules—in direct contradiction to the law—"driven, determined and subjected" means freedom indeed; for with Christ, God is unthwartable in his regard for us. That is what is meant by grace as God's favor (*Favor dei*), which allows Paul to give another unsurpassable promise: "If God is *for us*, who is against us?" (Romans 8:31 NRS).

Favor Dei: Grace and Law, Not Grace and Nature

If the Holy Spirit's proper work is removed from the law, then Grace must also utterly be taken away from the legal scheme, either as it was refined subtly by scholastics like Thomas Aquinas, or as it was made excessive by the Nominalists (who believed in a natural power that could merit God's grace or favor). The Holy Spirit's creation of faith as the divine work of grace is not done by making a change within the old person; grace is not a cleaning out, mending up, or any kind of re-working of the old creature. The *Favor of God* is a promise, not a law. This makes all the difference in the Lutheran teaching. In his chapter on grace in the *Loci*, Melanchthon drew the contrast:

> They [Scholastics of all types] have shamefully misused that sacred word 'grace' by using it to designate a quality in the souls of the saints. The worst of all offenders are the Thomists who have placed the quality 'grace' in the nature of the soul, and faith, hope and love in the powers of the soul . . . But we . . . lay down this language for grace, following the usage of Scripture, that grace is the favor of God . . . toward us.

Grace is God's favor applied to us by a preacher in the form of the forgiveness of sins, which is always on account of Christ taking those sins. Aquinas also said grace was first and foremost God's election, choice or "favor," but he proceeded to lay out a series of add–on "graces" of secondary nature in which the sinner was moved under the auspices of law to the final goal of perfection. Melanchthon cut off all those other "graces," or "gifts," for a reason—so that the Holy Spirit was truly free to make faith *entirely apart from law*. Law is not the origin of righteousness, nor is it the final goal of righteousness; only the *promise* of Christ concerns faith, and only faith is righteousness. The law, as Paul argued in Romans 7, is irrelevant to one who has died to the law, and so the law plays no role in faith.

Treating grace as *Favor dei* always seems to people in the old, legal scheme to be a fiction, and to leave out any real change in a person, or to be too restrictive regarding the many ways that Paul and others in the Bible speak of God's grace. They say that grace cannot only be forgiveness of sins, it must also be growth, development, power, charisma, and the like—or one has assumed merely a subjective perspective (a forensic declaration in a court of law) that has no basis in reality—even if the "subjective perspective" is God's. But Paul says, "For you did not receive the spirit of slavery to fall back into fear, but you have received the Spirit of sonship by whom we cry, 'Abba! Father!'"(Romans 8:15 translation altered). The Favor of God is not the effect of a cause in us—a power that we can possess, manipulate, or present to Christ on the last day as evidence of righteousness. When God favors a sinner he naturally gives gifts, just as Jacob favored Joseph and gave him a coat of many colors. God overflows with gifts, but Melanchthon puts the Lutheran teaching simply: "The gift of God is *the Holy Spirit himself* . . ." This Lutheran teaching of the Holy Spirit agreed with the suggestion by Augustine (which was almost never accepted by anyone until Peter Lombard) that grace is not a *fruit* of faith, or a *cause* of an effect, but is the Holy Spirit himself in *person*. Paul had said it: "The Spirit himself testifies . . ." (Romans 8:16 translation altered). Why was this so unpopular before Luther? Because the Holy Spirit dwelling personally in a sinner does not leave much room for the old person—specifically for the free will to make its own choices. Where the Holy Spirit dwells personally and fully, free will is crowded out. That made Paul's words unpopular throughout the history of theology, but Lutherans pulled them out of storage and applied the personal gift of the Holy Spirit as a hedge against thinking of grace according to the mode of Aristotle—as a cause of an effect in us. The Lutheran teaching of the Holy Spirit also opposed picturing grace in the Platonic sense of participation of a lower being in a higher being—as is found in the language of "deification" (being made like God).

Yet the Lutheran teaching went beyond the musing of Lombard as to whether God's gift is simply the Spirit in person, or some quality of the person, and so it goes beyond Augustine as well. The point of the Lutheran teaching is that the Holy Spirit in person is the gift I receive—entirely and utterly *apart from the law*. Neither Augustine nor Lombard ever went so far.

One of the great modern writings on the Holy Spirit is from the Danish theologian Regin Prenter (1907–1990), called *Spiritus Creator*. It came at a crucial time, since the Spirit had regained pride of place in theology once Hegel (1770–1831) determined how to make change-through-time (history) into law's primary feature in opposition to Kant who had identified the unchanging (eternal) aspect of law as the central point of religion. Though it was indeed essential that the moral episode of Lutheranism helped to rediscover history (and so the Holy Spirit), Hegel had simply made things infinitely worse than the Enlightenment's concentration on universal nature. He had found the German, idealistic secret that it was more important to make law *infinite* than it was to make it *permanent*; it was more important for the legal scheme to make law *endless* than it was to make it *changeless*. Both Kant and Hegel posed their legal, moral projects as extensions of the spirit of Lutheranism, but whatever themes they borrowed missed the point of Luther's teaching on Spirit—that Christ brings an end to the legal scheme entirely, and the Holy Spirit comes into history in preaching, first in baptism. Luther was too revolutionary for the Enlightenment, the Romantics, and the Idealists combined.

Against Hegel's new idealism in theology, Prenter made two central points about the Holy Spirit. One is that because of the Lutheran argument for the real presence of Jesus Christ in the Lord's Supper (ubiquitously present in his body as well as his divinity), there is an equally important argument for the real presence of the Holy Spirit—personally, spatially, temporally—and in whatever other ways humans construe the reality of a presence. The Holy Spirit is really present in faith, and is not a puff of smoke, a force field, a thought, a movement of history, a supernatural being or any other "spiritualizing" means of identifying the Spirit. Most especially, the Holy Spirit is not the progressive development of law to fit new historical situations. So what if the Holy Spirit's presence leaves no room for "free will" to fulfill the law—it is more important to have the gift of the Spirit than a mythical being that never accomplished a single thing in all history.

Prenter's second argument is that this presence of the Holy Spirit chases out any "idealistic" notion of the Spirit, which means the Spirit is not there in a split universe of lower material and flesh so that humans either participate in his higher "spirituality" or are the cumulative effects of the Spirit's cause to help you accomplish works of law. The Spirit is really present by means of the promising word. By that word he creates brand new things—and accomplishes once and for all the real destruction of the old—in faith itself and alone. This means that the Spirit's real presence is not under the umbrella of God's eternal law—either as the paternal law of unchanging origin, or as the infinite law of the Spirit that adjusts law to new purposes as time progresses. God is neither the law as Father (changeless), nor as Spirit (constantly changing). Jesus is not a new Moses. There is no eternal law in the new creation, or any continuation, fulfillment, completion, or perfection of law—Spirit means *no law at all* in the new life. The law is eternal, it is true, but either *eternally ahead* of a sinner without Christ, or *eternally behind* a sinner as fulfilled and over. Therefore the person of the Holy Spirit dwelling with a person has nothing to do with law. The Holy Spirit concerns himself with one and only one thing: the promise of Christ (the forgiveness of sins), to which faith clings. Paul repeated a question in Romans that he had earlier put in Galatians: if Abraham was reckoned righteous by faith in the promise—what do you think happened to you in baptism? You received the Holy Spirit, whole hog, without any further ado.

The Lutheran teaching on the Spirit ruins the law as the guide for the will, leaving us with the *Simul*, whereby I see and feel the old Adam with his sins, but trust that the promise is already an accomplished fact in the eyes of the Father. Faith turns Christian life entirely into a sure and certain *hope,* "an anxious longing" (Romans 8:19)—not because we are unsure, but like children in the back seat of a car, we want to get to our destination immediately. That is what heirs do, they wait on tenterhooks under a harsh taskmaster until they come into their inheritance, and thus "we are saved by hope" (8:24)—not love.

It is not sufficient to understand the Lutheran teaching here by simply saying that the Holy Spirit personally is the gift of grace instead of a human quality, nor is it sufficient to conclude that God's favor is his "self-giving," though these are of course true. What is really needed is to say that God's self-giving in the preached promise is the end of law. The Holy Spirit himself is the gift of grace so that the legal scheme is destroyed, along with the legal schemer inside. The *Simul* is the result of the work of the Holy Spirit dividing the old Adam from the new Saint forever. The Holy Spirit's grace is His presence as Creator to the dead sinner—entirely free from the law—bestowed freely and fully in baptism.

Prayer: Defiance of Death

This is what Paul meant when he said that "we are debtors, not to the flesh . . . but the Spirit" (Romans 8:12 translation altered). We are indebted to the Holy Spirit. Now if this debt were according to the law it would have to be paid in full, and because it cannot be, it would mean death. But indebtedness to the Spirit is an odd debt, because the Spirit is a strange lender. Unlike the law, debt to Spirit increases your bank account rather than emptying it. Spirit-debt is not what you owe; rather it is what is paid out to you, just as Christ said, "to all those who have, more will be given" (Luke 19:26 NRS). What we learn by this debt is that the opposite of law is not chaos; it is the favor of God given in the Spirit. Debt to Spirit is life abundant; debt to law is death. For this reason being "driven" by the Spirit is not a slave-spirit (Romans 8:15), it is a spirit of being a child-inheritor. The mistake of Kant's Enlightenment, and the moral episode of Lutheranism, was to think that true freedom meant "autonomy"—being a law unto oneself, which meant not having any authority that could impose itself heteronomously. Instead, Christian freedom is the freedom to call upon the almighty name of God in time of trouble, so we cry, "Abba, Father!"—since we know we are speaking to a beloved Father whose favor we have, not an impersonal, spiritual force who stands outside and is unknown and unpreached to us. We are not forced to seek scraps from God's table in the form of signs; when we have his favor we have all we need.

The cash value of Spirit-debt is a strange non-worldly (eschatological) power to defy death rather than deny it—and of such is prayer: "Likewise the Spirit helps us in our weakness; for we do not know how to pray as we ought, but the Spirit himself intercedes for us with sighs too deep for words" (Romans 8:26 NRS). We do not know how to pray because the law cannot teach us to pray; yet beyond the law, where the Spirit is at work, there is another, free prayer that emerges. The Spirit takes the promise made by Christ, and uses it for prayer by teaching us to depend upon the promise—against our own feeling. We do not know how to pray as we ought because previous to the promise we had only one relation to God through the law. In that case, we prayed economically as a kind of trade—you give me this and I will give you that—in the form of *sacrifice*. That kind of prayer depended upon our own righteousness, and so never really got off the ground. But now, faith frees us to pray in a different way, changing prayer from something defensive and meek into something offensive and bold. It moves from praying in line "with" your old self, and allows you to pray *against yourself*. Christ taught not to pray as the proud Pharisee, nor to despair of prayer, but to pray precisely for what God promises to give: forgiveness of sin. Faith does not pray like a victim, it prays like a free lord of all, subject to none. For this reason, it is essential to know that the Holy Spirit is the one who intercedes for the saints, who are *Simul* (Romans 8:28) – "according to the Will of the Father." Luther says that when Christians pray we hear only our own sighing, but we are "hardly aware" of it, since we listen only to the Word.

This kind of praying gives an entirely different relation to death than we had in the legal scheme. There we could only hope to stave off death as long as possible to give ourselves more time for amendment of life. In that mode, death was not a defeated enemy, it always loomed over everything we did and said, and ultimately, as philosophers have long noted—death is denied, and philosophy from Socrates onward was an attempt to face the truth of death squarely—it always wins in the end and we are to prepare ourselves accordingly. But as a Christian you are freed to "consider yourself dead to sin, so that you do not let sin reign in your mortal bodies" (Romans 6:12). It is not the law, however, that unleashes you to "reign in your mortal body;" instead Paul refers everything to the word of baptism, and the key is to learn how to *use* the baptism. A promise initially appears useless (especially when you really need help) since it is not a "thing" able to be used in the old world like food is used when one is hungry. It is, however, the source of hope for the new creature, a kind of umbilical cord in the womb for a child very much alive, but not yet delivered. The promise of baptism gives the life of faith its characteristics, which are *certainty* that scoffs at skepticism (the Holy Spirit is no Skeptic), and *boldness* (*parresia*) of public speech to talk back to your enemies of law, sin, and death and tell them where to go. As we have seen, prayer that comes from baptism is courage to pester God when the promise appears moribund. That is why Christ said prayer was like a woman who goes to the Judge's home at night and gets no response, but continues to knock and carry on until the Judge rouses himself and opens his window just to stop the noise saying, "What do you want?" But instead of asking an unjust judge for vindication, one is asking the Just God for forgiveness which overcomes death. A promise gives the ground to nag and pester the Promisor. Boldness and courage are the bases of the two great modes of Christian life: confession and prayer. Confession publicly defends itself on the basis of the promise against all detractors; prayer turns to God in lament and praise—demanding and thanking ahead of time—even though there is no basis for receiving anything according to the righteousness in the self. Lament and praise depend utterly upon the promise of forgiveness that turns to death with a brand new tool. No longer does one deny death, but defies it. When we do so on the basis of Christ, defiance enslaves death and frees us from the final enemy—death.

In this way praying ceases to be selfish and trivial—seeking to have the old Adam declared righteous—and becomes patient in suffering and cosmic in scope. It is helpful to know that the whole Creation is groaning—just as we sigh and groan, because when death and sin subjected us, they also subjected the whole world with all its creatures. The apocalypse of creation is what creation awaits—and what an irony that hope is, since creation then awaits its own destruction in eager anticipation—but God subjected it to futility with a purpose in mind, it was done "in hope" (Romans 8:20). The whole creation's hope is precisely not found in itself, which is why it groans like it is in childbirth. Yet no child is forthcoming, because creation is not its own Mother. That is the old pagan belief in Mother Nature, or earth-mother, that she could produce life from herself. But creation cannot do so, since it was given birth by the Creator Spirit using divine words. Creation's only hope is our hope, that death is in fact defeated already in Christ, and we only await its revelation to the eyes. The hope of creation is *new* creation.

As we have already argued, faith is a surprising struggle, and so the Lord's prayer is the strange practice of living life in the crucible of God's destroying wrath—while floating safely like Noah in the Ark unable to see dry land but trusting that the promise holds even while death consumes us. Christ gave the Lord's Prayer to teach us how to pray against ourselves—that is against our feeling that the promise has failed us. Luther taught this form of offensive prayer in the Small Catechism (Lord's Prayer, fifth petition) that encapsulates Paul's argument in Romans 7 and 8 regarding the *Simul* in this prayer. We pray, "Forgive our debts, as we forgive those indebted to us,"

What is this? Answer: We ask in this prayer that our heavenly Father would not regard our sins nor deny these petitions on their account, for we are worthy of nothing for which we ask, nor have we earned it. Instead we ask that God would give us all things by grace, for we daily sin much and indeed deserve only punishment. So, on the other hand, we, too, truly want to forgive heartily and to do good gladly to those who sin against us.[3]

The pattern of this teaching is clear: "We" are the baptized; sins remain and we ask the Father not to reckon them, though we have no basis in our own righteousness to make the claim. So we seek grace, that is Christ, who has already taken our sins and forgiven us—in order that the good can flow from us by the Holy Spirit (not by the law). This is a prayer against our old selves, and for Christ's promise to rule.

The most contrary of experiences in prayer is to learn to defy one's own death. Death, like sin, is governed in Christian lives by the joy of scoffing, ridicule, and sarcasm. The power of faith that makes praying possible is to laugh at death when the whole world cowers at its feet; it is to dismiss death, not because of one's own power, but because Christ has conquered it. Sarcasm is the basis of the vibrant new life of the Christian and the primary mode of prayer—which it freely applies to the powers of this old Aeon: "Where, O death, is your victory? Where, O death, is your sting?" (1 Corinthians 15:55). Ridiculing death is now no longer howling at the moon; it is calling upon the name of the one man, Jesus Christ, who has defeated it and who gives us the power to sneer at death rather than deny it. We wait patiently because we know that God is working death to our old creature, but soon we will experience only the new in resurrection. Prayer steps out of our self-referential lives—our own experience, wishes, desires, goals, and conjectures about the future (not knowing what to ask for)—to let God work the fulfillment of the promise in us. Once baptism's promise is in place, Paul the preacher plucks a growing host of unparalleled promises from it that form the basis of the sarcasm of prayer: "If God is for us, who is against us?"; "Who shall bring any charge against God's elect?"; "Who shall separate us from the love of Christ?" These belong to the baptized who are "being killed all day long, we are accounted as sheep to be slaughtered" (Psalm 44:22 and Romans 8:36 NRS), and yet Paul concludes with the prayer that will be said at most of our own funerals: "For I am sure that neither death, nor life, nor angels, nor principalities, nor things present, nor things to come, nor powers, nor height, nor depth, nor anything else in all creation, will be able to separate us from the love of God in Christ Jesus our Lord" (Romans 8:38–9 translation altered). The one who is righteous by faith *shall live*, and so we defy death.

Chapter 10

The State of the Promise

Romans 9–11

And though it last into the night,
And up 'til tomorrow,
Yet shall my heart hope in God's might,
Not doubt or take to worry.
Thus Israel must keep his post,
For he's born by the Holy Ghost,
And for his God must tarry.

Martin Luther, *Out of the Depths*

Using the Promise: Confession and Lament

An American President gives the nation an address each year called "The State of the Union," and rhetoricians seek to identify the *status* of an argument. Paul now concludes his preaching on justification with an address on the state of the promise. A promise is no sooner given than it is attacked by the powers and principalities of the old Aeon (like the law) who either do not recognize the promise as God's or oppose it precisely because it is God's as with Satan—whom God will shortly crush (Romans 16:20). To attack the weakest point of the promise, these enemies attack the receiver as unworthy (Romans 6 and 7), but since the promise is tailor-made for sinners, eventually the strong point must be assailed, who is God—the maker of the promise (Romans 9–11). Since God cannot be attacked in his stronghold—in himself (*iustitia dei*)—the weak point is God in his word (*deum justificare*), and because that word is put in the world's history via preachers, the point of attack is God's faithfulness to a promise made to *unfaithful* people. Does God keep a promise, forever? What happens when his people are unfaithful to that same promise? Who wins? The answer focuses on Israel's unfaithfulness, but everyone in the church of Rome depended for their life upon the answer—Jew and Gentile. Are they, as church, people of law who must fulfill the law in order to inherit the promise, or are they people of promise whose future is determined by God's trustworthiness, not their own?

Until this point in his letter Paul has told the dramatic story of baptism—what led to it and what follows, but with the question of God's faithfulness, the story must now stretch over all history from Adam and Eve to the final crushing of Satan's head. Paul's narrative is not like Aristotle's notion of a story, which always has a beginning, middle and end. Paul's is a fractured narrative, broken into unbridgeable, contrary Aeons at the point of Christ's death on the cross. There is no continually existing subject (as the legal scheme requires) to carry the story through—on earth or in heaven. But there is an "order," and we are following it just as Luther taught in his German Bible's introduction to *Romans*:

> Follow this epistle in its order. Concern yourself first with Christ and the gospel, so that you know your sin and his grace. Next, strive with your sins, as taught in Chapters 1–8. Then, when you come to Chapter 8, under cross and suffering, providence in Chapters 9–11 will rightly teach you what a comfort they are. For apart from suffering, cross, and pangs of death, we cannot manage providence without hurt and secret anger against God. So Adam must first be dead before he allows it, before he drinks the strong wine. See to it you do not drink wine while a suckling . . . . Every doctrine has its measure, time, and age.[1]

Once the promise has been delivered in Romans 8 ("If Children, then heirs, and so fellow heirs with Christ . . . Who can bring a charge against the elect? It is God who justifies . . ."), the time has come to wean from milk and drink wine. After one has died in baptism it is finally safe to take up the doctrine of election. As I have argued, a promise is to be used, and now Paul proceeds to show us how to do that—first by *confessing*, then by *praying* in Romans 9–11.

He confesses in the form of an oath at a public trial: "I speak the truth in Christ, I do not lie, and my conscience bears me

witness in the Holy Spirit" (9:1 translation altered). His confession
is that the promises he preached are valid because their stock does
not depend upon the receiver but the giver. In capitalist slang, we
say the promises are "money" because God backs them. What if
Israel was unfaithful? God is faithful and he will out. What if Israel
tripped over the stumbling stone of Christ? "It is not as though
God's word has failed" (9:6 NRS). Paul says this in entire solidar-
ity with his people Israel—"brothers, kinsmen"—he calls them.
Baptism did not separate him from them, it brings him nearer
than ever before. In fact, his love is so great that he, like Moses of
old, is willing to substitute himself for his people: "Forgive their
sin—but if not, blot me out of the book that you have written"
(Exodus 32:32 NRS). Paul says, "I could wish that I myself were
accursed and cut off from Christ for the sake of my people according to the flesh" (Romans 9:3 NRS). He is willing to reverse
his own baptism and its union with Christ to take the curse of
unfaithfulness upon him—but baptism cannot be reversed! That is
the point. Paul cannot take their curse—because the curse is
already taken by Christ. Besides, Israel has had from its beginning
the great advantage of the word of God, just as Paul argued in
Romans 3: "They are Israelites, and to them belong the sonship
and the glory and the covenants, and the act of giving of the law,
and the worship, and the promises" (Romans 9:4). It is the promises (ἐπαγγελίαι) that have all Paul's attention here, since they
are at issue in the baptism, and the baptism is at issue as to whether
or not it has divided Paul from his brothers—it has not—and as
to whether it can be reversed—it cannot (just as the promises to
Israel cannot be reversed once Christ has come). What if some are
unfaithful?—God is faithful.

Once he has made this confession, Paul then prays. His prayer
is boldness itself in the face of contrary experience, and extends
for the next three chapters: "I ask, then, Has God rejected his
people? Impossible . . . O the depths of the riches, wisdom, and
knowledge of God. How unsearchable are his judgments and how
unfathomable his ways!" (11:1,33 translation altered).

Biblical historians have been too quick to unlink Chapters
9–11 from all the prior material. Käsemann said, "no part of the
epistle is so self-contained as this," and C. H. Dodd thought it was

imported from elsewhere, but in fact we have here the closest link.
In Romans 8 Paul gave the irrevocable promise: "If God is for us
who is against us? He who did not withhold his own Son but gave
him up for us all, will he not also give us all things with him?"
(Romans 8:31–2 NRS). He ended that sermon with the repeated
refrain of the Psalm: "For your sake we are being killed all the day
long; we are regarded as sheep to be slaughtered" (Psalm 44:11
and 22). That is the great, national lament of Israel calling upon
God's faithfulness in the most strident, aggressive, and bold form:
"In God we have boasted . . . yet you have rejected us . . ." (Psalm
44:8–9). Who dares pray to God this way? Israel, and only Israel,
because she has the promises.

There is no greater advantage on earth than to receive God's
word. This makes Israel bold to justify God—not in himself,
but in his words (deum justificare). But a promise also means great
suffering, since everyone in the old Aeon wants to destroy this
promise—even the holy law gets drawn into the attack. Yet Paul
is even bolder than the Psalmist. He teaches Israel—and all the
baptized—to pray this lament before God not on the basis of their
own righteousness: "we have not forgotten you or been false to
the covenant . . ." (Psalm 44:17), but as the unrighteous—and still we
make a claim on this God: "Rouse yourself! . . . Awake! . . . Why
do you hide your face? Why forget our affliction? (Psalm 44:23–4).
On what basis do we assail God if not righteousness by the law?
On the basis of righteousness by faith alone—because God is
faithful to his promise despite what we have done or left undone.
Paul turns Chapters 9–11 into the way hearers of the Gospel
lament by the groaning of the Spirit—boldly, with assurance in the
promise and against contrary experience.

Lament is only possible when you have a promise; it is only
needed when the promise is nowhere in sight. Anthropologically
the attack on the preached gospel comes in the form of the attack
on the Simul—why are we still suffering and threatened by sin,
death, and devil if we have faith (Romans 7)? Put theologically,
the attack on the promise is made as an attack on the hiddenness
of God apart from his word, "Why dost thou hide thy face? . . .
Rise up, come to our help! Deliver us for the sake of thy steadfast
love!" (Psalm 44:23–6)

In the city of Rome there were surely Jews and Gentiles in the church—but regardless of nation, everything now turns to the matter of whether God has reneged any promise made to Israel—so this promise has become the testing point for all believers. Is Paul not saying that if the Gentiles are included—necessarily the Jews are driven out, effectively reversing Psalm 44:2, "you with your own hand drove out the nations, but them [Israel] you planted; you afflicted the peoples [Gentiles], but them you set free." Isn't all of history, just as Hegel thought, a struggle between contrasting spirits, or religions? Isn't Paul simply reversing the power structures on earth as in a coup d'état; if Jews rule Gentiles are enslaved, if Gentiles rule Jews are destroyed? This would be true if righteousness came by law; but it comes by faith. A new Aeon has come and the law has ended; promise now reigns alone.

How does a promise function differently than a law? How is God faithful to a promise? Are there limits to God's faithfulness? Is there some covenant or agreement that God will do so much work—if humans do their part? Or does God have enemies too great for him that can void the promise? Paul now answers: "It is not as though God's word has failed" (Romans 9:6 NRS). If God cannot be faithful to the promise to Israel, how will he ever be faithful to Paul's "free" promise without any law that was given to *ungodly* people who have no zeal, are not running, and who give no effort to the law? The Gentiles have now been put in exactly the same place Jews have occupied for years—chosen by God yet showing no benefit for it—no glory, only the cross. Romans 9–11 is Paul's answer to the most basic attack on the promise—this benefit gives me no benefit! Life is promised, and I have only death. Yet, the ground of God's promise is found in nothing outside of that promise itself. One does not make a lament on the basis of one's own righteousness—but only on God's: "Deliver us for the sake of thy steadfast love"—that is God's trustworthiness, faithfulness, willingness, and power to keep the promise (Psalm 44:26). So anyone who hears Paul's sermon must conclude: be faithful to us, not on our account, but only on yours. This lament (though it comes with great suffering) is the fulfillment of the first commandment that says we should have faith, but it fulfills it without any commandment at all—only with Christ.

The Modern Escape from Justification

The current great divide in theology between Biblical historians and Reformation theologians began with F. C. Baur in 1836, who identified Romans 9–11 as the center of the letter because he thought those chapters did not expound a *doctrine* of justification, but revealed a *historical* controversy between Jewish and Gentile Christians, which in turn emerged from the deepest of all historical controversies between Jew and Gentile. Hegel had taught Baur that history is dialectical in the sense that it proceeds out of the controversy of opposites seeking resolution that takes up both positions synthetically—although in a previously unknown higher key, conceptuality or spirit. This form of historical thinking caused Baur to reject the longstanding Lutheran scholastic development which treated Paul's letter to the Romans (as he aged) as "a compendium of doctrine." As the allegorical episode developed in Lutheran scholasticism in the seventeenth century and beyond, its method was a non-historical, non-dialectical, logical system that developed thoughts deductively from first principles. Allegory translates Scripture's words into a more suitable idiom or worldview, but this created a crisis of faith by the nineteenth century.

F. C. Baur's groundbreaking thesis was simple: Paul's letter is understood not as timeless, logical ideas (Lutheran, scholastic doctrines), but as a particular historical controversy within the Roman congregation between two primitive religious groups, Jews and Greeks, each of whom has a contrary "spirit"—each of whom wants to shape the new Christianity. It was Baur's (mistaken) contention that Paul entered the fight in Rome against the predominant *Jewish*-Christian position, so that Paul was supposed to be arguing for something called Christian "universalism" against Jewish "particularism." The fault of Jews was held to be belief in predestination or election as a tribal prerogative that excluded every Gentile. Instead, Baur thought Paul argued for a universal inclusion of Gentiles into Israel and her covenant election by God. Paul was then seen by Baur as one of Hegel's great men of history, who rose above the old Jew/Gentile controversy by using the higher principle of *universal inclusion*. But the question was, What is the universe supposed to be included into? Into Israel? No—into the universal, eternal law.

This Hegelian, historical thesis had the effect, as Ernst Käsemann put it, of "removing from its hinges . . . the traditional Protestant doctrine of justification . . ."[2] so that the chief doctrine of the Reformation was reduced in two generations (as with Wilhelm Wrede and Albert Schweitzer) to a contextual, hyperbolic, polemical position momentarily assumed by Paul (and just as easily dropped) to argue against stingy Jewish-Christians who would not open the door to Gentiles—as Gentiles. How the mighty has fallen! Käsemann is also correct that "the failure of the Reformation to integrate chapters 9–11 into their message of justification was thus avenged."

The answer to Jewish particularism by law is not universalizing the law. Paul has argued throughout that *freedom from the law* is the Gospel's gift. Indeed, by rejecting the Lutheran teaching on justification the Biblical historians have naturally returned to the position of claiming that the law is the way to righteousness. Baur was correct that Romans 9–11 is the heart of the letter to the Romans, and that Paul is making a polemical argument in the midst of controversy in Rome. But what Paul delivered in the midst of this struggle within Rome's church was not a mere polemic or debating position; he delivered a controversial *sermon*. As usual the problem with preaching the gospel always boils down to whether the promise of the forgiveness of sins is "all there is?" What about the law? That is a problem shared, albeit in different ways, by both Jews and Greeks. Therefore the key to Chapters 9–11 is how the preacher, who just delivered a sermon in Chapter 8 that announced death's end (and who wants again to do so in person when he arrives in Rome, God willing) is the means used by the Holy Spirit to elect the faithful. Predestination means the unthwartable determination of God to send a preacher with a promise, and that the promise—all by itself—establishes righteousness. Righteousness has no legal basis in the person; it lies entirely in the word. What Paul is arguing in these chapters is not Christian universalism vs. Jewish particularism; he is arguing that God who is just in himself (*iustitia dei*) has now come to be justified in his words—*deum justificare*. The meaning of all history is the arrival of the preacher at a particular time and place—like Rome—and the hearing of faith.

Israel: Elected and Elector

Now, who are the elect? The legal scheme thinks one thing, the Gospel another. Psalm 44 was given by Paul to "the nations" (as well as Israel) because Israel always was righteous in exactly the way Gentiles are newly made righteous—by faith, not the righteousness of law. This is a consistent teaching of all Scripture about the *Remnant* in Israel and the nations elected by the preacher.

To whom has God made his promises? "Isaiah cries out concerning Israel: 'Though the number of the sons of Israel be as the sand of the sea, only the Remnant will be saved'" (Romans 9:27 NRS). The prophet Isaiah had already spoken that word in opposition to a popular belief that the "Remnant" was anyone who managed to remain in Zion once Judah's punishment was complete. Paul simply states what Israel has always known: "For not all who are descended from Israel belong to Israel." So Paul goes through the steps to make this clear even to Gentiles, who wonder from afar about God's faithfulness to unfaithful people. Just being Abraham's seed does not mean a promise is made to you. Ishmael was Abraham's seed as much as Isaac. Accordingly, Abraham was greatly distressed when Sarah wanted Ishmael and Hagar thrown out, but God agreed with Sarah, since it was not Abraham's parentage that made Isaac into Abraham's son, but the fact that Isaac received a divine promise and Ishmael did not: "in Isaac shall your descendents be named" (Genesis 21:12). Ishmael got a nation, but Isaac got the name of Abraham's heir. Therefore, a distinction must be made between children of *flesh* and children of *the promise*; election is by promise, not flesh.

Then, lest you think that it was having the correct *mother* in Sarah that made the difference, Paul continued, for Isaac's sons also were sons of the same father—and the same mother (Rebecca)—twins to be exact—yet before the children were born "and had not done anything good or bad, in order that God's purpose of election might stand, not by works, but by the One doing the calling, Rebecca was told: 'The elder shall serve the younger'" (Romans 9:11–12, translation altered). This is God's predestination: Is not Esau Jacob's brother? Nevertheless God's word says: "I have loved Jacob; but I have hated Esau" (Malachi 1 and Romans 9:13 NRS).

215

What can be said to this? "Is God unjust?" Yes, for a person caught in the legal scheme, but Paul answers outside that scheme: "God forbid." The promise depends upon God's faithfulness, and God's faithfulness depends upon God's election. Election is none other than God's favor (חן or χάριν)—the very words Melanchthon used to translate grace. Paul pointed out (Romans 9:15) that it was Moses who pleaded with God (after receiving the law!) to learn how he had managed to get God's favor so that he might know how to find it again when he needed it: "Now if I have found favor in your sight, show me your ways, so that I may know you and find favor in your sight. Consider too that this nation is your people" (Exodus 33:13). God hid Moses' face in the cleft of the rock, and preached his name: "The Lord"—meaning "I will have mercy on whom I have mercy, and I will be gracious to whom I will be gracious." What Paul is saying here is that God is faithful to his promise because that is *who he is*—faithfulness is not an effect of a cause; it is God's name. Luther made this the cornerstone for teaching the commandments. Before you can call on the name of the Lord (second commandment) or worship him (third commandment) you must have the name of the Lord given in the form of a promise, and that name is: *I want to give to you.* In the *Large Catechism* Luther is explicit:

> What this means is: "See to it that you let me alone be
> your God, and never search for another." In other words;
> "Whatever good thing you lack, look to me for it and seek
> it from me, and whenever you suffer misfortune and
> distress, crawl to me and cling to me. I, I myself, will give
> you what you need and help you out of every danger.
> Only do not let your heart cling to or rest in anyone else."[3]

Of course God is free, but the point of predestination is that God is *gracious*—finding favor with whom he finds favor—and never failing in his promise. Who can account for God's baptism in the present? It does not fit the Jew as something righteousness according to the law. It does not fit the Gentile as gracious initiation into the people of the law. This promise from God fractured "the people" according to any legal scheme, just as Hosea had preached: "Those who were not my people I will call 'my people,' and her who was not beloved I will call 'my beloved'" (Romans 9:25 NRS). This applies to Israel as much as to the Gentile nations, and is why Isaiah had preached, "Though the number of the sons of Israel be as the sand of the sea, only the Remnant will be saved" (Romans 9:27 NRS).

Now the effect of God's favor upon those who do not have it is hardening of the heart. Cain was hardened, Esau was hardened; God hardened Pharoah's heart who looked upon the promise to Abraham as his own curse. God did not give, he took away from them. When Luther's fellow Reformer, Erasmus, objected to Paul's use of this verse, Luther suddenly had his eyes opened to a persistent problem in the church: "For the scripture says to Pharaoh, 'I have raised you up for the very purpose of showing my power in you and that my name might be proclaimed in all the earth'. . . . he hardens the heart of whomever he chooses" (Romans 9:17–18 NRS). Erasmus was offended, and went right back for solace to the first theologians in the Christian church, Origen (c. 185–254) and Jerome (c.347–420), who said this must be a "trope," so that a moral interpretation in line with the law must be used at this point in order that God would work "as the agent who merely provides an opportunity" to Pharaoh.[4] For Erasmus, "I will harden Pharaoh's heart" then must mean "I will permit it to be hardened." What Exodus 4:21 really meant was that God provided opportunity for an exercise of free will, and Pharaoh then hardened his own heart. Luther quickly grasped the enormous problem; Erasmus' way of reading Scripture was to say that on one hand, grace was God temporarily restraining himself from acting, while sinners work fitfully toward repentance using their free will. Wrath, or hardening, on the other hand, was God acting unilaterally to remove "possibility." When you extend this thought out to its logical conclusion, mercy then becomes God *doing nothing* so that humans have potential, and wrath was the reverse—God *doing everything*, acting unilaterally without any external cause or reason.

Election and predestination are properly the Gospel, not the law, but they will work terrible hatred of God when the promise is hid from view. For Paul everything depended upon the faithfulness of Christ to his promise in baptism—but he was met with the substantial question—Does this Christ not mean the very destruction of the promise to Israel? Is the Father then not forced—through

217

love of the Son—to abandon his promise to Israel? What if Christ ends up hardening the hearts of any in Israel according to the flesh? Should God not rebuke his Son as the cause of failure for God's own promise to Israel? For this conundrum Paul put together two sermons of Isaiah: "The Lord placed in Zion a *precious corner stone* in which His congregation should build faith" (Is 28:16), and "the *stone of stumbling* for Israel" (Is 8:14). God hardens the hearts of those (even in Israel) who had zeal, though it was unenlightened, with his Son Jesus Christ—because law is not by faith, but by works. The zealous, like Paul, have stumbled over the cornerstone (9:31–2 NRS). But the Remnant, also like Paul, remains in Israel (9:27), and the Lord is faithful to his promise: "If the Lord of hosts had not left us a Seed, we would have fared like Sodom and Gomorrah." Israel from the beginning was not a people of the law; they were a people of the promise—the Seed, who is Christ.

Predestination as Pastoral Care (Romans 8:29–30)

Without a preacher, predestination is horror; with a preacher it is the greatest comfort, and for this reason the Lutheran teaching on predestination is actually its pastoral care of the soul (*Seelsorge*). The preached word of promise is not only the presence of Christ and the gift of the Holy Spirit in person, but is the unthwartable destination of the Father to get through to his sinners. When people are suffering and dying, they need to hear that God's promise cannot fail. The Formula of Concord addressed predestination in its eleventh article because fights among Calvinist and Lutheran preachers were beginning to break out, as in Strasbourg (1563), and Lutherans seemed restless about the prominence of divine election in Luther's own writings—especially *The Bondage of the Will*. It was Martin Chemnitz who provided the pastoral conclusion to God having mercy on whom he will: "This teaching offers the following beautiful, wonderful comfort ... to guarantee my salvation so completely and certainly—because it could slip through our fingers so easily through the weakness and wickedness of our flesh or be snatched . . . by the devil and world."[5] This means that predestination is not a doctrine, or thing to be believed; indeed, the point is that it cannot be believed in, but when joined with a promise from Christ the effect of predestination is priceless.

Normally Romans 9–11 is taken as the *locus classicus* of the doctrine of predestination, but the real theological struggle over how to teach predestination occurs back in Romans 8:29–31 (NRS):

> We know that in everything God works for good with those who love him, who are called according to his purpose. For those whom he foreknew he also predestined to be conformed to the image of his Son, in order that he might be the first-born of many brethren. And those whom he predestined he also called; and those whom he called he also justified; and those whom he justified he also glorified. What then shall we say to this? If God is for us, who is against us?

Theologically three distinctions have been made in these verses, each producing opposed teachings on predestination. Augustine distinguished salvation *in re* (present reality) and *in spe* (future hope) precisely so that salvation would not be certain. Augustine pictured salvation as a pilgrim's journey, which is only begun by *prevenient* grace (election in baptism), but it cannot be finished without a second, *persevering* grace that is also predestined. To baptism's grace must be added the second grace of perseverance, and in-between the journey's start and the finish the pilgrim must have faith that is sure of the first grace of baptism, but not of the final. This made faith a middle ground between despair (that would come if you knew for certain that you were *not* predestined for salvation) and pride (that would come if you knew for certain that you *were* predestined). Romans 8:24 says: "For in this hope we were saved," and Augustine took that verse as the necessary preamble to "those whom he foreknew, he predestined . . . ." By this reckoning, salvation cannot be given *in re*, in the present reality of life, it must be given only *in spe*—in hope that lies ahead in the unknown future. Augustine wrote in *City of God*, "We are saved in hope . . . we do not yet possess a present salvation, but await salvation in the future."[6] Faith in the present is not yet salvation, for that would short-circuit the pilgrimage which must always be

Calvin?

219

walked on the tightrope between despair and pride. Augustine placed Paul's eschatological distinction into a larger teleological, legal one, so that certainty is sin—and doubt (in medium doses) is beneficial. Faith has no security, and therefore depends entirely upon the unknown decisions of God.

Luther was raised on this Augustinian picture, but recognized that Paul made predestination exactly synonymous with justification because he had preached the gospel in Chapter 8, not law. Paul was giving the very best comfort to the Roman church that leaves no room at all for doubt. For Luther the key teaching in Paul's letter to the Romans is the certainty of faith. Faith is certain precisely because it is not a power of humans, but depends only upon God's faithfulness to the promise—precisely while the recipients are unfaithful. Hope does not yet see its glory, but faith already has Christ and so salvation is secured *in re*—in fact. This meant that for Luther, predestination was dealt with by distinguishing the law/gospel, not reality/hope. Wondering if God has chosen you or not is fruitless, and yet that proves to be an addictive fear that makes one hate and flee God, much as Oedipus did in Sophocles play or Jonah did in Scripture. However, if predestination comes with a preacher, and faith is given a promise in which to believe, then faith's certainty in the trustworthiness of the promise is salvation *in the present*. Certainty rests in the promise, not in the power of faith to persevere, or in God adding another grace to baptism. Luther's *Bondage of the Will* is actually a devotional, pastoral-care book meant to help people like Erasmus who are flummoxed over their salvation. At least Luther tried to preach directly to the unfortunate fear monger.

But a third, influential. alternative arose with John Calvin (1509–1564). He retained Augustine's notion of salvation in two parts, but he rid faith of insecurity by treating Paul's statement as an *ordo salutis* (ordered steps toward salvation). The first step is a predestination—outside of time—that is uncertain, until, secondly, an "inner call" is added that anchors faith's assurance of salvation. Instead of a preacher with a promise in the form of an external word, Calvin substituted the Holy Spirit—who is understood to give this second, certain gift of an *inner call* based on the verse: "For those whom he predestined he also *called* . . ." (Romans 8:30).[7]

This proved fateful for the relation of Lutherans and Reformed, and occupied much of the Lutheran scholastic period (sixteenth century) that tried to explain why Lutherans differed substantially from Calvinists. Because Calvin's reading of Paul affected preaching at its core, it also affected the sacraments, most noticeably the Lord's Supper—which used the bulk of the time and effort for distinguishing Lutherans from Protestants.

Calvin agreed with Luther that the assurance of faith is certain, and he agreed with Augustine that faith, to be true, must persevere to the end. Yet Calvin made an inference, that if a person has faith in the present moment—and comes to know it through the Holy Spirit giving an "inner call"—then that person necessarily will persevere and has therefore necessarily been predestined. He concluded that the preached word of promise is always general (e.g., "Everyone who calls upon the name of the Lord shall be saved." Romans 10:13), and therefore it can deceive us, since we can never be sure it belongs to us in particular; however, the inner call cannot deceive us. Calvin then made this into an *ordo salutis* in which the word must have a pledge, or seal added: "God by his call manifests the election which he otherwise holds hidden within himself." But this effectively replaced the promise with the call. Inner call was in time surrounded by various means of identification, but all of them refer to some inner movement of the Holy Spirit accessible through the individual's experience—the very thing the Lutherans referred to as enthusiastic. Suddenly, the human *experience* was added to the preaching of Christ, and the table was set for the whole revolution of subjective experience in theology.

This is why Lutherans and Calvinists differ on the basic matter of catechism and preaching. Calvin taught the internal matter of *how one knows* when she has faith or not. Luther taught the external matter of which promises are to be believed. For him, promises that come from a preacher are God's justification, predestination, call, and glory all at once. Lutherans have had a difficult time following Luther at this point. The luminary of Lutheran orthodoxy, John Gerhard, was going through the typical Lutheran work of rejecting Roman teaching on faith as "unformed without love and merely implicit," but when he turned to speak of the Lutheran teaching, he took up the term *fides specialis* in order to make Luther's and Melanchthon's point that it is not general faith or "historical faith" that saves—for even the Devil has that. *Fides specialis*, Gerhard wrote,

> is that by which the sinner, converted and regenerated, *applies to himself* individually *the universal promises* in reference to Christ the Mediator, and the grace of God accessible through Him, and believes that God desires to be propitious to him and to pardon his sins, on account of the satisfaction of Christ, made for him and all men's sins. It is therefore called special faith, *not because it has any special promise as its object* . . . but on account of the application by which, under the *universal promise* of the grace of God and the merit of Christ, it reaches him *individually*.[8]

Undoubtedly all the typical Lutheran themes are present in this definition of faith: promise, application, the satisfaction of Christ, forgiveness of sins, and mostly the application of the pronoun— but all these were put back into the legal scheme, and out came a very different understanding of these words than Luther's own. The promise became a "universal" idea, and the application became a self-application of an "inner" movement; the pronoun moved from the "you" of preaching to the "me" of self-reflection. Down this path lies the bitter abandonment of the sole consolation of the external word of preaching in predestination.

Christ the End of the Law

In the tenth chapter Paul reaches two conclusions that summarize his Argument (the one who is righteous by faith shall live). First, "Christ is the end of the law" (Romans 10:4) and second, "faith comes by what is heard" (Romans 10:17). The end of the law was a shock to Paul, for he had a special zeal for it—but it was not "enlightened." Loss of the law at first seemed to be the loss of all meaning in life and religion, but then became a new life entirely. When Schleiermacher (1768–1834) attempted to classify Christianity as a type of religion he called it a "teleological type," rather than an ontological type (like the mystical religions of Asia)—even though he is famous for describing the experience of faith as "feeling." That means that Christianity has a goal, and the goal is legal (or as Kant called it a moral imperative).[9] But in fact, the law's end ruins Christianity as a teleological religion, since Christ crucified cannot be a desirable goal for anyone. "For freedom Christ has set us free" sounds like gibberish in the legal scheme, but it means there is no goal humans must reach in Christ's new kingdom; instead, once the law ends, one can truly begin to live—freely—without any purpose in the sense of a path to perfection.

Paul's word for the end of the law is τέλος, meaning both a thing that is over and done with, and something that has been completed or fulfilled—so that when a runner crosses the finish line the race is over and done, but it has also been completed. Something stops; yet, something was accomplished. So it is with the law. It is only over and done with when it has been done. The masterpiece of this work was Luther's *Antinomian Disputations* that were scholarly debates with the antinomian Agricola. We can take his last four of his Second Set of Theses (1538) in reply to Agricola to make the point:

45. For the law, as it was *before Christ,* certainly accused us; but under Christ it is placated by the remission of sins; and then it is to be fulfilled in the Spirit.
46. Thus *after Christ* in the coming life, there it will remain as fulfilled, when what it demands in the meantime is brought about—the new creature.
47. For never will the law be removed in eternity, but it will remain, either as to be fulfilled in those damned or as fulfilled in those blessed.
48. These true disciples of Satan [Agricola's Antinomians] seem to think that the law is something temporal that has ceased under Christ, like circumcision.[10]

Starting with the last thesis, law does not end like a creature's life ends one day—or even as circumcision ended. That would merely be a temporal ending to law—in the old Aeon—but that cannot happen, since the law is eternally the divine word governing this

223

old world. Secular versions of the end of the law (utopia) never work—in fact they turn out to be imaginary explorations into what would happen if the law really was done—but it clearly is not. When Luke says, "the law and the prophets were until John" (Luke 16:16), he is not speaking about a moment when the law died in the ongoing salvation history of God's people. The law remains eternally, but it is not an eternal law in the sense of ruling or making any demands of Christians—nor is it the very mind of God itself. Law is not ended by temporal disappearance, but by being drawn into Christ, and so historicized by the cross. Ever since Christ's incarnation, death, and resurrection the law must now be identified as either *before Christ*, or *after Christ*. There is no sense to law without this designation once Christ has come.

Physicists, for example, would find this most confusing, since the law is abstract and universal for them—not historical as something that Christ's cross would change forever. How strange to think of laws of gravity as before or after Christ, but here Luther holds that law must refer to Christ—and him crucified—or one will not grasp its end. *Before* Christ the law accused us (Thesis 45); *Under* Christ, the law's accusation is forgiven (not imputed), and the Spirit's work fulfills it in us in the strange double work—by putting us to death and raising a new creation. *After* Christ, the law remains forever—but *fulfilled*. This is a surprise, especially to sinners, since no one could have expected that the law would be completed, fulfilled, done *for us* (even in us), but *not by us*.

Luther imagined a conversation like this: "The law says to a certain person: 'Render what you owe; God has given the law that you might fulfill it, yet you have not fulfilled it, therefore you have an irate God and strict Judge.'"[11] Now before Christ, this would be the end of the conversation with the law, and God's wrath would have the final word. But Luther continues, "Meanwhile the law does not say in what way or by whom that person can fulfill it. It cannot show him who fulfills it, until the Gospel comes and says: 'Christ has done it.'"

When the Gospel comes, law is historical—behind you—like a race that has already been completed—even though it was not completed by you. How did Christ do this? First, he knew no sin; the law had nothing to do with him. Then he became sin, taking the sins of the world upon him; then he became the total preoccupation of the law, until its accusation was used up in the cross. Luther says, "It is therefore no longer necessary that the law require its fulfillment and the prophets preach about Christ the future Fulfiller of the law, because he appeared in his time and was made a curse in order to free us from the curse of the law (Gal 3:13)."[12]

Those without Christ still have every bit of the law accusing them daily. Even the faithful struggle because of the *Simul*, "To be sure [the law] also accuses and threatens the pious (faithful), but it is unable to drive them into despair and damn them." What the law demands, which we cannot give, is that we be a new creature or have a new heart. This is what Christ accomplishes. First he rids us of the old creature—the law was *established* for this purpose, it is not discarded, but it surprisingly brings death instead of justification. Then, thesis 46 says the law demands faith, and faith requires a whole new creature, but this very thing is what Christ has arrived to give and the Holy Spirit to make. The law is eternally in the past for those who have been put to death in baptism; it is a memory. Their future is without any law, since a good heart does the works of the law—without any law at all—perfectly freely.

Faith Comes by What is Heard (Romans 10:17)

Paul had a second great conclusion to his argument: faith comes by what is heard (Romans 10:17 NRS). Justification, the end of the law, comes only by means of hearing a promise. Rather than talk about promises abstractly, Paul proceeded to give the eschatological, messianic promise of Joel 2 to the congregation in Rome: "For everyone who calls upon the name of the Lord will be saved" (Romans 10:13); and Paul then proceeded through his great theo-logic:

But how is anyone to call on him in whom they have not believed? And how are they to believe in him of whom they have never heard? And how are they to hear without a preacher? And how can they preach unless they are sent? As it is written, 'How beautiful are the feet of those who preach good news' (Isaiah). (Romans 10:14–15, translation altered).

225

From now on we do not listen to the law; we listen only to the preacher who, Luther said, spoke in this way: "Listen. The law, which formerly required of us what is impossible, no longer has any right to demand anything from us, because we have Christ . . . he now 'is the end of the law for righteousness to everyone who believes'" (Rom 10:4).[13]

Lutherans have put this in the form of their two basic teachings in the Augsburg Confession: "we cannot obtain forgiveness of sin and righteousness before God through our merit, work, or satisfactions, but that we receive forgiveness of sin and become righteous before God out of grace for Christ's sake through faith," (article 4) followed immediately by the 5th article on the preaching office:

> To obtain such faith God instituted the office of preaching, giving the gospel and the sacraments. Through these, as through means, he gives the Holy Spirit who produces faith, where and when he wills, in those who hear the gospel. It teaches that we have a gracious God, not through our merit but through Christ's merit, when we so believe.[14]

Preaching is God's predestination. Paul used Deuteronomy 30 "the word is near you," just this way. Moses' original use of this word concerned the law, and he thought it meant there was no longer any need to go find the law in a voyage *over* the sea or going *down* to the depths since now it had come near in the tablets of stone. But for Paul, once Moses is silenced and Christ ends the law for faith, "up" and "down" describe *Christ's* ascent into heaven and descent into hell. This is the crucial matter of the *presence of Christ* around which all of Lutheran theology circulates. Descent into hell is legally inappropriate for the infinite God, and ascent into heaven is impossible for a finite man. The communication of attributes nevertheless accomplished both at once. Christ's ascent into heaven is normally taken as "escape" or absence, consequently whenever Christ's presence is considered following his "humiliation" (as theology calls Christ's descent) and his "exaltation" (to the right hand of the Father) it is spiritualized in a pagan sense. Christ's body is removed from his presence, and more importantly, God himself is removed from the word that is preached. Then the word becomes a mere sign that points to an absent thing. When the question arises, where can I find Christ? the answer is obscured "spiritually" into such ideas as "the church," or "the faithful heart," or perhaps even in a sacrifice of the mass. Instead, Paul answers the question, Where is Christ now? by putting the preacher where Moses' law once was: "the word is near you . . . that is, *the word we preach*" (Romans 10:8 translation altered). For this reason Luther's theology is often called a "theology of the Word." It was Käsemann who observed that Paul is the first to link Christ's presence with the preached word, which was later used by the evangelist John in the Farewell Discourses, and so dispersed throughout the New Testament. John says Christ will be present always not through *remembrance*, or the imitation of his life, but "for the words that you gave to me I have given to them . . . sanctify them in the truth; your word is truth" (John 17:8, 17).

When Paul says, "For God has imprisoned all in disobedience so that he may be merciful to all," (Romans 11:32) he is not stating universal truths that must be acquired inwardly by the elect. He is giving the preacher the authority to preach the law and the gospel to specific people who are presently ungodly sinners—Jew and Gentile alike. The fact that the Holy Spirit uses nothing but this preached word to apply a mercy that has no end is unsearchable and inscrutable—but rich and glorious indeed. Faith comes from hearing (*fides ex auditu*) and how shall you hear without a preacher, and how will you have a preacher unless one is sent by the Holy Spirit?

Chapter 11

The Fruit of Faith

Romans 12
> *Fruit of faith therein be showing*
> *That thou art to others loving;*
> *To thy neighbor thou wilt do*
> *As God in love hath done to you*

Martin Luther, Jesus Christ our Savior

Faith Active in Love

Once a sinner has been made purely passive, then the active life begins in earnest. Justification by faith is a new creature clinging only to Christ instead of the law, and from this new tree the Holy Spirit produces fruit in the form of love that pours out its life in the body for the neighbor: "A good tree cannot bear bad fruit, nor can a bad tree bear good fruit" (Matthew 7:18 NRS). For the first time good works and love are not a goal and mere potentiality, but actual and present, emerging organically, freely and spontaneously (albeit hiddenly). Paul says "For in Christ Jesus neither circumcision nor uncircumcision accomplishes anything, but faith!—active through love" (Galatians 5:6 translation altered).

Luther composed a classical statement on good works in his *Preface to the Romans* which later became ensconced as the heart of the Lutheran teaching in the settlement of the "Majoristic" controversy (*Formula of Concord* IV, 1580) that sought to make good works a legal requirement for salvation: "Faith is a divine work in us which changes us and makes us to be born anew of God. It kills the old 'Adam' and makes us altogether different people, in heart and spirit and mind and all powers; and it brings with it the Holy

Spirit." Luther was describing the new creature (which Paul called "transformed"), and so he continued,

> O, it is a living, busy, active, mighty thing, this faith. It is impossible for it not to be doing good works incessantly. It does not ask whether good works are to be done, but before the question is asked, it has already done them, and is constantly doing them ... Faith is a living, daring confidence in God's grace, so sure and certain that the believer would stake life itself on it a thousand times .... And this is the work which the Holy Spirit performs in faith. Because of it, without compulsion, a person is ready and glad to do good to everyone, to serve everyone, to suffer everything, out of love and praise to God, who has shown this grace. Thus, it is impossible to separate works from faith, quite as impossible as to separate heat and light from fire.[1]

In order for good works to flow a person must die to the law, since a relation to the law interposes itself between a lover and the beloved, between creatures and their Creator, and between a person and her neighbor. Love is always relational, it is between people, not a quality that resides in an individual soul, and that relation will either be immediate or it will be a relation to the law first—and only secondarily to another person. This is the meaning of Jesus' parable of the Good Samaritan in Luke 10. Two men representing obedience to the law, a Levite and a priest, pass by a wounded man specifically because of their higher calling to remain clean according to the law. The Samaritan, without a proper relationship to the law, simply "looked at him and loved him" (Luke 10:33). The Samaritan was not good because he loved; he was good—and so loved, apart from the relationship to the law. Once the law is removed as the relation between sinner and God the law is also removed from the relation to the neighbor, and love flows freely, organically producing fruit from a good tree.

But not only is faith active in love for an individual, but the fruit of faith is also the *church* where the newly created are gathered together by Christ: "My sheep hear my voice" (John 10:27). God's word of the gospel creates new individual creatures called Christians, and a communion of such creatures called the church.

Paul's Appeal

The first two sentences of Romans 12 express the evangelical teaching on good works. The first sentence concerns works as non-cultic sacrifice: "I appeal to you therefore . . . by the mercies of God, to present your bodies as a living sacrifice . . . ." The second marks the *Simul* as the distinction between being conformed and being transformed: "do not be conformed to this world, but be transformed by the renewing of your minds." Being *conformed* and being *transformed* are two opposite passivities, the first confines the person to this old world and the legal scheme, and the second marks the transference to the new world and the new teaching on good works. Good works follow faith as definitely as $2 + 3 = 5$, and nevertheless contribute nothing to faith; Justification remains faith *alone*. The Holy Spirit is trusted to produce good works in the body that Christians no longer need in order to manufacture righteousness. Once the body has been freed from the rigid requirements of merit, it becomes pliable for the purpose of helping the neighbor.

Morality is ruined in the process; after all, how does one make an appeal for good works once the legal scheme is bankrupt? This is rarely understood in Paul's letters so that a "parenetic" section is believed to be appended to the meaty theological prelude, or a section on "ethics" follows the articles of "dogma." But after articulating how faith is given through preaching, Paul seamlessly says: "I appeal to you therefore . . ." Because the law has indeed ended in Christ, *therefore* the appeal is made. To what or whom is Paul appealing? Is it a free will? If that were so, then all the talk of justification by faith alone would be for naught. Paul appeals to dead people to trust what Christ has said. So Paul's appeal is not legal, unlike Moses' appeal to Israel or that in Rudolph Bultmann's famous formula: "become what you are!" Paul's appeal is not teleological, trying to activate potential or to get you to the goal of righteousness—because righteousness is already given in faith.

The appeal is made because faith is a struggle—not *to do*, but *to trust* (in perfect passivity) that Christ does not lie (*pugnat fides*).

Non-cultic Sacrifice

Lutherans ruin the idea that good works have any standing before God, but does that mean that there is no such thing as a good work? God forbid! A real good work must first have the doer removed as its cause or purpose, or, to say it in reverse, good works must be taken away as the object of a person's trust. God does not need good works, he does not collect or count them or hold them in a treasury; good works are for the person who needs them, whom Scripture calls, "the neighbor." Paul makes this case in dramatic form by identifying a new, non-cultic sacrifice that makes up "your spiritual worship." Paul's appeal says, "present your bodies as a living sacrifice." When people have no preacher, the universal relation of sinners to God is sacrifice: *do et des*. One gives a token/sign to God, destroying one part of creation (plant, animal, or person) that is used as a symbol by burning the sacrificial victim in order to placate God's wrath; then when peace has been re-established, one eats the remainder of the sacrifice in a cultic meal that establishes communion through this symbol with the God and one's enemies. This is called "worship," in which God is imagined to have been given his due (*deum justificare*).

However, justification by faith alone has answered this question "what is due God?" without any cultic use of sacrifice to appease God's wrath, and also without good deeds in the form of merit. When the preacher comes with the words that kill and make alive (the law and gospel), faith trusts what Christ says is true. What then happens to Christian worship? It is "cultivated"— torn up for new planting, or made non-cultic so that sacrifice to God is removed. Christ is the end of all that old worship because he is the end of the law so that worship must now be in spirit and truth (John 4:24). Yet sacrifice does not disappear; it takes an entirely new direction. Before Christ's arrival the direction of sacrifice was from the sinner up to God—vertically. "But now," it is made horizontal, and is a sacrifice *acceptable* to God—but *made* to the neighbor. The sacrifice does not give in order to get back; those who have died in a death like Christ's do not need to hoard merit so that God's wrath will end. God's wrath is over, so that sacrifice has become love that gives itself over to the other. There is no sacrificial victim as a piece of creation burned in token of one's sorrow and willingness to change; it is a *living* sacrifice, Paul says, because only your living is useful for the other. Christian worship is now holy, not in the cultic sense of separating off from the evil world and keeping "clean," but by doing the exact reverse— entering into the world in its worst muck since holiness now is whatever the Holy Spirit brings forth as fruit from a good tree, and a good tree does not eat its own fruit; it produces it for others.

Consequently your body is not lined up before God for a final judgment, but is made as a present to the neighbor. Such a body is not the flesh, which works to destroy faith; it becomes the factory by which the Spirit manufactures good works for neighbors in need so that the body comes out of the new creature in the form of fruit. The source and vitality of the fruit comes from the tree already being good from the roots up, and the hardest part of this sacrifice is not to get the free will to do what the law requires; it is to trust the resurrection when one is being killed all day long by good works. In the end, there is nothing you gain from this sacrifice—and so the spiritual worship is to "let goods and kindred go, this mortal life also," as Luther said in his famous hymn *A Mighty Fortress*—without a legacy or estate or even a body that endures in this old world. Furthermore, these acts of love for the neighbor are hidden from the doers—since the new life is hid in Christ (Colossians 3:3)—otherwise they would attempt to make an ethics of them.

Thus, even the Christian adaptation of Israel's sacrifice in the canon of the Mass had to come to an end in Lutheran worship. Just as Paul entered the Corinthian church to put an end to its celebration of Eucharist without the proclamation of the death of Christ or the true spiritual worship of good works given to the neighbor, so Luther ended the use of the Canon of the Mass in the form of the eucharistic prayer as an "unbloody sacrifice," or even as a sacrifice of praise. Instead the Lord's Supper was *preached* in the words of Christ's institution: "In the night in which he was betrayed . . ." and the body and blood in the bread and wine were distributed to the sinners who trusted this word, "given and shed for you for the forgiveness of sins." The Lord's Supper is non-cultic because it is the preaching of the word in which God gives himself to sinners.

Even Christ's own sacrifice is revealed as non-cultic, since from the beginning the precise receiver of the sacrifice of the cross has been unclear: did the Father need to receive Christ's sacrifice in order to cease his wrath? Did the law—or perhaps Satan—require payment? Was it done instead of our failed sacrifices? Was Christ's sacrifice really once and for all, or only for those sins up to that time? In recent days, Gerhard Forde (1927–2005) suggested we would do well to follow the book of Hebrews (13:13) when it says that we must go "outside the camp" for worship, since Christ was crucified outside the gate of the city and temple—that is, we are to understand the cross as non-cultic. Forde suggested we think of Christ's crucifixion as an accident like those stories of someone stepping in and taking the blow of an oncoming truck while throwing an endangered child to safety.[2] That is a "sacrifice" of life, as even our common language says, but not in the form of a temple sacrifice. So Christ could rightly be said to have died for our sakes, without attempting to explain the cross as something the law required, or even something that God needed for his own purity's sake. The accident of Christ's death was caused by us sinners who, like the truck driver, are determined to get to our highest goal at whatever speed necessary, even at the cost of the neighbor's life.

The Greek word's root for spiritual (logos) is helpful to understand that this new worship is *logified* worship (τὴν λογικὴν λατρείαν ὑμῶν), the worship that results from hearing the word from the preacher—which is therefore logical (rational worship) because it comes not from the illogical sacrifice of appeasement according to the law, but from the proclaimed word (*logos*) of forgiveness that operates outside the law. In this way priesthood was also freed from the law as a non-cultic Royal Priesthood—shared by all the baptized who trust the promise of Christ. Presenting the body as a living sacrifice was always linked by Luther with Peter's saying, "Like living stones, you yourselves are being built into a spiritual house, to be a royal priesthood, to offer sacrifices acceptable to God through Jesus Christ" (1 Peter 2:5 translation altered). Peter notes that proclamation belongs to all the baptized and not to a holy priesthood as set aside by a law, and Paul agrees that the fruit of that proclamation is good works so that priesthood is now exercised as non-cultic good works for the neighbor.

Good Works and the Cross

Luther once wrote an open letter to the people of Latvia and Estonia when he heard that the evangelical teaching had spread to those lands. In it he summarized evangelical theology in three layers: first the foundation, which is *faith* in Christ's blood—apart from any merit or deed of law—that makes God favor us so that we have peace with God. Second, we then are free to lay aside traditions of humans being as our form of worship, and "do nothing except *love* the neighbor." That leads to the third matter: "if you hold to this pure doctrine and abide in it, you will not escape *cross* and persecution, for the evil spirit cannot endure it . . ."[3] From faith good works come in the form of love, and from love comes the cross. The reason Lutherans do not rightly produce a new ethics is that they remove *teleology*, the striving after the good, and in its place is the teaching of *suffering*. Aristotle is rejected, who says that good works make a person good; instead, a good person does good works. Person precedes work. Good works have nothing at all to do with making anyone righteous. In fact, good works hinder righteousness, as the opponents of George Major (and the Majoristic controversy) like Amsdorf, Flacius and Gallus argued, "that works are not only loss and rubbish . . . but even harmful,"[4] that is, when people take their eyes off the prize of Christ and trust their works instead of the promise they cease being a living sacrifice and become a blood sucker.

When Paul runs through his "appeal," what he is doing is assuring faith that even—and especially—when the fruit is not seen, there is plenty produced by the Spirit. Christ taught the same thing, that the left hand would not know what the right is doing. The primary effect of good works for the doer is that they meet persecution, cursing, weeping, and disharmony—in short evil (Romans 12:17). When Paul appeals to Christians he is preparing them so that one's faith is not shocked by the body's own death: serve, be patient in suffering (Romans 12:12). The Christian does

234

not resist evil with evil, but absorbs it, turning the other cheek and so overcoming evil with good (Romans 12:21). The goal of life is the death of the body in the most useful manner possible for the neighbor so that Luther once preached, "For the world never has enough of this life, while the experienced Christian is ready to be removed. What the world seeks he avoids; what it avoids, he seeks."[5]

Conforming means going back to thinking that there is one person who is measured by the law. The preacher reminds faith that suffering is not proof of the failure of faith's promise; in fact, it is the only "evidence" God gives in the old world that his will is being done. So Paul removed the fear of death so that the good works could flow by assuring us, "Bless those who persecute you . . .", for what is impossible for humans is precisely what the Holy Spirit produces.

Faith and Love

When Paul illustrates the kind of fruit faith produces, he comes back to love—which the law demanded, but could never deliver: "Let Love be genuine . . . love one another" (Romans 12:9, 10 NRS). Love can only be *fruit*, it cannot take the place of the tree of faith. But there is a constant attempt in the legal scheme to substitute love for faith. It is central in Lutheran theology to distinguish faith from love, since love is the common place for synthesizing gospel with the law in the most dangerous confusions, such as thinking, "You will be righteous when you love as God loves." Because of this temptation, Lutherans have had to make a consistent argument against grace and against love. The best example is given in Melanchthon's fourth article of *Apology of the Augsburg Confession*, written in defense of that Confession after its rejection by Rome (1530). After compiling his long lists from Scripture and the Fathers stating that faith alone justifies, Melanchthon observed that this Lutheran argument got nowhere because Roman theology interpreted every one of Scripture's statements of faith as a reference to "formed faith."[6] Melanchthon concluded, "where does this end but with the abolition of the promise again and a return to the law?" By an act of *synecdoche*, "ingenious people, seeking a method, imagine it is the law, just as the philosophers in ethics imagine it is moral precepts" in which the effect and cause are treated as one, every reference in all of Scripture to faith was reinterpreted as actually being about love.[7] Love—by bare definition—fulfilled the law, faith did not. No wonder the article of justification was buried under a pile of love.

In the fight against love, Melanchthon had learned from Luther to use Luke's story of the woman in the house of a Pharisee who anointed Jesus' feet from an alabaster jar. The Pharisee, Simon, was found outstripped by the woman not only in faith, but also in his pride—the righteousness of the law (which is love). Jesus said to the woman, "Your faith has saved you; go in peace" (Luke 7:50 NRS). Her faith came from the preached word heard earlier: "Your sins are forgiven," and this finally revealed what Jesus meant when he told Simon, "Her sins, which were many, have been forgiven; *hence* she has shown great love" (Luke 7:47 NRS). Love, it turns out, is either understood in relation to the law—in which case it is a work and cannot bear our trust—or it is simply what happens when Christ has forgiven a sinner.

Love is a freedom of the *Spirit* which refuses to be bogged down in the letter of any law—including hierarchical lists of moral casuistry to which one could refer when two loves collide. Melanchthon chided Cicero (and the Scholastics) for putting love on such a sliding scale, as in his *De officiis* where he posed the question of what love demands in the extreme case of a shipwreck when one comes upon a single plank in the water already held by a wise, old man. Such imaginary conundrums are an indication that law has interceded between persons—so that people sit about dreaming up extreme cases of "what if"—while actual situations in the middle of life are ignored: "Away with such stupid questions which hardly ever arise in actual human affairs!"[8] When the law does not intercede, neither does a supposed "free will"; instead the Holy Spirit is set free to work love as actual neighbors have need. Here love ceases being a virtue of the moral kind (Aristotle), or of the "theological" kind (as the Scholastics understood Paul's "faith, hope and love abide, these three, but the greatest of these is love" 1 Corinthians 13:13). Love is not greatest because it sits highest on a moral ladder. Love is the greatest because in eternal life it alone remains forever even when faith and hope no longer exist—without any law demanding it.

The Church

Once love is put in its proper place, then the church as an assembly can also be given proper place since it also is the fruit of faith—not the maker of faith. Church is the assembling of sinners by the preacher's words of law and gospel. Where there is true preaching there is true church, and so the "church is the creature of the word" (*creatura verba*). Before a positive description of the church could be given, Luther had to free evangelical teaching of the sense that the church was bishops—as the Jesuit Robert Bellarmine (1542–1621) put it—as visible as "the Republic of Venice."

In his 1520 *Address to the Christian Nobility of the German Nation concerning the Reform of the Christian Estate,* Luther sought to tear down three "walls" used to protect the Roman papacy from church reform and the fall of Christendom. The first wall was the Vatican's defensive attempt to raise itself above kings by saying that *spiritual* authority was higher than *temporal* authority. But Luther asserted that both are "estates" given by God and neither rules the other in their distinct kingdoms. The second wall of protection resisted Scripture by saying that the Pope alone had the right to interpret Scripture. Interpretation was then made into a power to add human tradition to Scripture, or invent new laws, which produced a whole industry that buried Christ beneath pious traditions. Luther's argument was not to share interpretation democratically, but that Scripture was clear and interpreted itself when law and gospel were distinguished. Scripture always drove away from law and toward Christ alone as our righteousness. Luther put in place of the Pope the distinction of law and gospel as set forth in the text of Scripture. The third wall of defense was the Pope's assertion that he was the only one who could call a church council to address the evangelical teaching. Lutherans prepared their chief public confessions with the hope of such a council, including the Augsburg Confession and the Smalcald Articles, and consider themselves still awaiting such an event. To the contrary, the Council of Trent (1545–1563) became for Lutherans a sectarian meeting of papal theologians who aimed at rejecting the evangelical teaching.[9]

In his own commentary on Romans, Melanchthon inserted a description of the church at this point in Paul's letter, concluding that "carnal opinions . . . imagine that the church is the papal state tied to the orderly succession of bishops, as kingdoms are upheld by an orderly succession of rulers. But with the church it is a different matter, for it is an assembly not bound to an orderly succession, but to the Word of God."[10] That Lutheran theology is a theology of the Word comes into sharp focus here. The preached Word makes the church, which word is solely authorized by the law and promises of Scripture. Justification and church depend utterly on God's faithfulness to that word: "That thou mayest be justified in Thy words" (*deum justificare*). Immediately there was no higher office in the church than that of preacher—which seemed ridiculous and dangerous to Rome, but Luther staked his life and the Reformation on that assertion already in his trial before Cardinal Cajetan following the posting the *95 Theses*.

It did not take long for questions to arise about the viability of such a church. Melanchthon observed, "But here the objection is raised: 'If the authority of the church is repudiated, then too great a license is granted to the wantonness of human mind. When the statements of the church have been rejected, many will think up new and impious interpretations of Scripture.'"[11] When it comes to interpretation, is it not necessary that diversity of opinion must finally be overcome by a single, earthly authority? The same issue was put in its modern form by Ernst Troeltsch when he called this Lutheran teaching "the sociological problem of Protestantism." He observed that the Word is not strong enough to provide consensus concerning the structure of the church and its authority, so Lutherans created a "Scripture and preacher" church that may have evolved to a higher level than the sacramental Roman church, but for Troeltsch, Lutherans retained the authority of a preacher over the inner faith of the individual (and over Troeltsch's preference for a "mystical and individualistic" church). It was the culmination of the long, legal episode in Lutheranism when Troeltsch asserted that no social structure can endure the ravages of time without the use of force—and that the preached Word is no such force. Lutherans were doomed to fail as a "church."

This same argument against Lutheran ecclesiology was made during the imposition of the Augsburg Interim (1548), when the Gnesio-Lutherans resisted re-catholicizing by using the slogan: "The Word remains forever" (1 Peter 1:25 and Isaiah 40:8). On that basis the Lutherans also asserted that the church remains forever in this world, however small a remnant it may become, as in the days of the Arians when the true church was reduced to exactly three faithful bishops. No higher authority exists in the church, or for that matter in the old world, than the preacher who is using the office of the keys to release sinners from wrath, law, sin, death, and devil. Signs of true church are therefore all acts of preaching: sermons that distinguish law and gospel, baptism, Lord's Supper, Absolution, the calling of a public minister from among the Royal priesthood, and suffering for the gospel—the exact opposite of any sign of glory or power in the world. The Lutheran teaching of the church was put simply in the *Augsburg Confession* (art. 7):

> The church is the assembly of saints in which the gospel is taught purely and the sacraments are administered rightly. And it is enough for the true unity of the church to agree concerning the teaching of the gospel and the administration of the sacraments. It is not necessary that human traditions, rites or ceremonies instituted by human beings be alike everywhere . . .

This preaching office, planted in the world by God, awaits another shockingly brief statement of churchly order put purposefully at a later point in the Lutheran confession: "that no one in the church should teach publicly or preach or administer the sacraments without a regular call" (AC, Article XIV). Lutherans travel very light when it comes to church structures; there is no command from God about the proper political structure of the new kingdom. The statement about the call, which meant ordination, is separated from the basic definition of the church because all baptized Christians are Royal priests who must be ready to exercise the office of the keys in the "mutual conversation and consolation" of Christians.[12] Many a sinner's confession is made out of earshot of a public preacher, and many are the absolutions given without the public office. However, it is dangerous to preach without a public call because of the constant attacks in the church by fanatics. The Church's necessary oversight of the gospel concerns how to call a person into the public work of word and sacrament by ordination in light of the demonic attacks on the church by self-appointed spiritualists who mask the law with a façade of grace. For this reason, and for good order in the body, public preachers cannot call themselves into service.

Fanaticism and Ecclesiastical Authority

The church is hidden as a poor, suffering, weak group (as judged by worldly power and glory), but it lives as faith does upon the promises of Christ: "For where two or three are gathered in my name, I am there among them" (Matthew 18:20). Anyone who places himself in the stead of Christ—as if he were absent—is then anti-Christ. Paul says church is "many members . . . though one body in Christ, and individually members one of another" (Romans 12:5 translation altered). Church, like love, is not an ethical admonition, and so it is placed in Paul's appeal to the "brethren" because the church is under siege—just as faith remains a struggle in this old world.

In fact, the church is "militant" as the scholastic Lutherans put it, because it is used by the Holy Spirit in battle against the powers of the old world: sin, death, and the devil. J. Gerhard wrote: "That is called the *Church Militant*, which in this life is still fighting, under the banner of Christ, against Satan, the world, and the flesh." Only heaven removes this fighting of church, where the church is at rest, "relieved from the labor of fighting and the danger of being overcome" (*Triumphant*).[13] It is essential to know that the church endures a unique attack that seeks to intercede between the hearers and the preacher that is called "enthusiasm," or *fanaticism*.

Fanatics think the Spirit speaks through them in order to add something supposedly left out of the sermon of the Apostle. The early churches, as historians like Ernst Käsemann have shown, were visited by apocalyptic, wandering prophets who would speak at worship gatherings of the church so that the churches had to learn to identify a true prophet from a false one (and at the very least a false prophet is one who stays too long and eats too much). Often, these preachers were not apostolic, so that Paul had to write letters like Romans to identify what is apostolic. It is also why Paul begins and ends his letters with his own external call, depending not on his own inner sense, but by the favor shown to him—who once persecuted the church, but now is "a minister of Christ Jesus to the Gentiles" (Romans 15:16 NRS). Fanatics are convinced they have the power of the Holy Spirit, but in fact have only called themselves, and do not know the gospel. Thus they think "too highly" of themselves and must be shut up. That is why Paul describes the church, which is the one body of Christ, as made up of many parts which do not have the same function or role. Paul had been around the block enough that he knew fanatics would infiltrate Rome, especially since the argument could be made that Paul is not *their* apostle, he did not start the church and so has no authority—a claim Paul admits on legal grounds: "Thus I make it my ambition to proclaim the good news, not where Christ has already been named, so that I do not build on someone else's foundation" (Romans 15:20 NRS); however, Paul has the authority of the content of the Gospel itself—and so he wrote "boldly by way of reminder, because of the grace given me by God to be a minister of Christ Jesus to the Gentiles in the priestly service of the gospel of God, so that the offering of the Gentiles may be acceptable, sanctified by the Holy Spirit" (Romans 15:15–16 NRS).

Churches are simply the creature of the preached word, which is the forgiveness of sin, and forgiveness of sin is the exercise of the office of the keys according to the promise: "I will give you the keys of the kingdom of heaven, and whatever you bind on earth shall be bound in heaven, and whatever you loose on earth shall be loosed in heaven" (Matthew 16:19 NRS). Thus, Luther said in his Smalcald Articles, a thirteen-year-old girl knows what the church is—it is the group gathered around the preacher according to the promise "he who hears you hears me" (Luke 16:16). Gifts differ, and they should be used, but if anyone has the gift of "prophecy" they must prophesy only in "proportion to faith," and those weak in faith (the subject of Chapter 14) should not preach—since weak faith means that the law continues to cling to the old creature as with those who are prophesying in Rome that the stronger faith eats only vegetables while the weaker eats indiscriminately, or that the holier observes religious days. The law always creeps in as the form of righteousness only to become the content of "new prophecy" whose form is: do this and you will be the true church! Without the light of Christ, the law conceives itself in terms of bringing salvation to the poor, disenfranchised, and needy, but Paul had been given much faith—and so he knew the freedom from the law—"nothing is unclean in itself; but it is unclean for anyone who thinks it unclean" (Romans 14:14 NRS). The church depends upon the freedom of the apostolic proclamation to keep the law in its place, and to preach the gospel apart from that law. Fanaticism cannot make that distinction.

Fanaticism is overcome only in the proper preaching of the law and gospel. The greatest tool for this purpose in the church is the external call, or ordination. Luther often noted that a proper call for a preacher today is not as it was for Paul, but in fact comes *through* humans, since public preachers are not Apostles—but are apostolic. To be one, holy, Christian and apostolic is to have the gospel preached to us. This living word (*viva vox evangelii*) of preaching itself is the successor to the Apostles—preached "for you," in the present. Those of us who come after the Apostles depend upon a *rite vocatus*, a regular call, which in church tradition is called "ordination." This rite was removed from the list of sacraments for Lutherans, since it uses a prayer rather than bestows a promise of Christ—as preaching does. Yet, despite coming through humans, this external ordination serves for the preacher's own assurance—and for that of the hearers—who inevitably undergo the attack of Satan following true preaching (can this sinner really give me the true word of God? Did I preach properly?). Otherwise one is always thrown back on the self for authorization, not the gospel, and so thrown into the temptation to become an enthusiast. The call is to a particular place (the congregation calls) so that a preacher does not claim authority by some notion of secret revelation, or have the temptation to flee when times are rough. Therefore the preacher's ordination is for good order so that not everyone demands the pulpit on the basis of their Royal Priesthood, and the church ends by constructing a tower of Babel. As Paul said: "I say this for your own benefit, not to lay any restraint upon you, but to promote good order and to secure your undivided devotion to the Lord" (1 Corinthians 7:35 NRS). You cannot call yourself. The temptation of a preacher is to be a spiritualist who receives new words from God not given in Scripture. What does God call a preacher to do? Preaching is God's command, not the congregation's own tradition. The preacher's call is not as Rabbi, Enthusiast, Spiritual Guide, Disciple, Prophet, or Community Organizer—What then is it? The call is to preach law and gospel. Even the office of over-sight—or bishops—which can be used for "good order" to see that the gospel is preached properly—is none other than the office of the keys like that used by any local preacher and held by the Royal Priesthood. So Melanchthon wrote in the Augsburg Confession (art. XXVIII):

> Many and various things have been written in former
> times concerning the power of bishops. Some have
> improperly mixed the power of bishops with the temporal
> sword. . . . Our people teach as follows. According to the
> gospel the power of the keys or of the bishops is a power
> and command of God to preach the gospel, to forgive or
> retain sin, and to administer and distribute the sacraments.[14]

The authority in the church must be distinguished from the authority of governments on earth, even though both come from God, which is Paul's next word of comfort.

Chapter 12

Temporal Authority and Its Limits

Romans 13–14

Herod why dreadest thou a foe
Because the Christ comes born below?
He seeks no mortal kingdom thus,
Who brings his kingdom down to us.

Martin Luther, *Herod, Why Dreadest Thou a Foe?*

Christ is a *Gemellus*: Two Kingdoms

Once Paul has made his appeal for the living sacrifice (Romans 12) the question arises: How does the non-cultic sacrifice of the body actually take place? Where is the fruit of the new tree born? When the law is not justifying, then we may freely speak of law's proper place in the old, limited world: "Do we then abolish the law because of faith? God forbid! On the contrary, we establish the law" (Romans 3:31 translation altered). Otherwise, fanaticism enters secular society as it does the church, through those who would *dominate* temporal government to bring justification to the ungodly, or would *abandon* the secular world as if they were Gnostics seeking escape. Melanchthon noted that "minds are greatly hurt by fanatical opinions that governments, laws, courts, and contracts are things thought out by human ingenuity and are only instruments of human greed . . . or exercising unjust power over the weaker."[1]

Instead, the fruit of love for the neighbor comes in the unromantic form of a call (*vocatio*) into an office (*vocation*) that organizes life in opposition to the forces of destruction. Love is born by children honoring parents, spouses being faithful, not murdering

244

our enemies or coveting, and so on (Romans 13:9), and—least romantic of all—by being subject to the governing authorities (Romans 13:1). Institutions are the way God gets good works done by sinners, and the way love happens. So the Lutherans "teach that lawful civil ordinances are good works of God" (*Augsburg Confession* XVI). Good works are mundane, old Aeon, "just doing my job," sorts of things; even those with no faith are used by God for good works since it is the receiver, not the doer, that determines when something is good. The two Aeons, old and new, are two kingdoms—both ruled by God. However, the kind of ruling God does in each is as different as the law is from the gospel. Those without faith in Christ are ruled by God in the one, old Aeon; those with faith (here is the key to Lutheran teaching) are ruled in *both* the old and new, and so are citizens of two different kingdoms at the same time.

The two Aeons overlap for a time, but they cannot be confused or synthesized. The bearing of good fruit takes place by the creature *of* the new Aeon *in* the old Aeon. This is what is meant by being "in the world but not of it," since the world is where the neighbor is found. As Christ did not count equality with God a thing to be grasped, but emptied himself, taking on the form of a servant, so "a believer is exalted once for all above all things and yet is subject to all things. Just as Christ does, he bears two forms in himself, for he is a *Gemellus*—a twin-born."[2]

Christians are not the only ones who make this living sacrifice of the body; indeed all people are being used in their vocations for this purpose—from the Mother of a child to the King of the nation; however, Christians are especially useful, living sacrifices since they are not afraid of death or confined by law. The freest person in any office is the most useful to the Holy Spirit for giving life to the world. Yet preservation and enhancement of life in the old world is not an end in itself; callings hold people in readiness for the arrival of the preacher and the coming of the new world. The old Aeon remains God's work, but is his "left hand," or alien work which serves the right hand's upbuilding of the kingdom of Christ. So for the sake of the temporal world, God establishes law and uses it for his purpose to limit evil and bring some momentary peace. Lutherans often call this the "first use" of the law. Even Christians undergo the sacrifice of the old body under the old law, and though it is not "good" in the ethical sense, it is still true that "in everything God works for good with those who love him, who are called according to his purpose" (Romans 8:28, translation altered). Law will not justify, but it will help the needy.

In this sense, Paul continues his appeal: "Let every person be subject to the authorities which are over you. For there is no authority except from God—and those authorities that exist have been instituted by God" (Romans 13:1 translation altered). As Melanchthon pointed out, "government itself is a good thing,"[3] and it must be obeyed. The "sword" is given to government so that it is obeyed, even though force does not appear "good" and was even implicated with Pilate in Christ's own death on the cross, so Christians need a clear word about divine rule in the world in order to recognize what God is doing while he is sacrificing them in their bodies ("that the works of God may be acknowledged"). They need a "testimony" that God permits—indeed requires— that the offices of government and its laws are to be used even by the godly. This is important when fanaticism inevitably fights against involvement in the institutions of government by Christians, but Christians are entirely free to use human reason as God's greatest gift in creation to participate in government.

For the Reformers, fanaticism emerged in two basic ways in the church. On the papal side, it appeared as monasticism that took Christ's words, "turn the other cheek" as renunciation of force belonging only to the truly religious saints. This *suppressed* good works for everyday sinners, and caused the monastic suspicion of government as an instrument of human greed. It also took the form of an increasingly active papacy that sought to *dominate* (or at least manipulate) the temporal state for its own noble ends. On the Protestant side, fanaticism took the form not of suppression, but *withdrawal* from the state in order to keep from holding an office that demanded use of force. This side of fanaticism replaced God's own good works with self-chosen works that had nothing to do with the way God manufactures love through earthly offices.

Melanchthon argued that Paul's definition of government is actually better than the political philosophy of Aristotle (government is the guardian of laws) because Paul added the "final cause" which is "for your good" (Romans 13:4 NRS). Melanchthon besmirched his own legacy on Romans 13 when he colluded with the Interim's (1548) confusion of the two kingdoms—agreeing that the Emperor had jurisdiction over Christian liturgy. Nevertheless, he was able to articulate the key Lutheran teaching on resistance: Rulers are God's *servants* for doing *good*. Rulers do not dominate, they serve, and what they serve is not merely another person, but the common good. The Lutheran teaching is no slave mentality. Melanchthon also saw that when Paul says, "subject to the authorities which are over you," he means—in your particular time and place—thus allowing different forms of government. The Gospel does not provide a Trinitarian shape for government, nor are Christians bound to Moses' form of government given to Israel. The authority placed over you is to be obeyed as long as it is in agreement with the laws of nature that are universal within the temporal world. Therefore, Lutherans appeal to the goodness of government, but immediately recognize its limit.

The One God's Two Ways of Ruling

"Love is the fulfilling of the law" (Romans 13:10), and so the proper setting for the discussion of Christian obedience to governing authorities is in the middle of Paul's appeal to love as the fruit of faith: "Owe no one anything, except to love one another; for the one who loves his neighbor has fulfilled the law" (Romans 13:8 translation altered). Once Christians are freed from thinking that love is fulfilled by good works, then love actually begins in earnest—by the Spirit not the free will. But love, and therefore worldly authority, are set within the larger eschatological reality of God destroying this old world, and establishing Christ's new kingdom: "Besides this, you know what time it is, how it is now the moment for you to wake from sleep. For salvation is nearer to us now than when we first believed . . ." (Romans 13:11 NRS). Temporal authority rules in this old world, but precisely because this old world is quickly coming to an end—it is temporal—there is a definite limit to this authority. This larger setting marks the two aspects of Lutheran teaching on earthly authority. One is the *refusal to use force* that is so often confused with "Lutheran quietism" (the charge made by Ernst Troeltsch and repeated endlessly).[4] The other marks the origin of the teaching of Christian *resistance* to authority. Lutherans hold both since Scripture teaches both, and they do so without confusion because they distinguish God's two ways of ruling in opposite, overlapping kingdoms.

Historically, most Lutherans abandoned their own best teaching on secular authority following the loss of the Smalcald War. The allegorical episode of Lutheran teaching in the seventeenth century became too comfortable with the rejection of papal authority in the church by means of a *territorial church* overseen by the state. This resulted from the assumption that the law was the one, eternal holistic background of God's work. The state and the church were then fit allegorically into a broader plan by which salvation was being won in this old Aeon, and church and state became too cozy. The moral episode of the eighteenth and nineteenth centuries did not improve this mistake by Lutherans, but turned the gospel into a "social gospel" project progressively creating the kingdom of God on earth; they substituted a teleological belief in the progress of society for Christ's eschatological new kingdom. That dream of social progress of church and society did not end until the First World War in Europe, and as Dietrich Bonhoeffer noted, never really ended at all in the United States.

The eschatological episode of Lutheranism in the twentieth century recognized that Paul was not presenting a formula for creating the kingdom of God on earth (vs. the moralists), but was describing what Schweitzer called "an interim ethic" that would hold between the time of Paul's arrival with the Gospel, and the end when Christ and the new kingdom would be seen "coming again." But Schweitzer abandoned this hope and ethic because Paul appeared to be wrong about the imminent timing of Christ's arrival in glory; Paul appeared to be an eschatological prophet who simply got it wrong like all such prophets with their sandwich boards predicting the immanent end of "temporal" society. The rediscovery of eschatology then fizzled into the existential emphasis on the present as the only real time for God's kingdom.

Before we can understand what Paul meant by "Let every person be subject to the governing authorities" (Romans 13:1) it is important to understand "Let us then lay aside the works of darkness and *put on the armor of light*" (Romans 13:12 NRS), which is

Paul's reference to the use of baptism. How does one use a baptism as "armor of light" in the struggle of faith? One must distinguish between the two worlds and the two persons "I" am—who reside in both kingdoms. There is the greatest possible difference between "this old, evil world" and Christ's new kingdom. The Christian resides in both worlds as long as the old Adam remains. The work of the devil is to confuse these two worlds by synthesizing them into one. He uses utopian hope in bringing peace on earth as easily as despair that peace will never come. Lutherans are even willing to call Satan a "Lord" of his own kingdom—though it is a shadowy kingdom of smoke and mirrors, dependent upon confusion between the law and the gospel so that the law is held up as the way of righteousness and the gospel is reduced to a content whose form is the law of love. The temptation of Christ in the wilderness reveals how the devil operates as if he had full rights over the world, and indeed claims unfaith as his kingdom's power. But Christ reveals that Satan is deposed with a mere word that promises Christ who justifies through the cross. Were there no "night," and no cosmic battle in which Christ is soon to crush Satan "under your feet" (Romans 16:20), or no eschatology of a new kingdom in these words of Paul, then Paul would indeed have set up the formula for tyranny on earth: "Therefore whoever resists authority resists what God has appointed" (13:2 NRS).

However, with this cosmic distinction of the battle between Satan and Christ, we learn that God fights the powers of Satan with two hands, not one. One is the right hand, which Paul has largely dealt with to this point in his letter, by which Christ is placed against Satan, and the old Adam is put to death with a new creature raised up in a world beyond the law; that is the kingdom of the preached word and faith that begins in baptism. But there is another left-hand work that is the alien work of God, by which God establishes the law in the form of the civil government to limit the chaos and destruction wrought by the demonic confusion of law and gospel. The shorthand in Lutheran theology for this teaching is "two kingdoms," but it really is a "three" kingdom eschatology by which God is opposing the lent power of Satan as ruler of this old world by establishing his own way of ruling by law in the world—and by creating a new kingdom by preaching where Christ rules without the law.

This means that Lutherans make a key adjustment to Augustine's picture of "Two Cities." For Augustine the temporal and eternal Cities were made up utterly of different individuals, and so the Cities were composed of *two different groups*—the damned and the saved—living in two opposite geographical locations. For Luther, every *Christian lives life in both* of God's kingdoms—the temporal and eternal—until the old world is utterly destroyed.

Without understanding this, Reformed theologians have depicted Lutheran theology as separating two kingdoms into static realms—one the inner, spiritual kingdom of faith that has no public voice; the other the outer, temporal world that is left to make up its own laws (or worse, simply equates state laws directly with divine law). Lutherans encountered this perception in the Barmen Declaration (1934) with the idea that both the temporal and the spiritual kingdoms are under the one and only rule of Jesus Christ—so that state governments are not given over to other—therefore ungodly—lords like Hitler. According to that teaching, if a government does not comport with the form of the Gospel of Jesus Christ's rule over everything, then it must be resisted.[5]

To the contrary, Lutherans distinguish the law and the gospel and in doing so have held that Romans 13 rightly calls for *submission* and *resistance* to governing authority. To understand this we can consider two formative historical events. The first when Duke George of Saxony attempted to suppress the Reformation by prohibiting sales of Luther's German Bible, and demanding that sold copies be handed over (with a refund!). Luther responded with a foundational treatise *On Temporal Authority* (1523). The second was the defeat of the Lutheran princes in the Smalcald War, and a gathering of Gnesio-Lutheran pastors and teachers (von Amsdorf, Gallus, Flacius) who held out for the evangelical cause and produced the *Magdeburg Confession* (1550) that established the basis for forceful resistance to the Emperor's assault.

When Duke George demanded that German Bibles be handed over, Luther had to consider the two basic Christian teachings on worldly power to determine how they fit together. The first is the Sermon on the Mount in which Christ gives the call to Christians to refrain from force: "But I say to you, Do not resist an evildoer. But if anyone strikes you on the right cheek, turn the other also" (Matthew 5:39). The second is the call for all to obey the power of the sword in Romans 13: "Let every person be subject to the governing authorities." The Medieval solution to the tension between renunciation and use of force was to separate Christians into two levels with two different ethical demands: The *commandments* (including obedience to authority) were required by all at a basic level, but the *evangelical counsels* of the Sermon on the Mount were a special ethics reserved for mature, committed saints who renounced any use of force.

Instead, Luther spoke of two ways in which God rules everyone: one form of ruling is by means of the *promise* that makes faith and whose kingdom is new and eternal. The second is the way God uses the *law* to establish external peace by means of the sword in the temporal, old kingdom. Neither of these ways of ruling was sufficient without the other. Instead of the scholastic distinction between levels of Christians, Luther then distinguished between *Christians* who do not need the temporal government at all since they live beyond the law, and *the rest of the world* who require the force of the sword to resist evil and preserve some peace. To Christians alone (all of them) belongs the renunciation of force.

Then Luther made a second alteration of the old teaching. Because of the *Simul* in which the old Adam clings for now to the new creature, the Christian sacrifices the body to the neighbor by means of earthly vocations. So, though Christians renounce force for their own sake, for the sake of the protection of the weak neighbor they will even volunteer (in Luther's striking illustration) to be the hangman if none other will fill such a divine office. There is an important distinction between person and office, in which the person of the Christian rejects force even if martyred; nevertheless, the Christian person is always called into an office—in fact a series of offices which are meant for the protection of the neighbor. Force is used as the office requires it, so for example, court judges do not give death penalties as a personal choice, but the office may require it. The problem, as Luther saw more clearly over time, is that the Christian person is *always* in an office in this old world, and so rejecting force even in the case of personal attack cannot be without abdication of an office as Mother, Husband, preacher or soldier at the same time. Nevertheless the distinction of person and office is not without purpose; indeed it is of the highest significance, so that there is not the inevitable pull of the old world into linking justification with the renunciation of force, or taking up force as if this could produce good works. Fanatics want to make renunciation into justification; secularists want to make the distinction irrelevant so that the life of faith is private—and eventually meaningless. Even if the distinction does not lead to martyrdom for a Christian, it preserves freedom from the confusion of love and faith, works and justification, and makes for a better, living, non-cultic sacrifice of one's earthly life.

Domination, Withdrawal, or Participation

The source of governmental authority is God, in the form of the sword. This first argument from Luther's *On Temporal Authority* leaves us with a significant political assertion. Luther recognized that rulers like the Pope and Duke George share a desire to *dominate* both of God's kingdoms—making of them one kingdom. One does it from the side of the church, which seeks to make the temporal government into a Christian empire and Christ into a new Moses (especially in the use of canon law). The other does it from the side of the temporal government that seeks to legislate over worship and faith by forbidding the German New Testament and the evangelical preaching. Both are fanatical positions that think of the church as a community of moral deliberation for shaping society into a Gospel form.

On the other side, the Anabaptist movements and monasticism taught *withdrawal* from civil responsibilities that demanded force and so corrupted the world—which are called "pacifism." But what is left beside these two false relations of the Christian to society? Luther's alternative was *participation*, just as Paul says in the parallel section of Galatians 5: "A little leaven leavens the whole lump." Participation is the means of the living sacrifice of the body. It happens not through some ethical commitment or inner motivation, but through *callings*. Vocations are God calling humans out of solitariness into service for the community, and as such they are not an inner calling, but are external offices instituted by God in order to provide service where there is actual need.

Luther adapted the church's traditional way of speaking of these offices in the form of three "estates," or divine orderings that concentrate sinners in groups to keep them out of trouble (and make them useful). The first estate is the Church, which was made for Adam and Eve so that their Creator could speak to them. The fact that the church comes into existence in the beginning of creation (rather than at Pentecost or at the Last Supper) has significance for identifying the unity of the church, and even the relation to the religions of the world—but here we note that a calling into the church means the office of preaching by which God speaks to creatures. The second estate is the Family, or household economy, including not only parent and spouse but business and finance. The second table of the Decalogue of Moses is largely concerned with this way of setting relations in place by which love is extracted for the good of the neighbor and for allowing social intercourse to flow. A natural affinity of mother for child, or husband for wife is normal—and conspicuously evil when not present. The final estate is the State itself which likely was made only after sin entered because force is its normal authority. In any of these estates webs of obligations are built between neighbors, so that all people, Christian or not, are drawn into them.

These institutions are known by their function, which gives limited—but essential—freedom in form to these offices, so for example a king is not necessary for a state, but the state is necessarily established by God to protect from violence and serve the enhancement of life. The Pope and bishops are not necessary for the church, but the church is necessarily established to get the word and sacrament out to sinners. As for participation in the state, Lutherans make a point of saying (Augsburg Confession XVI) that Christians are leaven in the loaf by holding public offices, working in law courts, imposing just punishments of the sword (including the death penalty), waging just war, serving as soldiers, and entering into legal contracts for law and business. They also participate in family life, and so are to "take a wife and be given in marriage" because marriage, not monasticism, has the word of God to adorn it.

Lutherans seek "ordinary saints," not the extraordinary who seek withdrawal or domination. These saints are used by the Holy Spirit for good works that form the glue of society, including those who are not Christian at all. The Augsburg Confession article 16 made this its public witness: "In the meantime the gospel does not undermine government or family but completely requires both their preservation as ordinances of God and the exercise of love in these ordinances. Consequently, Christians owe obedience to their magistrates and laws *except when commanded to sin*. For then they owe greater obedience to God than to human beings (Acts 5:29)."

Participation includes resistance; God instituted the governing authority as an office, but not all who hold the office do God's will, so it follows that not everything a government does is right. Nevertheless, Paul recognized that the office remains God's own; it is not taken away from God—who will use both good and bad persons for his purposes, as he once used evil King Cyrus for the sake of his own Israel. In Acts 4, it is noted that the kings of the world, including Herod and Pontius Pilate, were arrayed to do "what your power and will had decided beforehand should happen." Abused power is still the power created by God and resisting even bad persons ends up resisting God's establishment of the office so that one comes under God's own judgment and wrath: "Whoever resists authority resists what God has appointed, and those who resist will incur judgment" (Romans 13.2 translation altered). Medieval political theories of resistance, drawing only on natural law, were played out when it came to identifying a ground for resisting God's rulers on earth. It is true that as long as the old Aeon continues, God's established authority continues. The positive significance of rulers is that they are God's own servants, and God will use them—however strangely—to combat evil. Christians do not stand in opposition to earthly authority; in fact, they are often the only ones able to give the office the esteem and honor due it while it causes personal or communal suffering. So it was for Jesus with Pontius Pilate, which only shows that Christ was made to suffer God's wrath for us. Christians see that the ruler is a limited person finally able only to serve the wrath of God—which is indeed *alien* work, but divine nevertheless.

This is what Paul meant when he said that Christians are subject not only "because of wrath but also because of conscience" (13:5 NRS). We live in the old Aeon, as children of the New Aeon. Children of God stand to inherit the entire estate of the New Aeon, but while this old world remains they live under a harsh taskmaster. In time they will inherit the estate, this cannot be denied them, but they do not see it yet. Thus, even though such children cannot use the eternal kingdom, they live in harmony with it—in full anticipation of the future life—as one who will soon inherit everything. Christians do not, on the ground of their future inheritance, excuse themselves from any true human need, but they know where their hope lies and live freely with death already behind them, able to concentrate on making the most fruitful living sacrifice of the body available to them.

Participation by Resistance

Lutherans recognized early on that Romans 13 was speaking not only to lowly subjects, it was speaking—especially—to rulers because their office is God's, not their own. Individual rulers are quite dispensable; the office is not. Further, there is never only one person in the office of authority, there are many, and the difference between the "greater" and "lesser" magistrates became a central issue for Lutherans. Moreover, "rulers are not a terror to good conduct, but to bad," (Romans 13:3 NRS) is as much a statement to rulers as to the ruled—they are God's servants *for good* (13:4). The bookend for subjection in 13:1 is to pay "honor *to whom honor is due*" (13:7).

[handwritten margin note: If they do wrong then no honor is due them]

Participation has two components: one is *obedience* to the governing authority; the other is *resistance* to the governing authority at the necessary moment (without which obedience is never given). Obedience is not servile worthlessness, and resistance is not opposition to God in the false form of antinomianism (worldly anarchy). If we return to Luther's *Temporal Authority*, and Duke George's attempt to reclaim the New Testaments, we see that Luther developed the modern idea of passive resistance for Christians. He asserted that government should expect obedience in physical aspects of life—but not concerning faith and the preached word. Belief in Christ concerns the conscience of each person and does no harm to temporal authorities so that faith is free, and cannot be forced from the outside by anyone.

He then took up Romans 13:7, the other bookend for Paul's point: "Pay to all what is due them—taxes to whom taxes are due, revenue to whom revenue is due, fear to whom fear is due, honor to whom honor is due." Fear and honor identify a limit.

Ruling authorities are there not by their own behest, but as the servant of God to limit evil and stand for good. When these are confused, honor and fear are no longer due a ruler. Duke George had overstepped his limit by attempting to extend his temporal authority into the matter of faith and the word—so honor is not given in his case. Luther invoked the "*clausula Petri*" in this matter from Acts 5:29 and concluded that Christians should not submit to the Duke. The passive form of resistance meant not to hand over the Bibles—then to be ready to suffer whatever consequences might come for one's Christian person.

The second epochal event was the Magdeburg Pastors who established a further ground on which to resist authority with the use of force. This is the story of the imposition of the Interim law by the Holy Roman Emperor, Charles V (with the cooperation of the Pope), as the way to execute the Edict of Worms of 1521 that had long before made Luther, and evangelical preaching, outlaws of the state. Once Luther had died, and the Emperor was no longer occupied in war against the Turks, Charles determined to rid himself of the Lutherans and return the empire to one Catholic Church. To do this he had to stop evangelical preaching and reinstate the Roman Mass or liturgy, but the evangelicals would not stop preaching and their princes would not give them up, so Charles attacked the Smalcald League of Evangelical princes, and easily defeated them at the battle of Mühlberg on the Elbe river (1547). The Emperor had a law drawn up called "The Augsburg Interim" (1548) that would regulate church life and doctrine down to the details of the liturgy, and required acknowledgement of the Pope's rule of the church. Preachers who refused to reintroduce this Interim were banished, jailed, or even executed. Melanchthon at first opposed this Interim law, and then conceded to the notion that the Emperor had the authority to rule not only over the temporal kingdom, but the spiritual, churchly kingdom as well. Instead of distinguishing church and temporal government, Melanchthon offered a distinction between outer, public life (whether in state laws or the public liturgy of the church), and an inner, private life of the conscience. The Emperor could rule over anything public, including the public teaching of the church, but not over one's own thoughts or beliefs. Authority in the church was handed over to the secular government largely because

Melanchthon read Paul in Romans 13 without the distinction of kingdoms, and so once the Interim became an imperial law, he thought evangelicals had a sacred obligation to obey it—even when they personally, privately disagreed. Melanchthon did not remain silent, instead he chose a path of negotiation and compromise that he thought would guard the core of the Reformation, and so he proposed a way to "ward off dangers if we receive some rites which are not in themselves vicious . . . we are not too exacting with respect to such as are unnecessary . . . we know that much is said against this moderation; but the devastation of the churches, such as is taking place in Swabia, would be a still greater offense."[6] This came to be known as conceding in matters of "adiaphora" (indifferent matters), and precipitated a great Lutheran, intramural struggle called the "adiaphorist controversy." Are there really "indifferent" things like acceptance of certain legally imposed rituals in a "time of confession"? The Lutherans finally answered negatively:

> We also believe, teach, and confess that in a time when confession is necessary, as when the enemies of God's Word want to suppress the pure teaching of the holy gospel, the entire community of God, indeed, every Christian, especially servants of the Word as the leaders of the community of God, are obligated according to God's Word to confess true teaching and everything that pertains to the whole religion freely and publicly. They are to do so not only with words but also in actions and deeds. In such a time they shall not yield to the opponents even in indifferent matters, nor shall they permit the imposition of such adiaphora by opponents who use violence or chicanery in such a way that undermines true worship of God or introduces or confirms idolatry.[7]

There were two levels to this *adiaphora* controversy, each of which emerged from Paul's letter to the Romans. The first level is how one is *obligated* to confess true teaching—in words, actions, and deeds—without yielding to the government that wants to impose false teaching. That is a political problem concerning obedience to the established authority in Romans 13. The other level is the issue of dealing with differences of rites and customs within the church when there is no imposition from the outside—this is taken up in terms of the stronger and weaker in faith in Romans 14.

Regarding the political problem, the city of Magdeburg underwent a siege which they successfully overturned, leading eventually to a defeat and withdrawal of the Emperor and to the Peace of Augsburg (1555) that granted legal freedom to Lutherans in protected territories. It was the Magdeburg theologians—including especially von Amsdorf, Flacius, and Gallus—who worked out a theology of resistance in relation to Romans 13 that was to reverberate through history to the present by creating a revolutionary Lutheranism.[8] They did so by combining the distinction between God's two ways of ruling (the two Aeons), the three estates instituted by God for good works in the old world, and the recognition that Paul was not simply speaking in Romans 13 to *subjects* of a kingdom, but the *rulers* themselves. First, they argued that Charles V had no right to impose the Roman Mass because such matters of the church did not fall under his jurisdiction; the church was not his to rule. In fact, the church was God's first institution in the garden of Eden, and family (with the giving of male and female in marriage) was the second. Temporal government came late, after the arrival of sin, and its sword that limits evil is to be wielded on behalf of the church's freedom—not over the church as a vassal. Melanchthon was wrong in handing over his own office of teacher of the church to the emperor. This is the very ground on which Peter's confession was based: "We must obey God rather than humans."

Further, a ruler is to rule not at his own behest, but for the good of the subjects—that is "for good," not for evil, as Paul says. The Magdeburgers worked out a translation of Romans that kept rulers as the subject of the sentence, so that officials are the ones who ought to fear bad conduct even more than their subjects. Instead of reading, "For rulers are not a fear to good conduct, but bad," they translated: "The powerful *are commanded by God* to fear not good works but evil ones."[9] Then the Magdeburgers went further. When God institutes government, it is not in one office but many. God did not establish merely an office of king, and the king then created all other offices at his own whim. When God instituted government he instituted greater and "lesser magistrates," in a kind of mutually responsible web—the latter of which have their office not on loan from the emperor, but directly given by God with their own responsibilities to fill. When the Magdeburgers composed their public confession to Emperor and God (*Confession, Instruction and Warning* 1550), they followed Luther's example in the *Circular Disputation* and his *Warning to the Dear German People*, that a legal announcement of grievances or injuries should be made before force is used against a ruler. They legally cited the injury of an Emperor causing lesser magistrates to sin, since it is one thing to falsely impose one's self as king on the church; it is another to force local princes to do the same, especially against their own conscience and office. What this precipitated was a theory of resistance that called for use of any means available in the particular office one held. In this case the Smalcald League itself was upheld in its military opposition, and use of force against the emperor, because the lesser magistrates were not to be forced to sin against God's own church. Then the theologians went further still; the highest level of injury is:

> when the tyrants become so mad and delirious that they begin to persecute not only the persons of the lesser magistrates and subordinates in a legitimate matter, but in those persons the highest and most necessary right and at the same time our Lord God Himself, the institutor of these same rights; and do so not from frailty, such as might result from anger, but on the basis of a well thought-out design and a deliberate plan of destroying that right for all future generations.[10]

There is a right established by God that is the right for *faith to be free*. This is not just the obvious right to believe whatever you will (the American use of it), it was the right to have faith freed entirely from bondage to the law. This right came to them through the preaching of the gospel, and if it were taken away, then injury is done not only to the current citizens of Christ's kingdom—but to all future ones who will no longer be able to hear the gospel. What is more, it does injury to God himself, as if Christ were put back under the law and kept away from being Lord of his own, new kingdom because it opposes the Emperor! This is no longer a matter of rights based only on "natural law" (which was why the old Scholastics had difficulty limiting the King's power), but based upon the distinction between the old and new kingdoms. In his *Warning*, Luther had prophesied that "if this doctrine vanishes, the church vanishes." That is, the church would simply become a temporal organization that lost the gospel.

Then the Magdeburg theologians drew upon Luther a second time. The Interim was most notable for reimposing the hierarchy of authority in the bishops and Pope; the Magdeburgers resisted having the church ruled as a mirror image of the state. The full power in the one office of the church is the office of the keys, which is the power to forgive sins. This bestows the authority to give sacraments, ordain, make doctrinal decisions, and establish the temporal ordering of the church—but this authority was given to all Christians in baptism. In normal circumstances the believer delegates his office and authority to one preacher for good order and to oppose fanatics—but in emergencies (when the delegated authority is not preaching or acting freely), the individual may recall that authority and exercise it to preach and teach. The Magdeburgers reasoned—as it is true in the church, so it is true in politics and the economy of the family: "If those authorities lead men away from God, the duty of other authorities *and of parents* is dissolved."[11] Thus the ground was established even for *individuals* to use force in opposition to those authorities whose office is given by God. The Magdeburg Confession became a classic of authority and resistance despite being overlooked in the Lutheran scholastic and moral episodes—culminating in Ernst Troeltsch who appears to have known nothing of this history. One of the great historical struggles of Lutherans—between Pietists and State Churches over the issue of lay preaching—could have been helped by this history, but it was largely forgotten by the seventeenth century. It was different in the eschatological rediscovery of the twentieth century, when Dietrich Bonhoeffer's cousin and fellow fighter in the Church struggle of the Third Reich, Christoph von Hase, wrote a biography of the chief Magdeburg teacher—Flacius—with a rousing conclusion:

> The confusion in the evangelical camp was great. However, as a true pupil of Luther's there surfaced Matthias Flacius,

who with unbending courage defended the freedom of the Lutheran faith against all papal might and who coined the term *causa confessionis* to describe the situation . . . . Let us in our time prove as did the Magdeburgers in their day, 'that there are minds who love God's word, their fatherland, and their freedom.'[12]

It was the Magdeburg theologians who taught the world how to resist authority without denying that the offices are given by God, and that the offices are used by God for good, despite evil persons.

Romans 14: Faith, Love, and Adiaphora

The second level of the Adiaphora Controversy concerned the difference between private and public matters. The Interim law imposed by the Emperor required many of the old, Roman traditions to be followed in worship services right down to the kind of robe the priest should wear. Melanchthon and his students suggested that Lutherans could accept at least some of these human traditions because they were *adiaphora*. Flacius and von Amsdorf pointed out that when human traditions "indifferent" in themselves were being required—nothing remains adiaphora:

> All ceremonies and ecclesiastical practices, as free as they may be in and of themselves, become a denial of the faith, an offense, and the public initiation of godlessness when they are imposed with force or deception and however they happen, they do not edify but destroy the church of God and mock God. They are no longer adiaphora.[13]

As Paul stated, churches are characterized by "disputes over opinion" (Romans 14:1) because of fanaticism. When the dispute is about human tradition, which it always is, then a distinction must be made between the weak and the strong in faith. The strong are not the most pious according to the law; they are the ones who are most free in relationship to the law—knowing that nothing that comes from the outside can make you unclean, and that Moses is dead wherever Christ is alive. The weak in faith, however, still cling with one hand to the promise of Christ, and with the other to traditions of ceremonial law. Paul uses the example of one who believes he should eat only vegetables (perhaps attempting to model the original garden of Eden), and another who knew regarding food that he was free to eat anything. Melanchthon prefaced the warning about human traditions in the Augsburg Confession (XV) with "those rites should be observed that can be observed without sin and that contribute to peace and good order in the church, for example, certain holy days, festivals, and the like"; however, he also warned that "people are reminded not to burden consciences," and that traditions that "are instituted to win God's favor, merit grace, and make satisfaction for sins are opposed to the gospel and the teaching of faith."

Paul asks, "Who are you to pass judgment on the servant of another?" All Christians are Christ's servants, and one servant does not judge another. God judges—this is not a free-for-all—but the fact that you can leave the judgment to God is one key aspect of Christian freedom—the freedom not to have to judge others. The stronger can refrain from exercising freedom—to a certain extent—concerning traditions, and stop eating meat offered to idols (1 Corinthians), or stop eating meat altogether: "If your brother or sister is injured by what you eat, you are no longer walking in love" (Romans 14:15 NRS). But it is not love which will assure, or save you. The act of love for another Christian cannot become the new law by which the church exists, or by which justification is established before God. For this reason, Lutherans make a distinction between the way one treats a fellow Christian privately—and public teaching. Privately, one deals with the concerns of a fellow Christian about vegetarianism by using the "measuring stick of love" (*canon caritatis*) that goes beyond the negative form of the eighth commandment: "You shall not bear false witness against your neighbor." Love goes further—to "be a Christ" for such a one, praying for her, bearing the burdens that come with little faith, and always putting her actions in the best possible light.[14] But if such a person wants to turn her burden of vegetarianism into a law for the whole church—then a Christian must speak out publicly against her. It is one thing to confess to another Christian; it is another to turn and *teach* the faith falsely in public and impose it as a law for others, because then "little faith" turns <u>faith into a *law that justifies*</u>. Thus, when Luther took up the parallel part of Paul's earlier Galatians letter (Galatians 5: 9–10), he set down this distinction: "It is a matter for love to endure all things (1 Cor. 13:7), and to soften all matters. By contrast, it is a matter of faith to endure nothing at all and not to be soft toward anyone."[15]

This is the essential difference in the church between judging the other and refusing heresy (*damnatus*), which is something the papal theologians wondered whether the evangelicals could ever do without the hierarchy of the church. At Magdeburg the evangelicals showed themselves able to make a distinction which had become confused between the exercise of love for the neighbor and the necessity for pure teaching and preaching according to the distinction of law and gospel. But of course, in every generation there is a new form of the weakness of faith that attempts to show its strength in the church by imposing a new law—as if it were the way to unite the church or make it more pure. Paul was dealing with a small controversy in the church of Rome over a single vegetarian. He earlier had a much larger issue in Galatia concerning circumcision. In the first case, one makes the distinction between greater and lesser in faith; in the second, circumcision is condemned as a human tradition—even though it is written in Scripture as a sign for Israel—because it is not "indifferent," but a denial of the gospel. When does adiaphora cease being an "indifferent thing"? The Magdeburgers used three indications:

1. When a human tradition is demanded as necessary, then it stops being "indifferent" because this attenuates Christian freedom. If the vegetarian in the church at Rome were in a position to impose this as a requirement, then things would change: "Thus, Paul submits and gives in to the weak in matters of food or days and times (Rom. 14:6). But he does not submit to false apostles, who wanted to impose such things upon consciences as necessary even in matters that were in themselves free and indifferent."[16]

2. When a human tradition involves a denial of the truth, or an admission of a previous error for not having used

it in the past—as if suddenly the human tradition is treated as necessary in order to unite the church. This is none other than an attack on the truth of the Gospel as the end of the law.

3. And finally when any human tradition is an infringement on Christian liberty so that idolatry is demanded: "For weakening this article and forcing human commands upon the church as necessary—as if their omission were wrong and sinful—already paves the way to idolatry."[17]

In the end, Luther's dictum is most helpful: faith yields nothing; love yields all. When dealing with an individual, one distinguishes the weak and strong in faith and yields in love; when a teaching is imposed on others, then love is set aside and faith must be unyielding lest the gospel itself be lost.

Chapter 13

The Preacher's Sacrifice

Romans 15–16

To the Gentiles, you are health and happy light,
To see you then, feed them and make their eyes bright.
To your people Israel, you are praise and joy,
For you, honor and pleasure forever flow.

Martin Luther, *In Peace and Joy I Now Depart*

Doctrine and History

In the final two chapters, Paul discusses his own call as minister/
slave in just the way Christ is a minister/slave. Modern historians
of religion have attempted to shift the heart of the letter from
Paul's sermon in Romans 1:16–17 to these last chapters where
Paul discusses his mission in historical terms. Consequently, Luther
has become an object of scorn along with his presumed
"doctrine" of justification. For modern religion, Christ is not the
end of the law, but represents the Hegelian principle of history
that is assumed to open the way to freedom as the synthetic
resolution of the struggle between antithetical religious groups. /\/ PP
The great problem of life is then not human sin, but political,
religious struggles between Jew and Gentile "religions." However,
even if the Hegelian position were to be held, it is not Luther
these modern scholars actually oppose, but the preceding allegorical episode of Lutheranism and its treatment of justification.
Allegory translates the text of Scripture into another idiom, and
in the case of the orthodox in the century following Luther,
history seemed to threaten religion itself ever since the Western
church rejected the Augsburg Confession (1530). That rejection
caused the Western church to split into sects that fought in a
century of "religious" wars that devastated Europe. For this reason

alone, it was understandable that historical particularity of preaching would be feared, and that the greatest minds would attempt to translate the Reformation's discovery of the gospel into *universal* (trans-cultural), *eternal* (trans-historical) terms that apply to everyone, and so do not change with time. This gave birth to the modern notion of "doctrine" that is articulated in the grammar of eternal truths—but in fact this lost the eschatological character of the gospel's new creation, and put the gospel into the terminology of the law, because law appears to be the only thing eternal and universal in the world. Indeed, the mind of God itself was considered eternal, unchanging law, and so doctrinal collections or encyclopedias became the work of theologians who sought to map that divine mind, and thus the modern disparagement of "doctrine" was born. It took a century or two for the impact of removing history from doctrine to hit, but when it did there was a mighty wave of protest that continues to the present—especially against the Lutheran teaching of justification.

Baur (1792–1860), Wrede (1859–1906) and their company thought they were freeing the Reformation from the stranglehold of "doctrine," and freeing it for what they discovered in Idealism— the historical evolution of religions toward a higher goal. This trajectory allowed them to reject the doctrine of justification, which seemed to require suspension of critical investigation of the texts of Scripture in relation to their historical context because it was taught to them as the imposition of a universal, eternal law. The Biblical historians argued that Luther got Paul wrong, especially in the letter to the Romans. Luther was blamed for turning *Romans* into a compendium of doctrine—just like their Lutheran orthodox teachers wrote. What Paul was actually doing, they argued, was defending his personal mission against detractors, which was to create a higher form of religion based on love rather than Jewish particularism (covenant nomism), or Greek fatalism. What took doctrine's place for the tropologists was *history*—or narrative—that revealed and justified God's underlying plan in what appeared on the surface to be a chaos of events.

J. C. K. von Hofmann (1810–1877) summarized his theological work this way: "But how shall theology, in a time in which it has been declared to have lost its rights to its entire possession [universal doctrine that does not change with time], assure itself once again of its content, a content which is not doctrinal opinion, but history."[1] Doctrines are opinions of men, so the new Reformers thought; history deals with facts. But history's facts were in danger of being lost to radical historical criticism which cast doubt on the veracity of Biblical accounts of promises made by God. "Did God really say?" was the scholarly question put to Scripture itself (to say nothing of the doctrines collected in Lutheran textbooks). This position has become determinative among Biblical scholars to the present, and when it comes to Paul's *Romans* has produced a line of thought represented by Jacob Jervell (b.1925): "We have every reason to stress that justification by faith apart from the law is not the theme of Romans. That theme is treated in Galatians. The theme of Romans is this: the righteousness of God is revealed through faith apart from the law, first to the Jews, then to the Greeks, and at the end to all Israel."[2] Instead of doctrine, Paul's interest is believed to be setting forth the *stages of history* for God's plan of salvation. Therefore when Paul rehearsed his mission in Romans 15, and addressed greetings in Romans 16, it appeared to be a kind of theology of history rather than of Lutheran theological principles—and suddenly the conclusion of the letter took on central significance.

According to this theology, history operates from recognizable rules forming a continuum of cause and effect. Events not only unfold predictably from an original cause, but everything is organized toward a goal that progresses teleologically. Both these assumptions—origin and goal—bear the marks of the ethical episode of Lutheranism, sin being a deception about the divine plan that distorts the proper relationship to God that could have ended with perfection if Adam and Eve had only chosen better. For von Hofmann, God's consequent salvation has its goal in the appearance of Jesus the Savior, but prior to Christ's incarnation the concealed salvation history prefigures Christ's arrival in stages of history starting with "the family" of Abraham (from whom Christ descends), and the organization of the nation of Israel (since individual righteousness was insufficient to prepare Christ's way). When everything had been prepared, Christ appeared as the "archetypal world *telos*" in order to overcome the contradiction in God between his love as expressed for Israel and his wrath at sinners for being deceived by false goals. Unlike us sinners, Christ managed to keep his personal relationship to the Father intact despite coming under God's wrath at the cross—he "persevered" in a right attitude to God.[3] In this *heilsgeschichtliche* (salvation history) perspective, Jesus Christ was the historical realization of God's eternal will to love humans—who were misled by contrary spiritual forces, so they may be "transfigured" into a new relation with God as their proper goal. Christians are not left as "justified" individuals, but assembled communally into the final stage of the history of salvation, which is the life of the church.

This historical development (Abraham, Israel, Christ, faith, church) took the place of a series of doctrines as the "objective" objects of belief. What Hofmann in fact did was replace a mathematical type of universal law (as the foundation for orthodox theology) with a narrative or historical form of law that is oriented to a moral goal. His new development was to perceive that law was not changeless—it progressed over time toward the single goal of Christ as the mediator of a new relationship of God with sinners. The problem with this approach is that law, whether changeless or changing, is still the law alone. This type of argument has been picked up in more recent days by various "new" perspectives on Paul that believe they have rejected Luther and seek a new community that supersedes both synagogue and church. They are new in relation to Protestant orthodoxy, but not in relation to Luther—or Paul. Krister Stendahl (1920–2008) argued that it is not law or justification that concerns Paul, but the historical situation of Israel in God's plan of salvation: "In [Romans, especially Chapter 15] Paul reflects upon his mission within the total plan of God. He is not teaching, he is not instructing. The letter is . . . a kind of apology for or explanation of how he sees his own mission . . . to the Gentiles."[4] With variations in detail, one finds the same salvation historical picture in N.T. Wright (b. 1948), who argues that the Bible is a "great story"—or drama—that has five acts: (1) Creation, (2) Fall, (3) Israel as God's people, (4) The arrival and departure of the historical Jesus, and (5) The church that begins at Easter/Pentecost. This last stage is purported to be unfinished, and the Spirit gives power "to improvise a way through the unscripted period between the opening scenes and the closing one."[5] The goal of this "improvising church" is directed toward a "reworked chosen people of God"—a "model of what it means to be human" that is, a community "in which people from all kinds of backgrounds, with no natural affinity of kin or shared business, are welcoming one another and supporting one another practically."[6] The ideal, higher community would include both Jew and Gentile in a synthetic, ideal unity by means of the law of inclusive love. The legacy of this attempt thinks it must rid itself of "Lutheran" influence by the doctrine of justification that distinguished faith and love, gospel and law—because that teaching assumes that love does not save.

But this religious, communal dream is not Paul's conclusion to the letter to the Romans. Paul concludes with the living sacrifice of the preacher. The preacher presents a "living sacrifice" in the face of opposition from death, sin, and Satan—using both the words of law and gospel. The preacher must boast in Christ, not himself. "In Christ Jesus then," Paul says, "I have reason to boast of my work for God. For I will not venture to speak of anything except what Christ has accomplished through me to win obedience from the Gentiles, by word and deed" (Romans 5:17 NRS).

Christ's Mission and Paul's

The church is the one place on earth where Jew and Gentile belong together—not because they obey one law, but because they have the same minister/slave, the crucified Christ. Paul's final appeal is to this church which Christ serves as the fruit of faith: "welcome one another" (Romans 15:7 NRS). The church is the new kingdom, not the perfection of the old, and so the welcome is neither based on human virtues of acceptance nor of tolerance—nor even love, but upon having the one, true preacher who takes away the sin of the world. Christ's mission in being sent by the Father was first to serve the Jews, "that he might confirm the promises given to the patriarchs" (Romans 15:8 NRS). This confirmation is the great advantage of the Jews, who since Abraham have had the promises that made them God's chosen (not the commands), and in those promises that have their "yes" in Christ, God has sought to be justified (deum justificare) by faith. Though they came late to the banquet, Gentiles are also served by this same crucified minister. The promises were not given to their patriarchs, yet Christ came for the express purpose that Gentiles "might glorify God for his *mercy*" (Romans 15:9 NRS). The advantage of the Jews is that they can know God's steadfast love and faithfulness despite their sin, but the Gentiles are not complaining, since to them God's mercy is revealed—he chose them in baptism, despite having no prior promises. Scripture was opened to them to see that they too were included in the promises made to the patriarchs of Israel; Gentiles had only lacked a preacher, and so Paul ran through a sample of the many promises for the sake of Gentiles from Psalm 18 and 117, Moses in Deuteronomy 32, and the prophet—Isaiah 11. Mercy lacks history; it is straight out of the blue, but the glory (the burst of rejoicing that comes when the light is finally shone) is no less for the Gentiles since they are *lucky*—and yet also given the power of the Holy Spirit to "abound in hope" (Romans 15:13 NRS).

The New, and Last, Testament

By what authority does Paul preach to the far-flung corners of the world? Most especially by what authority does he preach in this letter to the Romans, which is after all a sermon (with its preparation, delivery, and aftermath)? Paul scrupulously noted that his "ambition" was to preach the gospel where Christ has not yet been named—not "building on the foundation of someone else" (Romans 15:20 translation altered). Perhaps Paul was a little sore that the Spirit did not wait for him to get to Rome, perhaps he knew what happened in the other churches when he did not arrive when people expected him so that they doubted the veracity of the preacher for being wishy-washy, but Paul knew his own calling clearly enough. His authority to preach came not from starting a church, but from his call as Apostle to the Gentiles—wherever those Gentiles were to be found. So Paul says, "I myself feel confident about you . . . nevertheless on some points I have written to you rather boldly by way of reminder because of the grace given me by God to be a minister of Christ Jesus to the Gentiles . . ." (Romans 15: 14–15, translation altered). Even the best congregation needs the preaching of the Apostle to the Gentiles. If it is by way of reminder, so much the better; if the sermon is new—then so be it. Paul gave the standard of preaching in the only way possible, not by giving a new law, but by boldly preaching Christ as the end of the law—regardless of who baptized or began them.

Paul did in the letter to the Romans exactly what he had previously done in Jerusalem to ensure that he was preaching the very same gospel as Peter, the Apostle to the Jews. Later in Antioch, when Paul learned that his fellow Apostle had stepped back from the Gospel they had agreed upon at the first council in Jerusalem, he did the only thing a preacher could do—he preached directly to Peter: "I opposed him to his face, because he stood self-condemned . . ." and said, "we ourselves are Jews by birth and not Gentile sinners; yet we know that a person is justified not by the works of the law but by faith alone in Jesus Christ" (Galatians 2:15, translation altered). Paul preached with confidence that in Rome all heard the same voice of the shepherd as he and Peter had—that the Gospel was indeed Christ, the end of the law for faith.

Assuming agreement on the gospel, only one thing was left to do. Back at the council in Jerusalem, Paul received the right hand of fellowship from the pillars of the Jerusalem church who then asked: "that we remember the poor, which I had already been eager to do" (Galatians 2:10, translation altered). Paul knew that such a request could never be an addition to the gospel, since the law had come to an end—but he also knew that the gospel always bears fruit, so that Paul gathered a collection from his poor Gentile churches to give to the poor saints in Jerusalem. It was this "service in material things," which Paul so dearly wanted to deliver—lest he appear to proclaim a gospel with no fruit and misled the simple. To this day, the repeated ground for rejection of the Gospel is that faith appears not to bear fruit. There was, therefore, much at stake in his delivery of the collection—indeed the reputation of the gospel was at stake. The reputation of the preacher was also at stake, since Paul was repeatedly attacked in other places—especially Corinth—for not following through on promises to arrive as scheduled, and so the argument went, "If he can't keep his own promises, how can we trust the promises he gives us from Christ?" Out of love, Paul wanted the poor to be helped in Jerusalem, and he wanted for there to be no side issue to derail the central matter of the gospel preaching.

271

Then Paul made a final confession. His living sacrifice of the body for the neighbor was not so much the money: "They were pleased to do this, and indeed they owe it to them; for if the Gentiles have come to share in the spiritual blessings, they ought also to be of service to them in material things" (Romans 15:27 NRS); Paul's sacrifice was as a preacher who would present the offering of the *Gentiles themselves*—the whole, sinful lot of them. Despite not being first in Rome ("often hindered," and attending to the Eastern mission from Jerusalem to Illyricum in Romans 15:19 and 22), the Romans nevertheless belong in Paul's big collection that he was presenting—not to the saints in Jerusalem—but directly to God: "so that the offering of the Gentiles may be acceptable, sanctified by the Holy Spirit" (Romans 15:16 NRS). Once his hope was fulfilled, and he had delivered the money offering to Jerusalem, he then sought prayers that he be freed to go and collect up all the rest of the Gentiles—stopping over in Rome on his way to the outer reaches of Spain. He assumed that the sooner he presented the full number of Gentiles in offering to God (as sanctified by the Spirit, lest you think this is a "good work" in the old Aeon's sense), the sooner the faithful of Israel will be got. Even Peter's apostleship to the Jews depended on Paul completing his own mission—yet, it was always "God-willing" for Paul, "so that by God's will I may come to you with joy and be refreshed in your company. The God of peace be with all of you. Amen." The doxology always came after he laid out his understanding of the mission.

But God had the last laugh, as Günter Bornkamm once wrote: "this letter, even if unintended, has in fact become the historical testament of the Apostle."[7] Even the great Apostle was able to present only a broken offering to God. The life of the Christian is hidden, and the work of the preacher in the form of the sacrifice of his hearers was graciously kept—even from Paul. Preachers never know what kind of offering they present to God in the end, so it is appropriate that the letter ends with Paul's greetings to his sisters and brothers who are serving with him—"chosen by . . . and working hard in the Lord" (Romans 16:12–13 NRS). Paul departed with the warning that faith is a particular kind of struggle against fanatic teachers who cause dissension—not because they are not Paul, but because they do not preach the gospel apart from the law. Then Paul delivered his last promise: "The God of peace will shortly crush Satan under your feet" (Romans 16:20 NRS).

The final doxology to God is the comfort that "my Gospel" (the one I, Paul, have just preached faithfully to you) is the revelation of the mystery kept secret for so many years but which has *now* been disclosed—because even you who are Gentiles finally have a preacher. And what was that disclosure of the long-kept mystery? It was that what the prophets promised in Scripture has now been fulfilled—with no law! "But now, apart from law, the righteousness of God has been manifested, and is attested by the law and the prophets, the righteousness of God by faith in Jesus Christ for all who believe" (Romans 3:21 translation altered).

God's plan included Paul delivering the whole offering to the poor saints of Jerusalem, and it included Paul presenting most of the Gentile world to God—but for that offering Paul was caught up short. Paul's letter served not only to preach to the Roman church in such a way that it would agree with him that this word of justification by faith alone is the gospel—it also serves for subsequent generations to determine whether what we preach is the gospel that frees, or a law that binds. Therefore, Paul's offering to God does not yet appear complete:

Oh the depth of the riches and wisdom and knowledge of God! How unsearchable are his judgments and how inscrutable his ways ... To him be the glory forever. Amen (Romans 11:33, 36).

Notes

Introduction

1   Pelikan, J. J. (Hrsg.); Oswald, H. C. (Hrsg.); Lehmann, H. T. (Hrsg.) (1972), *Luther's Works, Vol. 25: Lectures on Romans*. Saint Louis, MO: Concordia Publishing, p.135 (Hereafter LW).

2   LW 25:136.

3   LW 25:137.

4   Sasse, H. (1938), *Here We Stand: Nature and Character of the Lutheran Faith*. Trans. Theodore G. Tappert. New York: Harper & Brothers Publishers, p. 179.

5   LW 25:135.

6   Troeltsch, E. (1912), *Protestantism and Progress* (Rpt. 1986) Minneapolis, MN: Fortress Press, pp. 95–8.

7   Kolb, R. and Wengert, T. (2000), *The Book of Concord*. Minneapolis: Fortress (Hereafter BC), *Smalcald Articles* II.2, p. 301.

8   Forde, G. (1969), *The Law-Gospel Debate*. Minneapolis, MN: Augsburg, p.4.

9   Schmid, H (1899) *The Doctrinal Theology of the Evangelical Lutheran Church* 5th edn Philadelphia, PA: Lutheran Publication Society, p. 511.

10 Spener, J. (1964) *Pia Desideria*. T. Tappert, (trans.), Philadelphia, PA: Fortress, p. 95. The emphasis on the practical over the speculative forms of knowing God was shared by the orthodox as we see in Johann Quenstedt: "A distinction is made between theoretical sciences, which consist wholly in the mere contemplation of the truth, and practical sciences, which, indeed, require a knowledge of whatever is to be done, but which do not end in this, nor have it as their aim, but which lead to practice and action. We think that theology is to be numbered, not with the theoretical, but with the practical sciences." From his *Theologia Didactio-Polemica* (1685) Pt. 1, ch.1 sect 2, q.3 translated in Lund, E. (ed.) (2002), *Documents from the History of Lutheranism 1517–1750*. Minneapolis, MN: Fortress, p. 221.

11 LW 35:380.

12 Ibid.

13 LW 35:371.

14 The richest treatments of modern Lutheran theology work out of the proclamation. Wingren, G. (1960), *The Living Word: A Theological Study of Preaching and the Church*. V. Pogue (trans.) Philadelphia, PA: Muhlenberg Press, and Forde, G. (1960), *Theology is for Proclamation*. Minneapolis, MN: Fortress Press.

Notes

Chapter 1

1 Pauck, W. (ed.) (1969), *Melanchthon and Bucer* Philadelphia, PA: Westminster, p. 23. Hereafter cited as Melanchthon (1521), *Loci*.
2 Melanchthon (1521), *Loci*, p. 25.
3 LW 31:39 (Heidelberg Disputation, 1518).
4 LW 33:41.
5 LW 33:29.
6 Luther, M. (1957), *The Bondage of the Will*. J.I. Packer, O.R. Johnston (trans.), Grand Rapids, MI: Fleming H. Revell, p. 80 Cf. LW 33:37.
7 LW 33:139.
8 Luther, M. (1883), *Luthers Werke, kritische gesamtausgabe [Schriften]* J. F. K. Knaake et al. (eds), 65 + vols. Weimar: H. Böhlau, 1:12, 11ff. (Hereafter WA). Cited in Iwand, H.J. (2008) *The Righteousness of Faith According to Luther* V. F. Thompson (ed.), R.H. Lundell, (trans.) Eugene, OR: Wipf & Stock, p. 19.
9 Luther, M. (1961), *Luther: Lectures on Romans*. W. Pauck (trans. and ed.) Philadelphia, PA: Westminster, p. 30.
10 Melanchthon (1521), *Loci*, p. 20.
11 Ibid., p. 21.
12 The most noteworthy is the outcast Ludwig Feuerbach, who considered himself a devotee of Luther, Feuerbach, L (1967), *The Essence of Faith According to Luther*. M. Cherno (trans.), New York: Harper and Row.
13 Melanchthon (1521), *Loci*, 21.
14 Ibid.
15 Ibid., 22.
16 BC, 631.81 (*Formula of Concord*, Article VIII) quoting from Luther's *Confession concerning Christ's Supper* (1528), LW 37:218–19).
17 Melanchthon (1521), *Loci*, 25.
18 Cited in Grane, L. (1987), *The Augsburg Confession: A commentary*. J. H. Rasmussen (trans.), Minneapolis, MN: Augsburg, p. 74.

Chapter 2

1 LW 26:26.
2 Wrede, W. (1908), *Paul*. E. Lummis (trans.), Boston: American Unitarian Association, p. 123 and Schweitzer, A. (1931), *The Mysticism of Paul the Apostle*. W. Montgomery (trans.), New York: Henry Holt, p. 225.
3 Stendahl, K. (1976), "Paul and the Introspective Conscience of the West", in *Paul among Jews and Gentiles*. Philadelphia: Fortress, and Pannenberg, W. (1983), *Christian Spirituality*. Philadelphia: Westminster, pp. 13–30.
4 Aristotle (1984), *Rhetoric* 1366b 9–11 in *The Complete Works of Aristotle*, J. Barnes (ed.), Princeton, NJ: Princeton University Press, p. 2174.

Notes

5 "To have to respond for one's right to be, not by reference to the abstraction of some anonymous law, of some juridical entity, but in the fear for another. Was not my 'in the world' or my 'place in the sun,' and my home a usurpation of places that belong to the other man, already oppressed by me or hungry?" Levinas, E. (1998), "Bad Conscience and the Inexorable," in *Of God Who Comes to Mind*. B. Bergo (trans.), Stanford: Stanford University Press, 175.

6 LW 10:401.

7 LW 14:60.

8 LW 26:127.

9 Ibid.

10 LW 26:129.

11 *Romans* is set up on these two points, chapters 1–4 concern especially faith; and 5–8 one "shall live." See Nygren, A. (1949), *Commentary on Romans*. C. C. Rasmussen (trans.), Philadelphia: Fortress, p. 187.

12 Melanchthon, P. (1992), *Commentary on Romans*. F. Kramer (trans.), St. Louis: Concordia, pp. 71–3. Melanchthon points out that you should read Romans 1:17 as the conclusion of the great argument of Galatians, where Habakkuk served to defeat those who would add the law to faith.

13 LW 31:39.

14 LW 26:138.

15 See Holm, B. and Saarinen, R. in N.H. Gregersen, B. Holm, T. Peters, and P. Widman (eds), (2005), *The Gift of Grace: The Future of Lutheran Theology*. Minneapolis: Fortress Press.

16 Ritschl, A (1902), *The Christian Doctrine of Justification and Reconciliation: vol. III The Positive Development of the Doctrine*. H. R. Mackintosh and A. B. Macaulay (trans.), 2nd edn Edinburgh: T & T Clark, p. 21 and 139: "The justification of sinners by God depends on the condition of faith . . . conceived as the direction of the will to the highest end represented by God."

17 Tillich, P. (1963), *Systematic Theology*. Vol. III. Chicago: University of Chicago, pp. 224–5.

18 For the first, consider Hollaz (1646–1713) "The power and energy of faith are twofold, receptive, or apprehensive, and operative." For the latter, Hollaz says, "Faith is indeed considered a cause, but an impulsive cause subordinate, or an instrumental cause, organic and receptive . . . but by no means an effective cause of justification" in Schmid, H. (1899), *The Doctrinal Theology of the Evangelical Lutheran Church*. 5th edn Philadelphia: Lutheran Publication Society, p. 423.

Chapter 3

1 Otto, R. (1925), *The Idea of the Holy*. London: Oxford University p. 112.

2 This defense against wrath continues in the present, as in Wolfhart Pannenberg. See Paulson, S. (1994), "The wrath of God". *Dialog* 33, 245–51, and Ritschl A., (1902), *The Christian Doctrine of Justification and Reconciliation* vol. II (2nd edn), Edinburgh: T & T Clark 320ff and 572ff.

3 BC, p. 114 (*Apology* II. 14).

Notes

4 Elert, W. (1962), *The Structure of Lutheranism*, vol. I. Hansen, W. (trans.), St. Louis: Concordia, p. 39 quoting from Luther WA 10 I, 1, 472, 10 and 473, 19.

5 Leibniz G. W. (1985), *Theodicy: Essays on the Goodness of God and the Freedom of Man and the Origin of Evil*. A. Farrer (trans.), E. M. Huggard (ed.), Peru Illinois: Open Court, pp. 67–8.

6 Ibid., 51.

7 WA 40, I:256, 15, mistranslated in LW 26:148.

8 LW 33: 145, 126.

9 Ibid., 37.

10 Arndt J. (1979), *True Christianity*. P. Erb (trans.) London: SPCK, 104.

11 Johann Gerhard, J. (1995, 1996), *Seven Christmas Sermons (1613): Scripturally Saturated Sermons Celebrating the Birth of Christ*. E. M. Hohle (trans.), D. O. Gerger (ed.), Decatur, Illinois: The Johann Gerhard Institute, 99.

12 Bayer, *Luther's Theology*, p.108 citing WA TR 1:574. 8–19 (no. 1160).

13 Bultmann, R. (1951) *Theology of the New Testament* vol. I. K. Grobel (trans.), New York: Scribner, 41.

14 Seneca, *Naturales questions*. T.H. Corcoran, (trans.), Cambridge, Mass: Harvard University, vii.30.3.

15 WA 26:505.38–506.12, and LW 37,366 *Confession Concerning Christ's Supper* 1528.

16 WA 23:137.33 and LW 37: 60, "That These Words of Christ 'This is My Body,' etc. Still Stand Firm against the Fanatics," 1527.

17 LW 26: 95.

18 See Cleanthes' "Hymn to Zeus," in Barrett, C. K. (1963), *The New Testament Background: Selected Documents*. New York: Macmillan, pp. 63ff.

19 Philo, *De praemiis et poenis* cited in Käsemann, E. (1980), *Commentary on Romans*. G. Bromiley (trans.), Grand Rapids, MI: Eerdmans p. 39.

20 BC, *Small Catechism*, p. 352.

21 Luther, *Romans*, 26.

22 LW 31:39.

23 WA 40, I:256, 14–5 and LW 26:148 (translation altered).

24 WA 18:719 and 729, 14ff., and WA 1:354, 15.

25 Kolb, R. (2005), *Bound Choice, Election, and Wittenberg Theological Method* Grand Rapids, MI: Eerdmans, demonstrates how few Lutherans engaged Luther's argument up to 1580.

26 J. Gerhard in *Loci* XX, 178 cited in Elert, W. *Lutheranism*, p. 41.

27 See T. Harnack (1927), Luthers theologie mit besonderer beziehung auf seine versöhnungs- und erlösungslehre. München: Chr. Kaiser.

28 Elert, *Lutheranism*, p. 20.

Chapter 4

1 Käsemann. *Romans*, 92.

2 Luther, M. (2008), *Solus Decalogus est Aeternus: Martin Luther's Complete Antinomian Theses and Disputations*. H. Sonntag (ed. and trans.), Minneapolis: Lutheran Press, p. 153.

Notes

3 "Forgiveness is thus mad." Derrida, J. (2001), *On Cosmopolitanism and Forgiveness*. M Dooley and M Hughes (trans.), London: Routledge, p. 48.

4 Nygren, *Romans*, 156.

5 Pannenberg, W. (1977), *Jesus, God and Man*. 2nd edn L. Wilkins and D. Priebe (trans.), Philadelphia: Westminster, p. 287: "the formula of unity produced by Chalcedon in 451 bears the marks of a compromise."

6 Leo, (1988), 'Tome of St. Leo' in *Nicene and Post-Nicene Fathers*, vol. 14 series 1. P. Schaff (ed.) Grand Rapids, MI: Wm B. Eerdmans, p. 254.

7 Ibid., pp 254–5.

8 Schleiermacher, F. (1928), *The Christian Faith*. H.R. Mackintosh and J. S. Stewart (eds), Edinburgh: T & T Clark, p. 392.

9 LW 37: 211.

10 Chemnitz, M. (1971), *The Two Natures in Christ*. J.A.O. Preus (trans.), St. Louis: Concordia Publishing House, p 16.

11 Hegel, H. (1988), *Hegel Lectures on the Philosophy of Religion: One Volume Edition, The Lectures of 1827*. P.C. Hodgson (ed.) R.F. Brown, P.C. Hodgson, J.N. Stewart (trans.), Berkeley: University of California Press, p. 465 n. 199.

12 LW 26:278.

13 Forde (1984), "The Work of Christ," and Bertram, R (1992), "Luther on the unique mediatorship of Christ," in *One Mediator, The Saints and Mary* Anderson, H., Stafford, J., Burgess, J. (eds) Minneapolis: Augsburg, 249–62.

14 LW 26:278ff. (for the subsequent quotations)

15 Luther's notion of *kenosis* is more radical and free than the originator of the modern movement of the "self-denial of the eternal Logos," begun with Thomasius, G. (1886), *Christi: Person und Werk*. Erlangen: Andreas Deichert.

16 LW 26:39.

17 LW 26:34.

18 LW 26:152.

Chapter 5

1 Grane, L. (1987), *Augsburg Confession*, pp. 67–8.

2 LW 26:132.

3 Klug, E.F.A. (ed.), (1996), *Sermons of Martin Luther: The House Postils*. Vol. 2 Klug, Koehlinger, Lanning, Meier, Schoenknecht and Schuldheiss (trans.), Grand Rapids, MI: Baker Books, p. 451.

4 Melanchthon (1521), *Loci*, p. 71.

5 Olson, O. (2002), *Matthias Flacius and the Survival of Luther's Reform*. Wiesbaden: Harrassowitz Verlag, pp233ff.

6 Forde, (1969), *The Law-Gospel Debate*, p. 29.

7 Regarding normal human use of performative sentences Austin, J.L. (1962), *How To Do Things With Words*. 2nd edn J. O. Urmson and M Sbisa (eds), Cambridge, MA: Harvard University, pp. 6–7.

Notes

8 Mannermaa, T. (2005), Christ present in faith: Luther's view of justification. Minneapolis: Fortress.

9 Kolb, R. and Nestingen, J. (eds), (2001), *Sources and Contexts of the Book of Concord*. Minneapolis: Fortress Press, p.148.

10 Ibid., p.185.

11 Melanchthon (1521), *Loci*, p. 87.

12 In Reu, M. (1930), The Augsburg Confession: A collection of sources. Chicago, IL: Wartburg, p.52.

13 Melanchthon (1521), *Loci*, p. 97.

14 LW 25:274ff.

15 Kierkegaard, S. (1983), *Fear and Trembling* Hong, H. and E. (eds, and trans.) Princeton, NJ.: Princeton University.

16 Breen, Q. (1947) "The Terms 'Loci Communes' and 'Loci' in Melanchthon". *Church History*, 16, 197–209.

Chapter 6

1 LW 26:281–2.

2 Ibid., 282–4.

3 LW 31:40.

4 LW 26:133.

5 Nygren, A. (1953), *Agape And Eros*. Watson, P. (trans.), Philadelphia: Westminster.

6 LW 1:157

7 On the Lutheran teaching on justification and freedom from wrath see Mattes, M.C. (2004), *The Role of Justification in Contemporary Theology*. Grand Rapids, MI: Eerdmans, p. 184ff.

Chapter 7

1 Schweitzer, A. (1931), *The Mysticism of Paul the Apostle*. W. Montgomery (trans.), New York: Henry Holt and Company, pp. 17–18.

2 BC *Large Catechism* 14, p. 458.

3 Ibid., 29, p. 460.

4 Kolb, R. (2005), Bound Choice, election, and the Wittenberg theological method: from Martin Luther to the Formula of Concord. Grand Rapids, MI: Eerdmans, p. 117.

5 Bierma, L. (1999), The Doctrine of the Sacraments in the Heidelberg Catechism: Melanchthon, Calvinist, or Zwinglian?. Princeton, NJ: Princeton Theological Seminary, p. 28.

6 Muller, R. A. (1985), Dictionary of Latin and Greek Theological Terms Drawn Principally from Protestant Scholastic Theology. Grand Rapids: Baker Book House, p. 293.

Notes

1 Joest, W. (1956), *Gesetz und Freiheit*. 2nd edn Göttingen: Vandenhoeck and Ruprecht, pp. 93–8, and Forde, G. (2004), *A More Radical Gospel: Essays on Eschatology, Authority, Atonement, and Ecumenism*. M. Mattes and S. Paulson (eds) Grand Rapids, MI: Eerdmans, p. 128.

2 Ebeling, G. (1960), "On the Doctrine of the *Triplex Usus Legis* in the Theology of the Reformation," in *Word and Faith*. London: SCM, 62–78.

3 Sanders, E.P. (2001), Paul: A very short introduction. Oxford: Oxford University, and (1997) Paul and Palestinian Judaism: A Comparison of Patterns of Religion. London: SCM Press.

4 Luther, "Preface to Romans," in Dillenberger, J. (ed.) (1962) *Martin Luther: selections from his writings*. New York: Doubleday, p.21.

5 See Jersild, P. (1962), "Judgment of God in Albrecht Ritschl and Karl Barth," *Lutheran Quarterly* 14 no.4, 328–46.

6 LW 31:25.

7 Bayer O. (2008), Luther's Theology, pp 44ff.

8 Luther, M "Antinomian Disputations" in Sonntag, H. (ed. and trans. 2008), *Solus Decalogus Est Aeternus: Martin Luther's Complete Antinomian Thesis and Disputations*. Minneapolis, MN: Cygnus Series, Lutheran Press, p. 65.

9 Ibid., pp. 23–31.

10 Ibid., pp.104–5.

11 Ibid., p.75.

12 Troeltsch, E. (1992 rpt.), *The Social Teaching of the Christian Churches* Vol. 2. O. Wyon (trans.), Westminster/John Knox.

13 Tillich, P. (1963), *Systematic Theology*. Vol. 3, Chicago: University of Chicago, p. 227: "Radical doubt is existential doubt concerning the meaning of life itself." Paul's questions and Luther's have "no meaning" for him.

14 Bultmann, R. (1997), *What is Theology?* E. Jüngel and K. W. Müller (eds), R. A. Harrisville (trans.), Minneapolis: Fortress, pp.184–5.

1 BC, p.583: 11.

2 In Prenter, R. (1953), *Spiritus Creator*. Jensen, J. (trans.), Philadelphia: Muhlenberg, p. 180.

3 BC, p.358:15–16.

1 Translated in Harrisville, R. (1980), *Augsburg Commentary on the New Testament: Romans*. Minneapolis: Augsburg, 142.

2 Käsemann, *Romans*, 253.

Notes

3 BC, p. 387. Large Catechism, Ten Commandments I.4.

4 Erasmus, D. (1969), *On the Freedom of the Will*. Rupp, E.G. (trans. and ed.) in *Luther and Erasmus: Free Will and Salvation*. Philadelphia: The Westminster Press, p. 65.

5 BC, p. 648.

6 Augustine, *City of God* (19:4) in Schaff, P (ed.), (rpt. 1989), *Nicene and Post-Nicene Fathers*, First Series, vol. 2. M. Dods (trans.), Edinburgh: T & T Clark, p. 855.

7 Calvin, J. (1960), *Institutes of the Christian Religion* Vol 2. McNeill, J. T., (ed.) and Battles F. L. (trans.), Philadelphia: Westminster, pp. 966–7 (*Election is Confirmed by God's Call*) "Although in choosing his own the Lord already has adopted them as his children, we see that they do not come into possession of so great a good except when they are called . . . Even though the preaching of the gospel streams forth from the wellspring of election, because such preaching is shared also with the wicked, it cannot of itself be a full proof of election . . . But when the call is coupled with election . . . the very nature and dispensation of the call . . . consists not only in the preaching of the Word but also in the illumination of the Spirit . . . This inner call, then, is a pledge of salvation that cannot deceive us . . ." 3.24.1–2

8 Quoted in Schmid (1899), *Doctrinal Theology*, p. 420.

9 See Tillich, P. (1968), *A Complete History of Christian Thought*. New York: Harper & Row, pp. 95–7.

10 Luther, Solus Decalogus, p. 141.

11 Ibid., 51.

12 Ibid.

13 Ibid.

14 BC, pp. 39–41.

Chapter 11

1 LW 35:370–1.

2 Forde, G. (1984), "The Work of Christ" in Braaten, C.E. and Jenson, R.W. (eds), *Christian Dogmatics* Vol. II. Philadelphia: Fortress Press, p. 88.

3 Luther, M. (1955) "To The Christians in Riga, Tallinn, and Tartu, August 1535" in Tappert, T.G. (ed.), *Luther: Letters of Spiritual Counsel*. Westminster: John Knox Press, pp. 194–7.

4 BC, p. 580:37.

5 Luther, M. (1909) "First Sunday After Epiphany Romans 12:1–6," in Lenker, J.N. (ed.), *Sermons of Martin Luther* Vol. 7. Minneapolis: The Luther Press, p. 17.

6 BC, p. 138:109.

7 Ibid., p. 154:229.

8 Melanchthon, *Loci*, p. 148 "On Love."

9 Chemnitz, M. (1971–1986), *Examination of the Council of Trent*. Kramer, F. (trans.), St. Louis: Concordia.

Notes

10 Melanchthon, *Romans*, p. 242.

11 Ibid., 246.

12 BC, p. 319. *Smalcald Articles* III. 4.

13 Gerhard, J. *Loci Theologici* XI, 10 in Schmid, H. (1957), *The Doctrinal Theology of the Evangelical Lutheran Church*. Philadelphia: The United Lutheran Publication House, p. 587.

14 BC, p. 91:1, 5.

Chapter 12

1 Melanchthon, *Romans*, p. 216.

2 Luther, *Romans*, p. 359.

3 Melanchthon, *Romans*, p. 217.

4 Troeltsch, E. (rpt. 1992), *The Social Teaching of the Christian Churches* vol. 2. O. Wyon (trans.), Louisville: Westminster/John Knox.

5 Here lay the real law/gospel debate with Barth, and the reason Lutherans disagreed with the Barmen declaration (1934), which began not Christocentrically, but monistically (according to the law alone)—denying the distinction of law and gospel as anything but a material/formal distinction: "Jesus Christ, as he is attested to us in Holy Scripture, is the one Word of God which we have to hear, and which we have to trust and obey in life and in death." Hermann Sasse (1895–1976) is an example of a Lutheran who refused the Barmen declaration while opposing the Nazis and their takeover of the Christian church in Germany. Eberhard Jüngel is a Lutheran in favor of the Barmen declaration and Barth's rejection of the distinction between law and gospel in Jüngel, E. (1992), *Christ, Justice and Peace: Toward a Theology of the State*. D. B. Hamill and Alan J. Torrance (trans.), Edinburgh: T & T Clark.

6 Quoted in Bente, F. (1965 rpt.), *Historical Introductions to the Book of Concord*. St. Louis: Concordia, p. 99.

7 BC, p. 637:10.

8 Olson, O. (1972), "Theology of Revolution," *Sixteenth Century Journal* 3:1, pp. 56–79.

9 Whitford, D. (2001), *Tyranny and Resistance: The Magdeburg Confession and the Lutheran Tradition*. St. Louis: Concordia, p. 68. The German translation reads: 'Die Gewaltigen sind *von Gott* nicht den guten wercken sondern den bösen zufürchten *verordnet.*'

10 Olson, O. (1972), 'Theology of Revolution' pp. 73–4.

11 Ibid., p. 75.

12 Hase H.C.von (1940), Die Gestalt der Kirche Luthers: Der Casus Confessionis im Kampf des Maathias Flacius gegen das Interim von 1548. Göttingen: Vandenhoeck & Ruprecht. Quoted in Siemon-Netto, U. (1955), The Fabricated Luther. St. Louis: Concordia, p. 91.

13 Flacius, *Von wahren und falschen Mitteldingen* (A1b), quoted in BC, p. 638.n 313.

Notes

14 LW 33:88.
15 LW 27:38.
16 BC, p. 637:13.
17 Ibid., p. 638.

Chapter 13

1 Quoted in Forde, *The Law-Gospel Debate*, p. 13.
2 Jervell, J. (1991), "The Letter to Jerusalem" in K.P. Donfried (ed.), *The Romans Debate: Revised and Expanded Edition*. Peabody, MA: Hendrickson Publishers, p.59.
3 See Forde, *The Law-Gospel Debate*, pp.46ff summarizing von Hofmann's (1857, 1860), *Der Schriftbeweis* (2nd edn).
4 Stendahl, K. (1995), *Final Account: Paul's Letter to the Romans*. Minneapolis: Fortress, p. 12.
5 Wright, N.T. (2009), *Paul*. Minneapolis: Fortress, p. 172.
6 Ibid., pp.164–5.
7 Bornkamm, G. (1991), "Last Will and Testament," Donfried, K. (ed.) *The Romans Debate*, 16–28.

Index

Index

Index

Index

Index

Index

Index

Index

Romans 14:14 242
Romans 14:15 262
Romans 14:23 152
Romans 15 267
Romans 15:7 269
Romans 15:8 269
Romans 15:9 270
Romans 15:13 270
Romans 15:14–15 270
Romans 15:15–16 15, 241
Romans 15:16 241, 272
Romans 15:19 272
Romans 15:20 241, 270
Romans 15:22 272
Romans 15:27 272
Romans 15–16 265
Romans 16 267
Romans 16:12–13 272
Romans 16:20 208, 249, 272
Romanticism 64, 201

Salvation 7–8, 11–13, 23, 25, 28,
    58, 79, 95, 101, 107, 116, 119,
    128–9, 156–8, 163, 166, 175–6,
    180, 218–20, 224, 228, 242,
    247–8, 267–8
sanctification 32, 125, 128
Sanders, E. P. 176, 280n. 3
Sarah 136, 215
Sasse, Hermann 4, 274n. 4
Satan 100, 104, 138, 145, 150,
    208–9, 223, 233, 240, 242,
    249, 269, 272
satisfaction 41, 48, 58, 184, 222,
    226, 262
Schleiermacher, Friedrich 59, 65,
    96, 278n. 8
scholasticism 11, 45, 125, 134, 213
Schweitzer, Albert 13, 32, 35, 68,
    154–5, 158, 189, 191, 214,
    247–8, 275n. 5, 279n. 1
Scotus, John Duns 45, 66
Scripture 11, 13–14, 17–19, 28–9,
    38–9, 46, 49, 94, 106, 117,
    120–1, 128, 130, 136, 167, 199,
    213, 215, 217, 236, 273, 282n. 5

Selnecker, Nikolaus 194
Seneca 73, 277n. 14
sin 149–52
    baptism's freedom from 153–69
    law and 180–4
Smalcald Articles 60, 151, 168, 237,
    241, 274n. 7, 282n. 12
Small Catechism 58, 65, 76, 93,
    182, 206
Sophocles 22, 220
Spener, Philip Jacob 12, 274n. 10
Speratus, Paul 61, 69
Spinoza, Baruch 73
Stendahl, Krister 189, 191, 268,
    275n. 3, 283n. 4
stoicism 23, 33, 67, 73, 75, 83

testament
    New Testament 13–14, 27,
        88, 120, 131, 194–5, 227,
        255
    Old Testament 13–15, 17, 46,
        88, 181
theodicy 144
Thomas, the Apostle 101–2
Tillich, Paul 52, 59, 146, 189,
    276n. 17, 280n. 12, 281n. 9
transformation 30, 65, 190
Trinity 26, 28–31
Troeltsch, Ernst 7–8, 12, 189–90,
    238, 248, 260, 274n. 6, 280n.
    12, 282n. 4

Valla, Laurentius 67
vocation 89, 244–5, 251–2

Wilhelm Wrede 35, 191, 214, 265,
    278n. 2
Wisdom of Solomon 12:10–1 71
wrath of God 26, 41, 63–4, 66,
    70, 80–1, 84, 87, 143, 149,
    254
Wright, N. T. 268, 283n. 5

Zacchaeus 103
Zwingli, Ulrich 96–9, 166

293

Made in the USA
Monee, IL
25 September 2020